THE EVERYTHING®
GLUTEN-FREE BAKING
COOKBOOK

Dear Reader,

When I went gluten-free in August of 2007 there wasn't a single gluten-free bread, cookie, muffin, cupcake, or pizza within a fifty-mile radius of where I live. Now, six years later, the small locally owned drugstore in my tiny town (population 785) carries a gluten-free baking mix. The times have truly changed and *gluten-free* could almost be considered a household word. Yet, despite the better availability of gluten-free products, options are still limited and often the options available are much more expensive than their wheat-filled counterparts.

So why not try making your own gluten-free baked goods? Although still expensive, making most of your own gluten-free foods right in the comfort of your own home is definitely a more frugal option.

Please keep in mind that this isn't a gourmet cookbook . . . it's a book to teach you the very basics of gluten-free baking. I want you to feel comfortable baking an easy but great tasting gluten-free cake for your child's birthday. I want you to know that you absolutely can make a gluten-free piecrust or brownie or pizza or loaf of bread.

I'm a big believer in keeping things simple, using affordable, everyday ingredients, and creating recipes that make everyone, including children, happy! I hope soon after you've purchased this book it will be ingredient-stained, dog-eared, and sitting proudly on your kitchen counter. Happy gluten-free baking!

Carrie S. Forbes

Welcome to the EVERYTHING® Series!

These handy, accessible books give you all you need to tackle a difficult project, gain a new hobby, comprehend a fascinating topic, prepare for an exam, or even brush up on something you learned back in school but have since forgotten.

You can choose to read an Everything® book from cover to cover or just pick out the information you want from our four useful boxes: e-questions, e-facts, e-alerts, and e-ssentials.

We give you everything you need to know on the subject, but throw in a lot of fun stuff along the way, too.

We now have more than 400 Everything® books in print, spanning such wide-ranging categories as weddings, pregnancy, cooking, music instruction, foreign language, crafts, pets, New Age, and so much more. When you're done reading them all, you can finally say you know Everything®!

QUESTION

Answers to common questions

FACT

Important snippets of information

ALERT

Urgent warnings

ESSENTIAL

Quick handy tips

PUBLISHER Karen Cooper

MANAGING EDITOR, EVERYTHING® SERIES Lisa Laing

COPY CHIEF Casey Ebert

ASSISTANT PRODUCTION EDITOR Alex Guarco

ACQUISITIONS EDITOR Lisa Laing

SENIOR DEVELOPMENT EDITOR Brett Palana-Shanahan

EVERYTHING® SERIES COVER DESIGNER Erin Alexander

Visit the entire Everything® series at *www.everything.com*

THE
EVERYTHING®
GLUTEN-FREE BAKING COOKBOOK

Carrie S. Forbes

Avon, Massachusetts

To Nan and Grandma P: You both let me let lick the spoons, told me story after story about a handful of potato salad, the infamous Steelman girls' sweet tea, and the best pound cake ever made. You're both a huge part of who I am today and I'll forever be grateful.

An Everything® Series Book.
Everything® and everything.com® are registered trademarks of F+W Media, Inc.

Published by Adams Media,
a division of F+W Media, Inc.
57 Littlefield Street, Avon, MA 02322. U.S.A.
www.adamsmedia.com

ISBN 10: 1-4405-6486-8
ISBN 13: 978-1-4405-6486-4
eISBN 10: 1-4405-6487-6
eISBN 13: 978-1-4405-6487-1

Printed in the United States of America.

10 9 8 7 6 5 4 3 2

Library of Congress Cataloging-in-Publication Data

Forbes, Carrie S.
  The everything gluten-free baking cookbook / Carrie S. Forbes.
      pages cm
  Includes bibliographical references and index.
  ISBN-13: 978-1-4405-6486-4 (pbk. : alk. paper)
  ISBN-10: 1-4405-6486-8 (pbk. : alk. paper)
  eISBN-13: 978-1-4405-6487-1
  eISBN-10: 1-4405-6487-6
  1. Gluten-free diet--Recipes. 2. Baking.
  3. Baked products. I. Title.
    RM237.86.F66 2013
    641.81′5--dc23

2013016736

Always follow safety and commonsense cooking protocol while using kitchen utensils, operating ovens and stoves, and handling uncooked food. If children are assisting in the preparation of any recipe, they should always be supervised by an adult.

Many of the designations used by manufacturers and sellers to distinguish their products are claimed as trademarks. Where those designations appear in this book and F+W Media was aware of a trademark claim, the designations have been printed with initial capital letters.

Cover image and interior photographs
© Jennifer L. Yandle.

This book is available at quantity discounts for bulk purchases. For information, please call 1-800-289-0963.

Acknowledgments

To the readers of Gingerlemongirl.com: thank you! It's because of your incredible support and readership over the past six years that I've been writing a food blog that this book is a reality. I truly thank you for reading my words, making my recipes, and spending some of your valuable time interacting with me on Facebook and through e-mail. Your friendship, energy, and belief in my abilities help make my dreams come true every day.

To Clara, Heather, Tracy, Angie, Jaime, Cheryl, and Diane: Thank you for always being sounding boards and putting up with me through deadline after deadline. Your steady and faithful friendships keep me grounded, humble, and thankful (and usually hungry because we all love food :-P).

To Michael: Truly, I'm blessed out of my socks to be with you (as Nan would say) and I absolutely could not do what I love without you. Thank you for being my best and most helpful critic and for fixing all my computer problems, even at 2 A.M.! And I promise I'll make your favorite chocolate chip cookies soon. Promise!

Contents

Introduction

THERE ARE SO MANY different schools of thought on how to bake gluten-free. Some people prefer baking with a host of expensive, exotic flours. Some people prefer to bake using a kitchen scale for measurements instead of cups and teaspoons. Some people prefer to use only organic or vegan ingredients. Some people prefer to bake without grains or sugar. Each gluten-free cookbook you buy will have a unique "personality" depending on what the author or publisher feels is the best method of giving you a delicious end product. This cookbook is no different.

Instead of focusing on specific flour blends, this book teaches you basic baking techniques that can be used with just about any gluten-free flour that you prefer. Although I do list specific flours, you can adjust these recipes to work with the gluten-free flours you have on hand.

Bette Hagman wrote one of the first gluten-free cookbooks, *The Gluten-Free Gourmet*, back in the mid-1980s before many people had ever heard of gluten, let alone celiac disease. Ms. Hagman was a pioneer in the field of gluten-free home baking and many of the recipes in this book are inspired by her creativity and passion in the kitchen. Many of Ms. Hagman's recipes were based on the few gluten-free flours that were available during that time, mostly white rice flour, tapioca starch, and potato starch. As the demand and need for gluten-free recipes has risen over the past twenty years, more and more types of gluten-free flours have become readily available. Ms. Hagman had to purchase most of her flours through mail order. These days, with the convenience of the Internet, you can purchase nearly any ingredient you'd like with a few simple clicks or even at your local grocery store.

This cookbook is unique in that it contains not only gluten-free recipes, but dairy-free, egg-free, soy-free, vegan, and grain-free recipes as well. There's an entire chapter on gluten-free vegan baking for those who prefer (for health or lifestyle reasons) to bake without animal ingredients. I've also included a chapter for people who cannot tolerate grains or choose to follow a paleo-type or low-glycemic diet. The recipes in that chapter use blanched almond flour and coconut flour instead of traditional grain-based gluten-free flours.

Also unique to this book is a special chapter for using a homemade all-purpose gluten-free baking mix. The recipe for the basic mix is included and you can make it yourself, or you can use your favorite gluten-free baking mix instead such as Betty Crocker's Gluten Free Bisquick or Pamela's mixes. Included with the mix are over thirty recipes that you can whip up in less than ten minutes to create easy, delicious homemade gluten-free meals and baked goods.

If this is your first time experimenting with gluten-free flours and recipes, take a moment to realize that it's different than the wheat-based baking you are used to. One of the hardest concepts to grasp if you are an experienced "wheat" baker is that the texture and feel of gluten-free baking is very different (especially for breads and cakes). The chemistry and baking processes are unique and require new techniques to achieve the desired results.

I hope this cookbook will encourage you to experiment and play in the kitchen. Try a recipe exactly the way it's written the first time. The next time you make it? Add a different flavoring. Try a different gluten-free flour. Use the alternate baking suggestions in the sidebars. Don't worry about being perfect. If a recipe doesn't come out exactly right the first time, try it again. Gluten-free baking does take some practice, so be patient with yourself, take your time, and enjoy the experience!

CHAPTER 1

Gluten-Free Baking 101

This chapter will teach you everything you need to know to start baking gluten-free. You'll find the fundamental ingredients needed to make everything in this book, along with recommended basic baking equipment. If you want to learn how to make a "regular" recipe in some of the beginning chapters of the book egg-free or dairy-free, this is the chapter to turn to. Additionally, you'll find basic conversion charts along with tips and tricks on the best methods to recreate your old favorite wheat-based recipes.

What Is Gluten?

Gluten is the term used for several types of proteins found in wheat, barley, and rye. The proteins gliadin and glutelin are found in these grains and together form a substance called gluten. Gluten is a "storage protein," which means that it holds the key ingredients for these grains to continue proliferating.

Gluten is primarily found in foods such as traditional breads, pasta, cakes, muffins, crackers, and pizza. These grains are used in many baked goods because gluten provides excellent elasticity, structure, and texture. Gluten is what causes pizza to have a chewy, stretchy texture. It gives French bread its soft center and chewy crust. Gluten makes cinnamon rolls stretchy, soft, and light. Gluten helps give structure to bread dough when rising, so the bread becomes tall and stays tall after baking and cooling.

FACT

Did you know that there are *no* "typical" signs and symptoms of celiac disease, according to the Mayo Clinic? Celiac patients of all ages, genders, and races often report having a wide range of symptoms that can be anything from well-known signs such as diarrhea, constipation, or malabsorption of nutrients, to migraine headaches, brain "fog," loss of memory, joint pain, irritability, depression, neuropathy, or osteoporosis.

Avoiding gluten can be difficult for several reasons. The biggest reason is that many foods and food products contain gluten, but because gluten is simply a protein found in the ingredient itself, it's not listed on the package. By law the top eight food allergens must be listed on every food label in the United States. Wheat is one of the top eight allergens. The remaining seven foods are milk, eggs, tree nuts (such as cashews, almonds, walnuts), fish, shellfish, peanuts, and soy. However, in addition to wheat you also need to avoid these foods (most are derivatives of wheat) that also contain gluten:

- Barley
- Rye
- Triticale (a cross between rye and wheat)

- Bulgur
- Durum flour
- Farina
- Graham flour
- Kamut
- Seminola
- Couscous
- Spelt

Celiac Disease Explained

Celiac disease (also known as celiac sprue or gluten-sensitive enteropathy) is an autoimmune and digestive disorder that occurs in about 1 in 100 people in the United States. For people with this disorder, gluten can cause serious damage to their intestines if it is ingested. If you have celiac disease or gluten intolerance, gluten damages the "villi" in your intestines. Because the villi (fingerlike projections that contain most of the enzymes needed for digestion) are damaged for people with celiac disease, their bodies have enormous difficulty ingesting the healthy nutrients their bodies need such as fat, calcium, iron, and folate. Some of the symptoms of celiac disease and gluten intolerance include:

- Digestive problems such as bloating, vomiting, excess gas and/or pain, severe and/or chronic diarrhea, irritable bowel, weight loss, or weight gain
- Constant and/or severe headaches or migraines
- Low levels of iron (anemia)
- Skin rashes (also known as dermatitis herpetiformis)
- Bone or joint pain
- Depression and/or anxiety
- Seizures
- Infertility
- Unexplained fatigue
- Failure to thrive (often seen in children with celiac disease)

Most people have healthy immune systems that prevent the body from being harmed by gluten, but for those with celiac disease the only effective treatment is avoiding foods with gluten altogether.

To get tested for celiac disease and/or gluten sensitivity you need to visit your family doctor or a gastroenterologist, who will do a blood test to check for high levels of certain types of antibodies. If your blood test comes back with positive results for celiac disease, your doctor may then choose to do a biopsy of your small intestine to check for damage to the villi. A diagnosis is usually given using a combination of these diagnostic tests. Gluten sensitivity (as opposed to celiac disease) is sometimes diagnosed if a patient tests negatively for the disorder, yet his or her body reacts with symptoms that are similar to those with celiac disease. The most effective treatment for either condition is to avoid all foods with gluten by following a gluten-free diet.

When you're following a gluten-free diet, you not only have to learn to cook gluten-free foods, you also need to learn how to bake without gluten. Birthday parties need cake! Big breakfasts need biscuits, or pancakes, or toast. Sandwiches usually need bread to hold them together.

To make these foods you will need a few special ingredients such as gluten-free flours. The gluten-free flours used in this book are brown rice flour, sorghum flour, oat flour, arrowroot starch, tapioca starch, and occasionally cornstarch. Generally you will only need two or three of those flours per baking recipe. Sorghum flour and brown rice flour can be used interchangeably in these recipes. So if you prefer sorghum flour over brown rice flour, feel free to substitute.

In the low-glycemic chapter, in addition to arrowroot starch, blanched almond flour and coconut flour are used for gluten-free baked goods that have less impact on your blood sugar levels when eaten.

Why Bake Gluten-Free from Scratch?

You live in a very busy world. You're constantly running from one place to the next. If you're a parent, you're most likely shuffling children between school, sports practices, ballgames, band rehearsals, and dentist appointments in the midst of getting yourself back and forth to work—you're lucky if you get a hot meal on the table on an average weekday night.

Despite how busy and challenging your current lifestyle can be, learning how to make some of your own gluten-free foods from scratch can actually save you time in the long run. Not only are homemade foods healthier than their store-bought counterparts, they are generally cheaper as well. Gluten-free ingredients will most likely be more expensive than regular baking ingredients for a long time to come, but it's still cheaper to make most foods from scratch.

FACT

It's far more eco-friendly to make as many foods from scratch as you can. When you make your own baked goods or main dishes, you don't throw away extra, unnecessary packaging. You can make gluten-free baked goods as gifts during the holidays. Simply wrap tightly with a sheet of plastic wrap or parchment paper and tie with a simple ribbon. You save money, time, and excess paper and plastic that will likely be thrown away.

Homemade foods also contain less sodium, preservatives, and partially hydrogenated oils. When you make your bread, cake, muffins, and pizza crust at home you completely control what ingredients go into your food. You can add additional fiber or less sugar. You can decide to make a food egg-free or dairy-free.

Another good reason to make gluten-free foods from scratch is that many people who have gluten sensitivities also have additional food sensitivities or allergies. Most of the recipes in this book are gluten-free and soy-free already. Many of them also already contain dairy-free substitutes to make the recipes even easier.

The Science Behind Gluten-Free Baking

Gluten-free baking isn't nearly as scary as it first sounds. You do have to learn how to use a different set of ingredients, but once you have a few basic recipes under your belt you'll gain the confidence to continue trying new recipes and baking techniques. When you first begin baking, try making a simple quick bread such as the Ginger Lemon Muffins or the Apple Spice Bread in Chapter 2.

These recipes work similarly to wheat-flour recipes of the same type. Quick breads do not rely on gluten to give them structure and texture, as a yeast bread generally does. As a matter of fact, most wheat-based muffin or quick-bread recipes will tell you to mix the batter as little as possible, or "just until combined." This is because they do not want you to overwork or get the gluten proteins to develop in the batter. If a wheat-based muffin, cake, biscuit, or pie dough is "overworked" it means the gluten proteins have developed and become long strands, which in these types of baked goods creates a dense, tough texture.

When you are making gluten-free baked goods, the most challenging recipes are yeast breads. Wheat-based yeast breads are dependent on the gluten in flour. As those long strands of gluten protein develop while the bread is rising, they create air pockets in the bread structure. They need extra time to continue developing before baking, so they usually have a second rising time. Most gluten-free yeast breads do not.

QUESTION

Is xanthan gum a safe food to eat?
For most people food gums are safe to eat. Xanthan gum is actually used in a variety of commonly eaten processed foods such as most brands of ice cream, pastry fillings, and even salad dressings in very small quantities. Some people do have a sensitivity to gums and have to use alternative ingredients in gluten-free baking. Some of those alternative ingredients include plain gelatin, psyllium husks, chia seeds, or ground flaxseeds.

Gluten-free yeast breads are actually a wet batter before they become a "dough." If you are or were an experienced homemade yeast-bread maker, the texture of gluten-free batter will seem more like a thick cake batter and seem *way* too wet to create bread. Most gluten-free yeast breads also contain eggs (although you will find several vegan, egg-free yeast-bread recipes in this book). The eggs help replace some of the protein that would be found in the gluten proteins in regular wheat-based breads.

To help replicate the same chewy texture and structure as wheat bread, gluten-free baking often uses gums such as xanthan gum or guar gum. These gums, when mixed with a liquid, become gelatinous and sticky. That quality helps the gluten-free flour (in yeast breads especially).

Gluten-Free Flours

There are literally hundreds of different types of flours that can be used in gluten-free baking. To help alleviate some of the confusion that so many ingredients can cause, this book focuses on five basic gluten-free flours: brown rice flour, arrowroot starch, sorghum flour, blanched almond flour, and coconut flour. Occasionally this text also uses tapioca starch, oat flour, cornmeal, and cornstarch. This brief primer explains why these flours work so well in gluten-free baking.

Brown Rice Flour

This basic flour is both a whole grain and a starch. It includes the bran and the germ of the rice grain, which provide a small amount of fiber, nutrients, and protein. This flour has a very mild taste, although some people detect the slightest hint of a nutty flavor.

Arrowroot Starch

This "flour" is actually a powdery ground-up rhizome from a tropical herb. This is the most-used starch in this cookbook because it works well in "regular" gluten-free baking, vegan gluten-free baking, and low-glycemic gluten-free baking. In Ayurvedic herbal medicine, arrowroot starch is considered one of the less-irritating herbal foods and is used for people who have chronic bowl and bladder diseases because it doesn't cause as much inflammation as other foods can.

Sorghum Flour

Sorghum flour is a cereal grain used in many developing countries. It's a whole grain that has a high protein and fiber content. Some people who do not like the texture of brown rice flour like sorghum flour instead.

Why are so many different flours used in gluten-free baking recipes? Wheat flour has been preferred for centuries because of the special properties of gluten. Because gluten-free flours don't contain the unique elastic properties of wheat flour, they don't have the same ability to produce baked goods that are light, yet sturdy. Gluten-free baked goods often have a much better texture and taste when you combine a variety of flours that have different properties.

Blanched Almond Flour

Blanched almond flour is a lower carbohydrate flour with high protein, fat, and fiber content. The almonds have had the brown outer skin removed and are ground into a fine flour. Several different companies make brands of this flour, but for testing purposes in this book the best brand was Honeyville Blanched Almond Flour, for its great consistency and quality.

Coconut Flour

Coconut flour is also a lower carbohydrate flour that has high levels of protein and fiber. It is made from finely ground coconut meat that has had most of the fat and moisture content removed. This flour is very different from any other type of gluten-free flour and cannot be easily substituted for any other type of flour. It is often used in combination with other high-protein flours such as almond flour.

Tapioca Starch

This starchy powder is extracted from the roots of the cassava plant. This is a cheaper starch than arrowroot starch, and some people prefer it to arrowroot. You can use it interchangeably with arrowroot starch in most of the recipes in this cookbook.

Oat Flour

A whole-grain flour that can be bought from a few select companies in the United States, oat flour is easy to grind at home in your blender. Simply pulverize gluten-free rolled oats until they're soft and powdery. Some people who cannot tolerate gluten are also very sensitive to oats and oat flour, even though oats do not naturally contain gluten.

Cornmeal

This refined, but coarse, meal is usually ground from yellow corn (although there are white varieties as well). Buy a brand that has been tested for gluten content, as it's often processed in a plant that also processes wheat. Several brands are certified gluten-free.

Cornstarch

This soft, powdery starch is used in small quantities in a few of the recipes in this book as a thickener for fruit pies and some cake fillings. Most brands are naturally gluten-free, but always double-check the label.

Additional Gluten-Free Baking Ingredients

Many of the other baking ingredients you will use in this cookbook's recipes are naturally gluten-free. Most brands of plain sea salt, baking soda, baking powder, and sugar are all gluten-free. It's always important to check ingredients labels to make sure, however, especially with mixed products such as baking powder.

Although not technically flours, ground flaxseeds or chia seeds are used in some of the recipes in this book. Both of these seeds have a gelatinous quality that can help bind recipes and/or add additional fiber and omega-3 fatty acids. You can find these seeds easily online, at most health food stores, or upper-end grocery stores. As with all other ingredients, double-check to make sure they are gluten-free.

For yeast breads in this cookbook, I recommend what is called "instant yeast," "bread machine yeast," or "rapid-rise yeast." This yeast has been processed differently than active dry yeast, so the yeast granules are more porous. They do not need to be mixed with a warm liquid and sugar to be activated to start the rising process in the dough. This makes the recipes a bit easier and cuts out one step in the bread-making process.

When you try a recipe for the first time, make sure you read the ingredients and the directions carefully all the way through. You'll save yourself a lot of time and frustration by knowing for sure that you have all the correct ingredients and understand exactly how the recipe is supposed to be prepared.

Most baked goods contain some type of fat. The most common fats found in this cookbook are butter, light-tasting olive oil, and Spectrum Palm Shortening. Light-tasting olive oil is a great ingredient to use in baking. It's an easy replacement for butter, and although it's made from olives it does not have a strong flavor so it doesn't interfere with the taste of sweet baked goods. You can use canola oil instead if you prefer.

Spectrum Palm Shortening is a nonhydrogenated, all-natural version of shortening that was used to test many of the recipes in this book. It is more expensive than Crisco shortening, but many people consider the trans fats in Crisco to be unhealthy. However, you can use Crisco in place of Spectrum Palm Shortening in any recipe in this book, if it's a more frugal (and easier to find) option for you.

Lastly, when baking gluten-free recipes, you need a binder, which helps replace the action of gluten in baked goods. The most commonly used binder in gluten-free baking is xanthan gum. This is a powder made from a strain of bacteria grown on corn. When xanthan gum is introduced to a liquid, the mixture becomes thick and sticky. This quality helps give structure to gluten-free baked goods. If you're allergic to corn products, you can use guar gum in place of xanthan gum. A few recipes in this book use other ingredients as a thickener instead of gums. The low-glycemic chapter uses absolutely no gums, and the vegan chapter contains gluten-free breads that use whole psyllium husks to create their structure instead of gums.

Substitutions for Egg-Free and Dairy-Free Recipes

Many of the recipes in this book already contain dairy-free ingredient substitutions. The primary dairy-free ingredient used is almond milk. However, if you are sensitive to tree nuts you can use a different type of nondairy milk such as hemp milk (which is made from hemp seeds) or rice milk. You can also use dairy milk, if you prefer. Dairy ingredients are easy to substitute in general gluten-free baking. It's a little more tricky to substitute dairy when you are cooking main dishes than baking breads and sweet treats.

Following is an excellent list of dairy-free substitutes and how you can use them in your everyday gluten-free baking. Make sure to also try the recipes in Chapter 13 to see how easy it is to make all different types of gluten-free recipes dairy-free.

VEGAN DAIRY SUBSTITUTES FOR GLUTEN-FREE COOKING AND BAKING	
Type of Dairy	Substitutions
1 cup 2% or regular milk	1 cup almond milk, full-fat coconut milk, hemp milk, soy milk (if tolerated)
1 cup 1% or fat-free milk	1 cup rice milk or ½ cup almond milk mixed with ½ cup water
1 cup buttermilk	1 cup almond milk or hemp milk mixed with 1 tablespoon lemon juice or apple cider vinegar
1 cup heavy cream	1 cup full-fat coconut milk cream (skimmed off the top of full-fat coconut milk), 1 cup reduced nut milk
1 cup yogurt	1 cup coconut milk yogurt, 1 cup almond milk yogurt, 1 cup unsweetened applesauce or plain pumpkin purée
1 cup sour cream	1 cup full-fat coconut milk cream mixed with 1 tablespoon lemon juice or apple cider vinegar, 1 cup unsweetened applesauce or plain pumpkin purée
1 tablespoon butter	1 tablespoon light-tasting olive oil, 1 tablespoon coconut oil, 1 tablespoon Spectrum Palm Shortening
1 cup cream cheese	1 cup Tofutti (soy substitute, if you tolerate soy), 1 cup Daiya "cream cheese style" spread
1 cup shredded cheese	1 cup shredded Daiya "cheese" shreds, 1 cup Galaxy Vegan Shreds, ¼ cup nutritional yeast
1 cup grated Parmesan	1 cup blanched almond flour, ¼ cup nutritional yeast, ½ cup finely chopped toasted pecans or cashews

Eggs are a bit more tricky to replace in any type of baking. Eggs are a truly magical baking ingredient. They provide fat, protein, nutrients, and structure to baked goods. It can be quite a challenge to get baked goods to rise well without eggs. Keep in mind that egg-free baked goods are generally going to be a bit more dense than their egg-containing counterparts. Don't get frustrated; it takes a little time and patience to learn what substitutes work best with certain recipes.

ALERT

Remember, it's incredibly important to keep gluten-containing ingredients separate from gluten-free ingredients if you keep both in your home kitchen. A person with celiac disease or gluten sensitivity can become extremely ill very quickly if he or she eats the tiniest crumb of gluten. You must make sure during food preparation to make all food in a safe place away from any allergens that could come in contact with the food.

When baking egg-free, it's best not to attempt recipes that require more than two eggs. When you need more than two eggs, the integrity of the dish will be extremely compromised. For example, you probably don't want to attempt making an angel food cake without egg whites. Egg whites create structure and texture and are the base of the cake. It will be much easier to try other recipes instead, such as a simple yellow cake that only requires two eggs.

If you prefer to bake with higher-protein, lower-glycemic flours such as almond flour or coconut flour, remember these flours generally tend to work better with eggs. A handful of recipes in Chapter 12 do not contain eggs, or only contain one egg (which can probably be replaced), so if you want to experiment try those recipes first.

VEGAN EGG SUBSTITUTIONS FOR GLUTEN-FREE COOKING AND BAKING		
Egg Replaced	**Substitution**	**Works Best In**
1 egg	2 tablespoons potato starch	dense baked goods, savory or sweet
1 egg	¼ cup mashed potatoes	dense baked goods, savory
1 egg	¼ cup pumpkin or squash purée + ½ teaspoon baking powder	sweet baked goods
1 egg	¼ cup puréed prunes + ½ teaspoon baking powder	sweet baked goods
1 egg	¼ cup unsweetened applesauce or mashed bananas + ½ teaspoon baking powder	sweet baked goods
1 egg	2 tablespoons water + 1 tablespoon oil + 1 teaspoon baking powder	baked goods, savory (breads calling for 2 eggs or fewer)
1 egg	1 tablespoon ground flaxseeds + 3 tablespoons warm water	dense baked goods

1 egg white	1 tablespoon plain agar + 1 tablespoon water	whipped and chilled recipes calling for 1 or 2 egg whites
1 egg	¼ cup firm tofu, crumbled	for those who can tolerate soy, this is a good replacement for savory foods such as scrambled eggs

Information from www.peta.org/living/vegetarian-living/egg-replacements.aspx

Baking by Weight versus Baking by Volume

In the United States most home cooks bake using volume measurements rather than weight measurements. Many other parts of the world rely on weight measurements because they tend to be more accurate, especially for large-scale baking. However, the case can be argued that baking by volume is generally quite accurate as well, especially for recipes that most nonprofessional home bakers use.

The recipes in this cookbook are "small amount" recipes meant for average families of two to six people; they will work even with slight variations in volume measurements. These recipes were tested using the "scoop-and-sweep" method, meaning the measuring cup was dipped into the container holding the flour until it was overflowing and then swept clean at the top with the back of a butter knife. The only variations to this rule are with brown sugar and blanched almond flour. Those ingredients were "packed" into the cups before being "swept" clean at the top with the butter knife.

FACT

Until quite recently, cooking and baking recipes did not specify precise quantities of ingredients. For instance, recipes would call for "a pinch" of this or "a cupful" of beans. Or butter "the size of a duck's egg" or "the size of a walnut." In the United States it wasn't until Fannie Farmer introduced exact measurements in her 1896 *Boston Cooking-School Cookbook* that home cooks started using more precise measuring units for recipes.

Liquids in this book's recipes were measured using a glass (volume) measuring cup and small amounts of ingredients were measured with measuring spoons, again using the scoop-and-sweep method. This method usually works fine for most home cooks. If you need to triple or quadruple a recipe, it would be easier to use weight measurements, because the "slight" variations become big variations when recipes are industrial-sized. However, with basic smaller recipes, the slight differences in how each home cook measures should not make a significant difference in the end results.

For those who prefer to bake by weight, please refer to the following chart for basic weight conversions for the flours used in this cookbook.

GLUTEN-FREE FLOUR VOLUME/WEIGHT CONVERSIONS			
Type of Flour	¼ cup (weight in grams)	½ cup (weight in grams)	1 cup (weight in grams)
Blanched Almond Flour	28	56	112
Arrowroot Starch	30	60	120
Brown Rice Flour	40	79	158
Coconut Flour	28	56	112
Cornmeal	32	64	128
Oat Flour	30	60	120
Sorghum Flour	32	64	128
Tapioca Starch	31	63	125

CHAPTER 2

The Breakfast Table: Muffins, Biscuits, Sweet Breads, and Scones

Almond and Dried Cherry Granola

Sometimes you just want cereal for breakfast. If you make a big batch of this wholesome granola, you will have an easy, whole-grain, protein-packed breakfast cereal for weeks to come.

INGREDIENTS | SERVES 24; SERVING SIZE: ¼ CUP

5 cups old-fashioned, gluten-free rolled oats

1 cup slivered almonds

¼ cup mild honey

¼ cup canola oil

1 teaspoon vanilla

½ cup dried tart cherries, raisins, or dried cranberries

¼ cup unsweetened flaked coconut

½ cup sunflower seeds

3 tablespoons ground flaxseeds

1. Preheat oven to 250°F. Line a large baking sheet with parchment paper.
2. Place oats and almonds in a large bowl. Drizzle with honey, oil, and vanilla. Stir mixture to distribute syrup evenly. Add cherries, coconut, sunflower seeds, and ground flaxseeds. Stir to thoroughly combine.
3. Pour granola onto the lined baking sheet. Bake for 1½ hours, stirring every 15–20 minutes.
4. Allow granola to cool fully, and then store it in an airtight container for up to 1 month.

Ginger Lemon Muffins

*These gorgeous, aromatic muffins, with the bite of ginger and the zing of fresh lemon zest,
are a light, fluffy alternative to traditional blueberry muffins.*

INGREDIENTS | SERVES 12

1 cup brown rice flour

1 cup arrowroot starch

¾ cup sugar

½ teaspoon xanthan gum

1 teaspoon baking powder

1 teaspoon baking soda

½ teaspoon sea salt

½ teaspoon ground ginger

2 large eggs

1 cup almond milk

½ cup light-tasting olive oil

2 tablespoons freshly grated lemon zest

2 tablespoons lemon juice

1 tablespoon finely chopped fresh
ginger (optional)

Lighten Them Up

These muffins are fluffy and delicious as is,
but if you would like to reduce the overall
fat content, use only ¼ cup light-tasting
olive oil and ¼ cup applesauce in place of
the ½ cup of oil.

1. Preheat oven to 375°F. Place paper liners in a muffin pan. Spritz the paper liners with nonstick cooking spray and set aside.
2. In a large bowl whisk together brown rice flour, arrowroot starch, sugar, xanthan gum, baking powder, baking soda, sea salt, and ginger.
3. In a medium bowl whisk together the eggs, almond milk, olive oil, lemon zest, lemon juice, and fresh ginger.
4. Pour the wet ingredients into the dry ingredients and mix to combine. Scoop the batter into muffin pan. Bake for 15–18 minutes until muffins are golden-brown and a toothpick inserted in the middle comes out clean.
5. Store muffins in an airtight container in the refrigerator for up to 1 week.

Pumpkin Spice Chocolate Chip Muffins

Surprisingly, pumpkin and chocolate make a wonderful combination.
These muffins are perfect for the fall season, but you can make them year round.

INGREDIENTS | SERVES 12

⅔ cup brown rice flour
⅔ cup arrowroot starch
⅔ sorghum flour
¾ cup sugar
½ teaspoon xanthan gum
½ teaspoon baking powder
1 teaspoon baking soda
2 teaspoons cinnamon
½ teaspoon ground cloves
½ teaspoon ginger
¼ teaspoon salt
2 large eggs
1 cup plain pumpkin purée
½ cup light-tasting olive oil
¾ cup chocolate chips

1. Preheat oven to 350°F. Place paper liners in a muffin pan. Spritz the paper liners with nonstick cooking spray and set aside.
2. In a large bowl whisk together brown rice flour, arrowroot starch, sorghum flour, sugar, xanthan gum, baking powder, baking soda, spices, and salt. In a medium bowl whisk together the eggs, pumpkin purée, and olive oil.
3. Pour the wet ingredients into the dry ingredients and mix to combine. Fold in the chocolate chips. Scoop the batter into muffin pan. Bake for 18–20 minutes until muffins are golden-brown and a toothpick inserted in the middle comes out clean.
4. Store muffins in an airtight container in the refrigerator for up to 1 week.

Make Your Own Muffin Mix

To make these muffins even easier than they already are, whisk together all of the dry ingredients: brown rice flour, arrowroot starch, sorghum flour, sugar, xanthan gum, baking powder, baking soda, spices, and salt. Pour into a glass jar or a zip-top plastic bag, seal and voilà . . . a shelf-stable muffin mix. When you're ready to bake, add the eggs, pumpkin purée, olive oil, and chocolate chips and you'll have muffins in 20 minutes.

Oatmeal Raisin Muffins

These hearty whole-grain muffins make a wonderful "grab-and-go" breakfast.
Add ⅓ cup of chopped pecans or walnuts to the batter for additional protein and fiber, if desired.

INGREDIENTS | SERVES 12

⅔ cup brown rice flour
⅔ cup arrowroot starch
1 cup gluten-free rolled oats
¾ cup sugar
½ teaspoon xanthan gum
2 teaspoons cinnamon
½ teaspoon baking powder
1 teaspoon baking soda
¼ teaspoon salt
2 large eggs
1 cup almond milk
1 tablespoon vanilla extract
½ cup light-tasting olive oil
¾ cup raisins

1. Preheat oven to 350°F. Place paper liners in a muffin pan. Spritz liners with nonstick cooking spray and set aside.
2. In a large bowl whisk together brown rice flour, arrowroot starch, oats, sugar, xanthan gum, cinnamon, baking powder, baking soda, and salt. In a medium bowl whisk together the eggs, almond milk, vanilla extract, and olive oil.
3. Pour the wet ingredients into the dry ingredients and mix to combine. Fold in the raisins. Scoop the batter into muffin pan. Bake for 18–20 minutes until muffins are golden-brown and a toothpick inserted in the middle comes out clean.
4. Store muffins in an airtight container in the refrigerator for up to 1 week.

Fluffy Buttermilk Biscuits

These fluffy, light biscuits are perfect topped with jam and a slice of cheese.
Or, dip them in your favorite soup.

INGREDIENTS | SERVES 9

1 cup brown rice flour, plus more for rolling out the dough

½ cup arrowroot starch

1 teaspoon xanthan gum

2 teaspoons baking powder

1 teaspoon baking soda

½ teaspoon salt

1 teaspoon sugar

½ cup cold butter, cut into chunks

2 large eggs

⅓ cup buttermilk

Milk (optional)

Coarse salt (optional)

Make Savory Biscuits

To make these biscuits savory, add ½ teaspoon of garlic powder or Italian seasoning (or even both) to the dry ingredients. Or, try a tablespoon of chopped fresh chives.

1. Preheat oven to 425°F. Line a baking sheet with parchment paper, and sprinkle with some brown rice flour. Set aside.
2. In the bowl of a food processor, combine all the dry ingredients and pulse to combine. (If you don't have a food processor, combine all dry ingredients in a medium-sized mixing bowl.)
3. Add the butter and pulse until the butter is the size of a lentil/pea. (Or, use a pastry blender to cut the butter into the dry ingredients. Work quickly, because you want the butter to stay cold.)
4. Add the eggs and buttermilk, and run the food processor until the dough comes together in a ball. (Alternately, you can use a wooden spoon and stir until the dough comes together.)
5. Turn dough out onto baking sheet, and flour your hands with more brown rice flour. Working quickly, pat the dough down into a square shape, approximately 10" × 10" and ¾" thick. Using a sharp knife, cut the dough into 9 biscuits.
6. Gently rearrange the biscuits so they are not touching and have room to expand while baking. Gently brush the tops of the biscuits with milk, and sprinkle with coarse salt, if desired.
7. Bake for 14–16 minutes, or until golden-brown. Allow to cool for 5 minutes on a cooling rack before serving. You can store any remaining biscuits in an airtight container on the counter for 2–3 days.

Banana Chocolate Chip Scones

These scones are perfect as is, or topped with cream cheese or chocolate hazelnut spread.

INGREDIENTS | SERVES 8

1¼ cups brown rice flour, plus more for the baking sheet

¼ cup arrowroot starch

1 teaspoon xanthan gum

2 teaspoons baking powder

1 teaspoon baking soda

½ teaspoon salt

¼ cup sugar

6 tablespoons cold butter, cut into chunks

1 large egg yolk

1 small ripe banana, mashed (about ⅓ cup)

½ cup sour cream, plain yogurt, or unsweetened applesauce

1 teaspoon vanilla extract

½ cup gluten-free mini chocolate chips

1 large egg white

1 tablespoon warm water

3 tablespoons coarse sugar

1. Preheat the oven to 400°F. Line a baking sheet with parchment paper and sprinkle with some brown rice flour. Set aside.
2. Place all the dry ingredients in the bowl of a food processor. Pulse to mix the ingredients.
3. Add the cold butter and pulse until the butter is the size of a pea. Add the egg yolk, mashed banana, sour cream, vanilla extract, and mini chocolate chips. Pulse again, just until the dough comes together in a ball. Spoon the dough onto baking sheet.
4. Dust your hands with flour and quickly form the dough into a disk, about 10" round and ¾"–1" thick. Cut into 8 even wedges and move the wedges apart, so they are not touching each other. This will allow them to bake evenly.
5. Brush the tops of the scones with the egg white whisked with warm water. Sprinkle coarse sugar evenly over scones.
6. Bake for 18–20 minutes, or until the tops are a nice golden-brown. Remove from oven, and move scones to wire cooling rack for 15 minutes before serving.
7. Store in an airtight container once the scones are completely cool.

Vanilla Scones

Thick, puffy scones are perfect for breakfast, brunch, or an afternoon snack. If you don't have access to vanilla beans, use an additional teaspoon of high quality, pure vanilla extract for flavor.

INGREDIENTS | SERVES 8

1¼ cups brown rice flour, plus more for the baking sheet

¼ cup arrowroot starch

1 teaspoon xanthan gum

2 teaspoons baking powder

1 teaspoon baking soda

½ teaspoon salt

¼ cup sugar

2 vanilla beans, scraped, divided

½ cup cold butter, cut into chunks

2 large eggs

½ cup sour cream or plain yogurt

1 teaspoon vanilla extract

1 large egg white

1 tablespoon warm water

1 tablespoon coarse sugar

¾ cup confectioners' sugar

1 tablespoon milk or cream

How to Scrape Out a Vanilla Bean

Inside those long, dark, dried-out bean pods is a dark paste filled with tiny vanilla seeds. To remove the seeds from the pod, cut the bean in half lengthwise, separate the two pieces, and use the back of a knife to scrape out the seeds from the bean. Don't throw the pod out. You can place the scraped-out bean pod into a container with sugar and let it sit for two weeks or more. The vanilla pod gives the sugar a beautiful vanilla flavor and aroma. This sugar can be used the same way you would use any sugar, it just has a slight vanilla flavor.

1. Preheat the oven to 425°F. Line a baking sheet with parchment paper and sprinkle with brown rice flour. Set aside.
2. Place all of the dry ingredients, plus the seeds scraped from 1 vanilla bean, in the bowl of a food processor. Pulse to mix the ingredients.
3. Add the cold butter and pulse until the butter is the size of a pea. Add the eggs, sour cream, and vanilla extract. Pulse again, until the dough comes together in a ball. Spoon the dough onto your baking sheet.
4. Dust your hands with flour, then form the dough into a disk, 10" round and ¾"–1" thick. Cut into 8 even wedges and move the wedges apart, so they are not touching.
5. Whisk egg white with water. Brush the tops of the scones with the egg white mixture and sprinkle with the coarse sugar.
6. Bake for 13–16 minutes, or until the tops are golden-brown. Remove from oven and move scones to wire cooling rack for 15 minutes before topping with the vanilla drizzle.
7. Make the vanilla drizzle: In a small mixing bowl, stir together the seeds from 1 scraped vanilla bean, confectioners' sugar, and milk until the icing is smooth.
8. Place icing into a small zip-top plastic bag, and cut a small corner off the bag.
9. Place the parchment paper (that you baked the scones on) under the cooling rack that the scones are on. Drizzle icing onto the scones.
10. Serve immediately, or store in an airtight container once the scones are completely cool.

Sunday Pancakes

Pancakes are a weekend tradition in many families. Just because you're gluten-free doesn't mean you can't enjoy them too. These easy pancakes will be a favorite addition to your breakfast routine and can even be used as a gluten-free wrap for sandwiches.

INGREDIENTS | SERVES 4

1 cup sorghum flour
½ cup arrowroot starch
1½ teaspoons baking powder
1 teaspoon sugar
½ teaspoon sea salt
¼ teaspoon xanthan gum
2 teaspoons vanilla extract
1 cup almond milk
1 large egg
2 tablespoons light-tasting olive oil

1. In a medium bowl whisk together the sorghum flour, arrowroot starch, baking powder, sugar, sea salt, and xanthan gum. Make a well in the center of the dry ingredients and add the vanilla, almond milk, egg, and olive oil. Whisk together until you have a thickened batter.
2. Grease a large, heavy-bottomed skillet or nonstick pan with olive oil. Heat pan on medium-high heat until it's hot enough to make a drop of water sizzle. Pour ¼ cup of batter per pancake onto the hot skillet.
3. Cook until bubbles form on the top and pop and the edges are slightly dry. Flip with a spatula and cook the opposite side for 1–2 minutes.
4. Serve piping hot with butter or coconut oil and real maple syrup.

Hearty, Whole-Grain Pancakes

If you would like to add more fiber to these delicious pancakes, add 3 tablespoons of gluten-free rolled oats and 2–3 tablespoons of ground flaxseeds. Both will add fiber and plant protein, and the ground flaxseeds add heart-healthy omega-3 fatty acids.

Belgian Waffles

These waffles are a real treat! This recipe takes a little extra time and effort, as you will need to whip the egg whites and fold them into the batter. This helps give the waffles a super-light and crisp texture.

INGREDIENTS | SERVES 4

1 cup sorghum flour

¼ cup brown rice flour

½ cup arrowroot starch

½ teaspoon xanthan gum

½ teaspoon salt

2 teaspoons baking powder

1 tablespoon sugar

3 large egg yolks

3 tablespoons light-tasting olive oil

1½ cups almond milk

1 tablespoon vanilla extract

3 large egg whites, beaten until stiff peaks form

1. Preheat waffle iron according to manufacturer's instructions.
2. In a large bowl whisk together sorghum flour, brown rice flour, arrowroot starch, xanthan gum, salt, baking powder, and sugar.
3. In a smaller bowl whisk together egg yolks, olive oil, almond milk, and vanilla extract. Whisk the egg yolk mixture into the dry ingredients. Gently fold the beaten egg whites into the batter. Do not over mix, you don't want to "flatten" the air bubbles out of the egg whites.
4. Pour about ¼ cup of batter into the hot waffle iron and cook according to the manufacturer's instructions. It generally takes 2–3 minutes per waffle for large waffles, 1–2 minutes for smaller waffles.
5. Serve waffles piping hot with butter or coconut oil and real maple syrup.
6. Store any remaining waffles in an airtight container on the counter for 2–3 days. Waffles also will freeze well for up to 1 month.

Classic French Toast

French toast is one of those traditional breakfast recipes that's even better using gluten-free ingredients. Many brands of store-bought gluten-free bread are a bit dense, yet soak up liquids very well, making the perfect base for French toast. Feel free to use the homemade Basic Gluten-Free Sandwich Bread in Chapter 5 or your favorite store-bought gluten-free bread.

INGREDIENTS | SERVES 4

1 cup almond milk or other nondairy milk

3 large eggs

3 tablespoons sugar

1 teaspoon ground cinnamon

4 tablespoons light-tasting olive oil, butter, or melted coconut oil

8 slices gluten-free bread

1. In a large bowl with a wide bottom (large enough to dip a piece of bread), whisk together the milk, eggs, sugar, and cinnamon. If you don't have a wide bowl, you can also pour this mixture into a pie pan to prepare the French toast.
2. Heat a large, wide skillet on medium-high heat and add the olive oil, butter, or melted coconut oil. Heat for 3–4 minutes until the fat is sizzling.
3. Dip each piece of bread into the milk/egg mixture for 30 seconds on each side to soak.
4. Cook two slices of bread at a time in the hot skillet for 2–3 minutes per side until each side is golden brown. Repeat and cook all slices of coated bread.
5. Serve French toast piping hot with real maple syrup and additional butter or coconut oil.
6. Freeze any leftover slices in an airtight zip-top bag for up for 1 month. Slices can be reheated in the microwave for 30 seconds.

Popovers

These easy-to-make popovers can be enjoyed at breakfast or as a dinner roll. There's little flour in this recipe, so you can alter the gluten-free flours according to what you have on hand.

INGREDIENTS | SERVES 8

4 large eggs, brought to room temperature

1 cup almond milk

1 tablespoon honey

½ cup brown rice flour

½ cup arrowroot starch

¼ teaspoon salt

1. Preheat oven to 425°F. Place a muffin tin or popover pan in the oven while it's preheating to get it very hot.
2. In a blender, add eggs, milk, and honey. Blend for 10 seconds just to break up the eggs and mix them with the milk. Add the flour, arrowroot starch, and salt and blend for another 20–30 seconds, just until the flours are fully incorporated into the batter. Do not over blend.
3. Remove hot pan from oven and grease each cup with olive oil, nonstick spray, or butter. Pour batter into the hot muffin cups until they are about ⅔ full. Place the pan immediately back into oven and bake for 25 minutes. *Do not* open the oven while baking. (The popovers will fall if any cold air is introduced during the baking process.)
4. Remove the popovers from the oven after 25 minutes. They will be flaky and golden-brown. Prick each popover with a fork or a knife to release the steam from the inside. Serve immediately. They are delicious plain or with butter or coconut oil and jam.

Apple Oatmeal Breakfast Bars

These easy oatmeal bars filled with fresh fruit can also be served as a less-sugary dessert.

INGREDIENTS | SERVES 9

¾ cup brown rice flour

¾ cup arrowroot starch

1 teaspoon baking powder

¼ teaspoon salt

1½ cups gluten-free rolled oats

⅓ cup brown sugar, packed

¾ cup Spectrum Palm Shortening or butter

2–3 small apples, any variety, seeds removed, coarsely chopped or grated

2 teaspoons ground cinnamon

½ teaspoon ground nutmeg

¼ cup sugar

1 tablespoon honey

Breakfast Bar Variations

If you're not a fan of apples, use peaches, pears, blueberries, or other berries in place of the apples. You could also use 1 cup of pumpkin purée, butternut squash purée, or even cooked and mashed sweet potatoes in place of the apples.

1. Preheat oven to 350°F. Grease a 8" × 8" baking dish with nonstick cooking spray or olive oil, or line with parchment paper.
2. In a large bowl whisk together brown rice flour, arrowroot starch, baking powder, salt, rolled oats, and brown sugar. Using a pastry blender or a knife and fork cut in the shortening or butter until it resembles small peas throughout the mixture. Mix with a fork until you have a crumbly dough. Press half of the mixture into the bottom of the baking dish.
3. In a small saucepan mix together the chopped apples, cinnamon, nutmeg, sugar, and honey. Cook on medium heat for 8–10 minutes stirring every few minutes until the sugar is completely dissolved and the apples are soft. Pour the apple mixture over dough in the baking dish.
4. Sprinkle the remaining crumbly dough mixture evenly over the apples. Bake for 30–40 minutes until the tops of the bars are golden-brown. Allow bars to cool completely before cutting into 9 servings.
5. Store any remaining bars in an airtight container in the refrigerator for 2–3 days.

Easy Biscuit Cinnamon Rolls

These cinnamon rolls are yeast-free and don't have to rise before baking. They don't have the same texture as a traditional yeasty cinnamon roll, but they're just as delicious and a lot easier to make!

INGREDIENTS | SERVES 10

Gluten-free flour for dusting

Fluffy Buttermilk Biscuits dough (see recipe in this chapter)

3 tablespoons melted butter or coconut oil

½ cup sugar

1½ teaspoons cinnamon

¾ cup confectioners' sugar

2 tablespoons almond milk

1. Preheat oven to 400°F. Line an 8" × 9" cake pan or square pan with parchment paper and set aside.
2. Place a large sheet of plastic wrap, parchment paper, or wax paper down on a clean, flat surface. Dust the plastic wrap generously with gluten-free flour to help prevent the biscuit dough from sticking. Place dough on wrap and pat out into a 10" × 10" square or just into a large rectangle. Brush melted butter or coconut oil over the dough, leaving about ¼" around the edges of the dough unoiled. Sprinkle sugar and cinnamon evenly over the dough. Using the plastic wrap to help if necessary, gently roll up the square of dough into a large roll.
3. Using a sharp knife, cut the dough into 10 rolls. Place the rolls into cake pan. (It's fine if they are squeezed in side-to-side.) Bake for 20–25 minutes until golden-brown.
4. Allow to cool for 10–12 minutes.
5. In a small bowl whisk together the confectioners' sugar and almond milk to create a thin glaze. Drizzle evenly over the cinnamon rolls.

Ooey, Gooey Cinnamon Buns

Soft, gooey, yeasty cinnamon buns are perfect for special meals like Christmas morning breakfast! These buns rise beautifully, have a soft, doughy center, and will absolutely melt in your mouth.

INGREDIENTS | SERVES 8

Dough

¾ cup brown rice flour

¾ cup arrowroot starch

¼ teaspoon baking soda

2 teaspoons xanthan gum

2 teaspoons baking powder

½ teaspoon sea salt

2 tablespoons butter or coconut oil, melted

¼ cup sugar

⅔ cup almond milk

1 tablespoon rapid-rise yeast

1 large egg, room temperature

¼ cup light-tasting olive oil or canola oil

1 tablespoon vanilla extract

Filling

⅓ cup butter or coconut oil, softened

¾ cup packed brown sugar

2 tablespoons cinnamon

Icing

1½ cups confectioners' sugar

1½ tablespoons almond milk

Try a Different Type of Cinnamon

To give these cinnamon buns a slightly different flavor, try using a different type of cinnamon. You can find many varieties at gourmet spice shops and in most supermarkets. Some common "new" varieties are Saigon (Vietnamese) cinnamon, korintje cassia cinnamon, and Ceylon cinnamon. Each has a slightly different flavor and some are more spicy and hot than others.

1. In a large bowl whisk together the brown rice flour, arrowroot starch, baking soda, xanthan gum, baking powder, and salt. In a smaller bowl mix together melted butter, sugar, almond milk, and the yeast. Allow yeast mixture to sit for 5 minutes. Then stir in the egg, olive oil, and vanilla extract. Mix the wet ingredients into the flour mixture and stir until you have a very wet and sticky dough. Cover the bowl of dough with a towel, set in a warm place, and allow dough to rise for at least 1 hour. Chill the dough for 2–3 hours after it has risen; the dough will be much easier to work with if it's been refrigerated.

2. Gently roll out into a ¼" thick 12" × 12" square between 2 sheets of well-floured parchment paper or plastic wrap. Remove the top sheet of paper or plastic wrap and spread ⅓ cup of softened butter or coconut oil on the dough. Combine brown sugar and cinnamon and sprinkle over the buttered surface. Leave a 2" strip of dough uncovered at one end of the square. Using the bottom sheet of parchment paper or plastic wrap as an aid, roll up the dough jelly roll–style into a log.

3. Using a sharp, serrated knife, cut the log into 8 equal pieces and place the rolls in a large greased baking dish, leaving about an inch of room between each. Loosely cover the baking dish with plastic wrap and set in a warm place to allow rolls to rise for another hour.

4. When ready to bake, heat oven to 400°F. Bake for 18–22 minutes until the tops of the buns are golden-brown. Allow the buns to cool for 20–30 minutes.

5. Make the icing: In a small bowl mix together confectioners' sugar and almond milk. Drizzle generously over cooled cinnamon buns. If you or your family prefer more icing, double the recipe.

Brown Sugar Pecan Coffee Cake

This delicious, lightly sweetened yellow cake with a crumbly pecan and brown sugar topping is a wonderful (and quick) dessert.

INGREDIENTS | SERVES 9

Cake

½ cup brown rice flour

½ cup arrowroot starch

½ teaspoon xanthan gum

½ cup sugar

½ teaspoon sea salt

1½ teaspoons baking powder

1 large egg

⅓ cup melted butter or light-tasting olive oil

½ cup almond milk

1 teaspoon vanilla extract

Topping

1 teaspoon cinnamon

½ cup brown sugar

2 tablespoons brown rice flour

⅓ cup finely chopped pecans

2 tablespoons butter or coconut oil

1. Preheat oven to 375°F. Grease an 8" × 8" cake pan with nonstick cooking spray or olive oil, or line with parchment paper.
2. In a large bowl whisk together brown rice flour, arrowroot starch, xanthan gum, sugar, sea salt, and baking powder. Make a well in the center of the dry ingredients and mix together egg, melted butter, almond milk, and vanilla extract. Stir into the dry ingredients and mix together into a thick cake batter.
3. Pour batter into cake pan. In a small bowl mix together all of the topping ingredients into a crumbly mixture. Evenly sprinkle the topping over the cake. Bake 20–25 minutes until the cake is golden-brown and a toothpick inserted into the middle comes out clean.
4. Allow cake to cool for 15–20 minutes before slicing. Store leftover cake in an airtight container on the counter for 2–3 days. This cake freezes well for up to 1 month.

Blueberry Breakfast Cake

To turn this recipe into a blueberry breakfast cake, add 1 cup frozen or fresh blueberries to the batter. To the topping add 3 tablespoons of rolled oats in place of the brown rice flour and then bake as directed. Feel free to leave out the pecans if you're nut-sensitive or just don't like them.

Baked Chocolate Doughnuts

One of the things you might miss most when on a gluten-free diet is doughnuts. These quick doughnuts are baked, making them a (slightly) healthier option.

INGREDIENTS | SERVES 6

Doughnuts

¾ cup brown rice flour

¼ cup plus 1 tablespoon arrowroot starch

½ teaspoon xanthan gum

3 tablespoons cocoa powder

½ cup sugar

1 teaspoon baking powder

¼ teaspoon salt

2 large eggs

¼ cup light-tasting olive oil or canola oil

¼ cup almond milk

½ teaspoon apple cider vinegar

Frosting

1 cup confectioners' sugar

2 tablespoons cocoa powder

2 tablespoons butter or coconut oil, softened

1–2 tablespoons almond milk

1. Preheat oven to 375°F. Lightly grease a doughnut pan.
2. In a large bowl, whisk together all the dry ingredients.
3. In a smaller bowl, whisk together all the wet ingredients.
4. Pour the wet ingredients into the dry ingredients and stir until fully combined.
5. Spoon mixture into prepared doughnut pan. Bake 10–12 minutes, or until a toothpick inserted into the thickest part of the doughnut comes out clean.
6. Let doughnuts sit 5 minutes before turning them out onto a cooling rack. Allow to cool completely before frosting.
7. Make the frosting: Stir together confectioners' sugar, 2 tablespoons cocoa powder, butter, and enough milk to make the glaze the consistency you want. Dip cooled doughnuts into glaze and top with sprinkles, chopped nuts, or shredded coconut, if you prefer.

Mini Confectioners' Sugar Doughnuts

*Doughnut pans are a fun tool to have in your kitchen. If you only have
a large doughnut pan, this recipe will make 6 large doughnuts.*

INGREDIENTS | SERVES 8

2 tablespoons Spectrum Palm Shortening

⅓ cup sugar

1 large egg

2 teaspoons vanilla extract

¾ cup brown rice flour

½ cup arrowroot starch

½ teaspoon cinnamon

½ teaspoon baking powder

½ teaspoon baking soda

¼ teaspoon sea salt

¼ teaspoon xanthan gum

⅓ cup almond milk

1 cup confectioners' sugar

1. Preheat oven to 350°F. Generously grease a mini-doughnut pan with nonstick cooking spray or olive oil.
2. In a large bowl cream together the shortening and the sugar. Stir in the egg and vanilla and set aside.
3. In a small bowl whisk together brown rice flour, arrowroot starch, cinnamon, baking powder, baking soda, sea salt, and xanthan gum. Stir ⅓ cup flour mixture into the creamed mixture. Then add ⅓ of the milk and stir until incorporated into the batter. Repeat with the flour mixture and milk until all has been used.
4. Spoon batter into a large plastic zip-top plastic bag. Cut off a corner of the zip-top bag to make a ½" opening. Squeeze the batter into the doughnut pans. Bake 8–10 minutes. Remove doughnuts from pan and place on a wire rack to cool.
5. Once the doughnuts are cool, put confectioners' sugar in a large zip-top plastic bag. Add the doughnuts, seal the bag, and shake to coat all the doughnuts. Serve immediately. Doughnuts are best the day they are made, but can be frozen for up to 1 month.

Ultimate Monkey Bread

This sweet, sticky bread is a fabulous dessert, but many people
also serve it for breakfast on special occasions.

INGREDIENTS | SERVES 10

½ cup chopped pecans

1¾ cups brown rice flour

1½ cups arrowroot starch

1 tablespoon rapid-rise yeast

3 tablespoons sugar

½ teaspoon salt

1 tablespoon xanthan gum

¼ cup gluten-free instant vanilla pudding mix (dry)

1 teaspoon baking powder

½ cup water

¾ cup butter, divided

¾ cup milk

1 large egg, room temperature

1 teaspoon apple cider vinegar

2 tablespoons oil

1½ teaspoons vanilla extract, divided

½ cup rehydrated raisins (optional)

½ cup sugar

1–2 teaspoons ground cinnamon

1 cup brown sugar

2 tablespoons maple syrup

Pinch salt

2 tablespoons heavy cream

1. Place chopped pecans in the bottom of a Bundt cake or tube pan. Set aside. Do not use a pan with a removable bottom, as the syrup would run through and make a mess.
2. In the bowl of a stand mixer, whisk together the brown rice flour, arrowroot starch, yeast, sugar, salt, xanthan gum, vanilla pudding mix, and baking powder until combined. Set aside.
3. Put water and ¼ cup butter in a glass measuring cup and microwave just until the butter has melted. Remove from microwave and stir. Add milk, egg, vinegar, oil, and 1 teaspoon vanilla extract and whisk to combine.
4. With the stand mixer running (using the paddle attachment), pour the wet ingredients into the dry ingredients. Scrape down the bowl if you have to. Add the raisins (if using).
5. Allow to mix on medium speed for 3 minutes.
6. In a shallow bowl, stir together ½ cup sugar and cinnamon. Form the dough into ¾" balls and roll them to coat them fully with cinnamon-sugar mixture.
7. Place sugar-coated dough in the Bundt pan on top of the pecans. Do not tightly pack the dough into the pan; allow gaps between the dough. Repeat until all the dough has been formed, rolled in the cinnamon-sugar mixture, and placed in the pan. If you have any cinnamon-sugar mixture left, sprinkle it over dough in the pan.
8. In a small saucepan over low heat, melt ½ cup butter. Stir in the brown sugar, maple syrup, salt, and ½ teaspoon vanilla until the sugar is dissolved. Stir in the heavy cream. Pour mixture over the top of the dough.
9. If you want to freeze the dough, wrap the pan in 2 layers of plastic wrap and place in the freezer.

10. To bake immediately, allow the dough to rise for 20–30 minutes in a warm, draft-free place. Bake in preheated 350°F oven for 30–35 minutes. When you remove the Monkey Bread from the oven, allow it to sit in the baking pan for 5 minutes before turning it out onto a serving dish or plate. To do this, place the plate upside down on top of the baking pan, and (while wearing oven mitts) quickly turn the plate and baking pan upside down. Your Monkey Bread should release from the pan easily. If there are still pecans and syrup in the pan, spoon mixture over the top of the Monkey Bread. Wait 10–15 minutes before serving. This not only allows the syrup to cool, but also improves the bread's texture.

Zucchini Bread

People always seem to end up with extra zucchini in the summer months when it's prolific in backyard gardens. This bread is great as a light dessert or as a gift.

INGREDIENTS | SERVES 8

1 cup brown rice flour

1 cup arrowroot starch

1 teaspoon xanthan gum

1 teaspoon cinnamon

½ teaspoon cloves

2 teaspoons baking powder

½ teaspoon sea salt

2 large eggs

½ cup sugar

⅓ cup light-tasting olive oil or canola oil

⅓ cup plus 2 tablespoons freshly squeezed orange juice (about 1 large orange)

1½ cups grated fresh zucchini

1 cup chopped walnuts (optional)

1. Preheat oven to 350°F. Grease an 8½" × 4½" loaf pan with nonstick cooking spray.
2. In a large bowl whisk together brown rice flour, arrowroot starch, xanthan gum, cinnamon, cloves, baking powder, and salt.
3. In a smaller bowl mix together eggs, sugar, olive oil, ⅓ cup orange juice, and zucchini. Pour the wet ingredients into the dry ingredients and stir to combine. The batter should be like a thick cake batter, but not as thick as bread dough. If the batter is too thick, add additional orange juice 1 tablespoon at a time until it's the correct consistency. Fold in the walnuts, if desired.
4. Pour batter into loaf pan and spread evenly. Bake for 50–60 minutes until a toothpick inserted in the middle of the loaf comes out clean. Allow to cool for 20–30 minutes before slicing.
5. For any remaining leftovers, wrap the slices individually in plastic wrap, place in an airtight zip-top plastic bag, and freeze for up to 1 month.

Apple Spice Bread

*Applesauce and fresh apple combine in this delicious recipe to make
a quick bread that's perfect for a snack or after-school treat.*

INGREDIENTS | SERVES 8

1 cup sorghum flour

¾ cup arrowroot starch

1 teaspoon xanthan gum

¼ teaspoon salt

1 teaspoon ground cinnamon

¼ teaspoon ground nutmeg

⅛ teaspoon ground allspice

⅛ teaspoon ground cardamom

1 teaspoon baking powder

½ teaspoon baking soda

1 cup brown sugar

2 large eggs

2 tablespoons oil

1 teaspoon vanilla

½ cup unsweetened applesauce

1 cup of your favorite apple, peeled and grated

½ cup dried currants (optional)

1. Preheat oven to 350°F. Spray a 9" × 5" loaf pan with non-stick cooking spray and set aside.
2. In a large bowl, combine sorghum flour, arrowroot starch, xanthan gum, salt, cinnamon, nutmeg, allspice, cardamom, baking powder, and baking soda; mix well.
3. In a medium bowl, combine brown sugar, eggs, oil, vanilla, applesauce, apple, and currants, if using; mix well. Stir into dry ingredients just until mixed. Pour into prepared pan.
4. Bake for 50–55 minutes, or until deep golden-brown and a toothpick inserted in the center comes out clean. Let cool in pan for 5 minutes; remove to wire rack to cool completely.

Brown Sugar

Brown sugar can dry out quickly if kept in its original packaging. To make it last longer, buy a brown-sugar disc, a small pottery disc soaked in water. Pack the brown sugar into an airtight container and top with the disc. Make sure the cover is fastened securely. Store in a cool, dark place.

Lemon Poppy Seed Bread

This classic poppy seed loaf is a delicious bread to serve at a spring or Easter luncheon.

INGREDIENTS | SERVES 8

1½ cups brown rice flour

1 cup arrowroot starch

½ teaspoon xanthan gum

½ teaspoon sea salt

1 tablespoon baking powder

¾ cup sugar

3 tablespoons poppy seeds

¼ cup unsweetened applesauce

¼ cup light-tasting olive oil or canola oil

¼ cup fresh lemon juice (about 1 large lemon)

2 tablespoons fresh lemon zest

2 large eggs

¾ cup almond milk

1. Preheat oven to 350°F. Line a 9" × 5" loaf pan with parchment paper and grease with nonstick cooking spray.
2. In a large bowl whisk together brown rice flour, arrowroot starch, xanthan gum, salt, baking powder, sugar, and poppy seeds. In a smaller bowl mix together applesauce, olive oil, lemon juice, lemon zest, eggs, and almond milk. Pour wet ingredients into dry ingredients and stir thoroughly to combine.
3. Pour batter into loaf pan. Bake for 55–65 minutes until a toothpick inserted in the middle comes out clean and top is golden-brown. Allow to cool for 20–30 minutes on a wire rack before slicing.
4. Wrap leftover slices individually in plastic wrap, place in an airtight zip-top plastic bag, and freeze for up to 1 month.

Blueberry French Toast Casserole

Store-bought gluten-free bread is too expensive to waste if it becomes stale.
This recipe uses leftover or stale bread to make a delicious breakfast.

INGREDIENTS | SERVES 6

7 cups gluten-free bread, cubed

1⅓ cups almond milk

5 large eggs, whisked

1 tablespoon vanilla

1 tablespoon maple syrup

½ teaspoon salt

2 tablespoons butter or coconut oil, melted

3 tablespoons sugar

2 teaspoons cinnamon

1½ cups blueberries, fresh or frozen

1. Preheat oven to 350°F. Grease a 3- or 4-quart casserole dish with nonstick spray.
2. In a large bowl mix together the cubed bread, almond milk, eggs, vanilla, maple syrup, and salt. Pour mixture into the baking dish.
3. Drizzle melted butter or coconut oil over the casserole. Sprinkle cinnamon and sugar evenly over the bread. Top with blueberries.
4. Bake for 35–40 minutes until top of casserole is golden-brown. Allow to cool for 5–10 minutes before serving.

Do You Have to Use Almond Milk?

If you are not dairy-intolerant you can use any type of milk you'd like—regular milk, soy milk, rice milk, even coconut milk. Almond milk is a great nondairy alternative because it tastes good and has a consistent thickness that works well in gluten-free baking.

Cheesy Hash Brown Casserole

This is a perfect breakfast, brunch, or light supper recipe. You can put it together the night before, place in the fridge, and then pop in the oven for a quick meal.

INGREDIENTS | SERVES 4

1 package shredded hash browns, squeezed dry of all water

2 large eggs

2 cups shredded Cheddar cheese, divided

1 cup mayonnaise

¼ cup chopped onion

½ cup melted butter or margarine, divided

1½ cups gluten-free Rice Chex, crushed

1. Preheat oven to 350°F. Grease a 2-quart casserole dish with olive oil or nonstick cooking spray.
2. Mix together drained hash browns, eggs, 1½ cups cheese, mayonnaise, onions, and ¼ cup butter. Pour into casserole dish.
3. In small bowl stir together crushed cereal, ¼ cup butter, and ½ cup of cheese. Spread topping evenly over hash browns.
4. Bake for 40–45 minutes until casserole is golden-brown on top and bubbly around the edges. Allow to cool for 10 minutes before serving.

Ham and Cheese Oven-Baked Omelet

Eggs are one of the most affordable proteins available and they are naturally gluten-free. If you make a large family-size omelet like this on Sunday evening you'll have ready-made breakfasts all week.

INGREDIENTS | SERVES 4

10 large eggs

½ teaspoon ground mustard

½ teaspoon salt

½ teaspoon paprika

½ teaspoon ground pepper

½ teaspoon dill weed (optional)

1½ cups diced ham

1½ cups shredded Cheddar cheese

½ cup chopped green onions

1. Preheat oven to 350°F. Generously grease a large 2- or 3-quart casserole dish with nonstick cooking spray.
2. Whisk eggs in a large bowl. Add in mustard, salt, paprika, pepper, and dill weed. Stir in ham.
3. Pour egg mixture into the casserole dish. Sprinkle cheese and scallions over the top of the egg mixture.
4. Bake for 25–30 minutes until the omelet is set and a toothpick inserted in the middle comes out clean.

Amish Baked Oatmeal

*A regional dish from Lancaster, Pennsylvania, this simple baked oatmeal
is sweet and hearty. Serve cut in squares and drizzled with maple syrup
for breakfast, or for a unique dessert, serve it warm with ice cream.*

INGREDIENTS | SERVES 6

3 cups gluten-free rolled oats

2 teaspoons baking powder

1 teaspoon salt

2 large eggs, gently whisked

¼ cup butter, melted

¾ cup brown sugar

1½ cups milk

Room for Interpretation

As is, this simple oatmeal cake tastes like warm, salty butter and brown sugar. Yet you can make endless flavor variations with it. Add any combination of raisins, chocolate chips, sliced almonds, pecans, chopped walnuts, diced apples, dried cherries, dried cranberries, cocoa powder, vanilla, cinnamon, or freshly grated nutmeg to create your own unique adaptation.

1. Preheat oven to 350°F. Grease a 2- or 3-quart casserole dish.
2. In a large bowl mix together the oats, baking powder, and salt.
3. Make a well in the center of the dry ingredients and add the eggs, melted butter, brown sugar, and milk. Mix together thoroughly.
4. Pour oatmeal batter into baking dish. Bake for 40 minutes until the oatmeal is golden-brown and a toothpick inserted in the middle comes out clean. Cut in squares to serve.
5. This oatmeal is almost like a cake or brownie in texture. If you want a more creamy-textured oatmeal, add an additional cup of milk to the batter before cooking.

English Muffins

There's something incredibly comforting about this cornmeal-crusted, tender bread with big air pockets that soak up lots of butter and jam. Some English muffins are cooked on the stovetop, but these are baked, and a little less work.

INGREDIENTS | SERVES 8

Gluten-free coarse cornmeal, for sprinkling

½ cup sorghum flour

¼ cup brown rice flour

¾ cup arrowroot starch

1 teaspoon xanthan gum

½ teaspoon salt

1 tablespoon sugar

2 teaspoons rapid-rise yeast

1 teaspoon olive oil

¾ cup plus 1 tablespoon hot water

Make Your Own English Muffin Rings

You can buy metal rings to bake English muffins in, or you can make your own. Simply fold sheets of foil into 1" strips and staple them into a circle about the size of a tuna can. You can also use the metal rings from wide-mouth canning jars. Just place them top-side down on the baking sheet and add the dough.

1. Line a baking sheet with parchment paper and place 6–8 English muffin rings or foil rings on the parchment. Generously sprinkle cornmeal in the bottoms of the rings.
2. In a large bowl whisk together sorghum flour, brown rice flour, arrowroot starch, xanthan gum, salt, sugar, and yeast. Make a well in the center of the ingredients and add the olive oil and water. Stir together into a thick batter.
3. Divide the dough evenly between the English muffin rings. Smooth muffin tops by wetting your finger with water and then running your finger gently over the top of each muffin. Generously sprinkle additional cornmeal on top of each muffin. Loosely cover muffins with plastic wrap and set in a warm place to rise for 30–40 minutes.
4. Once the muffins have doubled in size, preheat oven to 375°F. Bake muffins for 15–20 minutes until golden-brown. Flip over the muffins after 8–9 minutes if you want them evenly browned on both sides.
5. Remove the muffins from the rings and allow them to cool for 10–15 minutes before eating. Break muffins apart with a fork to get the nooks and crannies of a traditional English muffin. These muffins are delicious toasted! Muffins are best on the first day. Freeze any remaining muffins for up to 1 month.

Bagels

This recipe makes four jumbo-sized bagels or eight smaller ones. To freeze, wrap them in plastic wrap and put them in a zip-top plastic bag before putting them in the freezer.

INGREDIENTS | SERVES 4

1 cup brown rice flour

½ cup sorghum flour

1 cup arrowroot starch

½ cup ground flaxseeds

1 tablespoon xanthan gum

1½ teaspoons salt

1 tablespoon rapid-rise yeast

2 tablespoons agave nectar or honey

1 teaspoon apple cider vinegar

2 tablespoons oil

1¼ cups warm water

2 teaspoons vegetable shortening, to grease your hands to form the bagels

1 tablespoon molasses

Sesame seeds, flaxseeds, chia seeds, onion flakes, garlic granules, poppy seeds, or coarse salt (optional)

More on Flaxseed

Ground flaxseed is a great topping for these bagels—it contains fiber and healthy omega-3 fatty acids, and adds stability and texture to gluten-free baked breads. You can grind whole flaxseeds using a coffee grinder. Store ground flaxseed in the fridge or freezer, so it doesn't go rancid quickly.

1. Line a baking sheet with parchment paper.
2. In the bowl of a stand mixer, mix all the dry ingredients together until well blended. In a small bowl, whisk together agave nectar or honey, vinegar, oil, and water.
3. With the mixer slowly running, pour in the wet ingredients. Then mix on medium speed for 3 minutes.
4. Grease your hands with the vegetable shortening. Take a quarter of the dough and form it into a bagel shape, using your finger to create a large hole in the center of the bagel. Place the formed bagels on the baking sheet. Give them plenty of space as they will grow a lot as they rise. Repeat to create 4 large bagels.
5. Place the baking sheet in a warm, draft-free place, and allow bagels to rise for 35–40 minutes, or until they are nearly doubled in size.
6. While the bagels are rising, fill a large pot three-quarters full with water. Bring to a rolling boil and add the molasses to the water. (The molasses will create a nice chewy outside to the bagel.)
7. Preheat the oven to 400°F. When the bagels have finished rising, gently place one at a time in the boiling water. Boil on one side for 30 seconds, flip, and boil for another 30 seconds. Remove bagels from water with a slotted spoon, and place on a cooling rack that has been placed over another baking sheet, allowing the water to drip off. Place boiled bagels back on the baking sheet. At this time, you can sprinkle the tops with whatever toppings you desire.
8. Bake the bagels for 20–25 minutes, or until they are golden-brown. Remove from oven, and allow to cool on a cooling rack for 10 minutes before eating. You can eat the bagels warm, or allow them to cool completely before storing in a zip-top plastic bag.

Breakfast Pizza

This quick breakfast pizza features a flat, crispy crust topped with traditional breakfast fare.

INGREDIENTS | SERVES 8

¾ cup sorghum flour

¼ cup arrowroot starch

¼ teaspoon sea salt

1 teaspoon rapid-rise yeast

½ teaspoon sugar

½ cup warm water

1–2 tablespoons olive oil

1 Roma tomato, thinly sliced

1 cup fresh spinach

2 large eggs, scrambled and cooked

6 slices bacon, cooked and crumbled

½ cup mild sausage, cooked and crumbled

1 cup shredded Cheddar cheese

1. Preheat oven to 400°F. Line a round pizza pan or a rectangular cookie sheet with parchment paper.
2. In a large bowl whisk together sorghum flour, arrowroot starch, sea salt, yeast, and sugar. Make a well in the center of the dry ingredients and add the warm water. Stir until you have a stiff round ball of dough.
3. Drizzle olive oil over the parchment paper and roll out the pizza crust onto the paper. Bake for 10–12 minutes until the crust is slightly brown and crisp on the edges.
4. Top the pizza with tomato slices, spinach, scrambled eggs, bacon, sausage, and cheese. Return pizza to oven and bake an additional 10–12 minutes until toppings are warmed through and the cheese has melted.
5. Allow pizza to cool for 5–10 minutes before slicing.

Quick Pizza Crust Mix

To create your own homemade pizza crust kit, whisk together sorghum flour, arrowroot starch, sea salt, yeast, and sugar. Put in a glass jar or a zip-top plastic bag and seal tightly. These dry ingredients can be stored in the pantry for 3–4 months. When you're ready to make pizza dough, add ½ cup warm water and mix together into a thick dough. Press out onto parchment paper that's been greased with olive oil and bake for 15 minutes at 350°F.

Cream Cheese Raspberry Danish

Thought you'd never eat a Danish again? Although this isn't a traditional short dough, it makes a wonderful Danish and you can fill these pastries with your favorite jam.

INGREDIENTS | SERVES 12

1 cup sorghum flour

1 cup arrowroot starch

1½ teaspoons baking powder

1 teaspoon xanthan gum

3½ tablespoons sugar, divided

½ teaspoon salt

⅓ cup butter or Spectrum Palm Shortening

⅔ cup plus 1 tablespoon almond milk, divided

½ teaspoon almond extract

4 ounces cream cheese, softened

¼ cup raspberry jam

Danish Glaze

To make a quick glaze for the Danish, mix together 1 cup confectioners' sugar with 2 tablespoons almond milk. If glaze is too thick, add more milk a few drops at a time until it's the correct consistency. Drizzle over cooled Danish and serve.

1. Preheat oven to 400°F. Line a large baking sheet with parchment paper.
2. In a large bowl whisk together sorghum flour, arrowroot starch, baking powder, xanthan gum, 2 tablespoons sugar, and salt. Using a pastry blender or a knife and fork, cut in butter or shortening until it resembles very small peas throughout the dry ingredients. Make a well in the center of dry ingredients and add ⅔ cup almond milk and almond extract. Stir into the dry ingredients until you have a thick, workable dough.
3. Divide the dough into 12 balls. Place the balls of dough about 1 inch apart on the baking sheet. Using a heavy glass, gently flatten each ball and using a spoon, make a round indentation in the center of the dough.
4. In a small bowl mix together cream cheese, 1½ tablespoons of sugar, and 1 tablespoon of almond milk. Add 1 teaspoon of the cream cheese mixture to each Danish. Then add 1 teaspoon of raspberry jam on top of the cream cheese mixture. Bake pastries for 10–12 minutes until lightly browned along the edges.
5. Allow pastries to cool on the pan for 15–20 minutes.

CHAPTER 3

Make It Easy: Baking with a Homemade Gluten-Free Mix

Homemade Gluten-Free Baking Mix

This mix is similar to a popular store brand that you can use to make biscuits and pancakes. However, this version is much cheaper. You can whip it up in just a few minutes and have it handy for any of the recipes in this chapter, or any recipe calling for that popular store-bought mix.

INGREDIENTS | YIELDS ABOUT 7 CUPS

3 cups brown rice flour
2 cups sorghum flour
2 cups arrowroot starch
2½ teaspoons xanthan gum
2 teaspoons salt
3 tablespoons baking powder
½ cup vegetable shortening or Spectrum Palm Shortening

Make a Healthier Mix

To make this mix even healthier add ¼ cup ground flaxseeds and ¼ cup brown rice protein powder or blanched almond flour. This will add fiber, omega-3 fatty acids, and healthy plant proteins.

1. In a very large mixing bowl (the bigger the better) whisk together the brown rice flour, sorghum flour, arrowroot starch, xanthan gum, salt, and baking powder. Whisk very, very well until the mix is thoroughly incorporated.
2. Using a pastry blender or a knife and fork, cut in the vegetable shortening so that it is well combined into the flour mixture. Pour the mixture into a large glass or plastic container with an airtight lid. This baking mix can be stored for up to 6 months in your pantry, or frozen and refrigerated for several months.

Easy Blueberry Muffins

You can whip up and bake these moist gluten-free muffins in less than 20 minutes. This recipe is for a small batch of six muffins, but it doubles easily for more.

INGREDIENTS | SERVES 6

1 cup gluten-free baking mix
¼ cup sugar
⅓ cup almond milk
1 large egg
1 teaspoon vanilla extract
⅓ cup frozen or fresh blueberries

1. Preheat oven to 350°F. Line a muffin pan with paper liners and grease them with nonstick cooking spray or olive oil.
2. In a medium bowl whisk together the baking mix and sugar. Make a well in the center of the dry ingredients and add the almond milk, egg, and vanilla extract. Stir until combined. Fold in the blueberries.
3. Spoon batter into paper liners until about ¾ full. Bake for 15–18 minutes until a toothpick inserted in the middle comes out clean.

Apple Cinnamon Muffins

This recipe is so easy to make, you could easily whip up a batch of these muffins on an average weekday morning. Perfect for sending with the kids to the bus stop or packing with lunches.

INGREDIENTS | SERVES 6

1 cup gluten-free baking mix

¼ cup sugar

½ teaspoon ground cinnamon

¼ teaspoon freshly grated nutmeg

⅓ cup almond milk

1 large egg

1 teaspoon vanilla extract

1 medium apple, peeled, cored, and chopped (about ½ cup chopped apple)

1. Preheat oven to 350°F. Line a muffin pan with paper liners and grease them with nonstick cooking spray or olive oil.
2. In a medium bowl whisk together the baking mix, sugar, cinnamon, and nutmeg. Make a well in the center of the dry ingredients and add the almond milk, egg, and vanilla extract. Stir until combined. Fold in the chopped apples.
3. Spoon batter into paper liners until about ¾ full. Bake for 15–18 minutes until a toothpick inserted in the middle comes out clean.

Banana Nut Muffins

Here's a recipe for a small batch of hearty banana muffins.
It's a perfect way to use that one leftover banana that never gets eaten.

INGREDIENTS | SERVES 6

1 cup gluten-free baking mix

¼ cup sugar

½ teaspoon ground cinnamon

⅓ cup almond milk

1 large egg

1 teaspoon vanilla extract

1 medium banana, mashed (about ½ cup)

¼ cup chopped pecans or walnuts

1. Preheat oven to 350°F. Line a muffin pan with paper liners and grease them with nonstick cooking spray or olive oil.
2. In a medium bowl whisk together the baking mix, sugar, and cinnamon. Make a well in the center of the dry ingredients and add the almond milk, egg, and vanilla extract. Stir until combined. Fold in the banana and nuts.
3. Spoon batter into paper liners until about ¾ full. Bake for 15–18 minutes until a toothpick inserted in the middle comes out clean.

Basic Pancakes

Pancakes can be eaten not only for breakfast, but also as a last-minute gluten-free sandwich bread, as "breakfast-for-dinner," or even as dessert when stacked between whipped cream and topped with cinnamon.

INGREDIENTS | SERVES 4

1 cup gluten-free baking mix
1 cup almond milk
1 large egg

1. In a medium bowl whisk together baking mix, milk, and egg. Mix until thoroughly incorporated into a smooth batter. This can also be done in about 30 seconds in a blender.
2. Grease a heavy-bottomed skillet or griddle pan with butter, oil, or nonstick cooking spray. Heat over medium-high heat until a few drops of water flicked onto the pan sizzle immediately. Pour about 2 tablespoons of batter per pancake onto skillet. Continue to cook on medium-high heat until bubbles form and pop on top of the pancakes, or until the edges appear dry. Flip and cook an additional 30 seconds to 1 minute, until the pancake bottoms are golden-brown. Serve piping hot with butter or coconut oil and syrup or jam.

Chunky Apple Pancakes

These pancakes have a little surprise of apple in each bite and are a delicious alternative to traditional pancakes. Add a few teaspoons of ground flaxseeds for even more nutritious goodness.

INGREDIENTS | SERVES 4

1 cup gluten-free baking mix
½ teaspoon cinnamon
1 cup almond milk
1 large egg
1 medium apple, peeled, cored, and chopped (about ½ cup)

1. In a medium bowl whisk together baking mix, cinnamon, milk, and the egg. Mix until thoroughly incorporated into a smooth batter. This can also be done in about 30 seconds in a blender. Fold in chopped apples.
2. Grease a heavy-bottomed skillet or griddle pan with butter, oil, or nonstick cooking spray. Heat over medium-high heat until a few drops of water flicked onto the pan sizzle immediately. Continue to cook on medium-high heat until bubbles form and pop on top of the pancakes, or until the edges appear dry. Flip and cook an additional 30 seconds to 1 minute, until pancake bottoms are golden-brown. Serve piping hot with butter or coconut oil and syrup or jam.

Gingerbread Pancakes

These little cakes are hearty and almost like cookies—a fun twist on the plain old pancake.
Serve with additional molasses or lemon sauce on top.

INGREDIENTS | SERVES 4

1 cup gluten-free baking mix
½ teaspoon ground cinnamon
½ teaspoon ground ginger
2 tablespoons molasses or brown sugar
1 cup almond milk
1 large egg

A Quick Lemon Sauce for Gingerbread Pancakes

The tang of lemon pairs perfectly with the sweet spiciness of gingerbread. Make a quick sauce for these pancakes by adding ½ cup sugar, 2 tablespoons cornstarch, ¾ cup water, ¼ cup lemon juice, 2 tablespoons of butter or coconut oil, and the zest from one lemon to a medium saucepan. Cook over medium heat, whisking constantly for about 5 minutes until the sauce has thickened. Serve immediately over pancakes.

1. In a medium bowl whisk together baking mix, cinnamon, ginger, molasses, ¾ cup milk, and the egg. If the batter is too thick add an additional ¼ cup of milk.
2. Grease a heavy-bottomed skillet or griddle pan with butter, oil, or nonstick cooking spray. Heat over medium-high heat until a few drops of water flicked onto the pan sizzle immediately. Pour about 2 tablespoons of batter per pancake onto skillet. Continue to cook on medium-high heat until bubbles form and pop on top of the pancakes, or until the edges appear dry. Flip and cook an additional 30 seconds to 1 minute, until pancake bottoms are golden-brown.
3. Serve piping hot with butter or coconut oil and syrup or jam.

Chocolate Chip Pecan Pancakes

Chocolate chip pancakes are a favorite of kids and chocolate lovers everywhere!
Feel free to use a different type of nut or leave the pecans out completely.

INGREDIENTS | SERVES 4

1 cup gluten-free baking mix

1 cup almond milk

2 tablespoons sugar

2 teaspoons vanilla extract

1 large egg

⅓ cup mini chocolate chips

¼ cup chopped pecans

A Fun Christmas Gift

In a clean half-pint glass jar layer the baking mix, sugar, chocolate chips, and pecans. Close with an airtight lid and tie a ribbon around the jar. Add a small notecard with instructions for adding milk, vanilla, and an egg and you have an easy, gluten-free Christmas gift.

1. In a medium bowl whisk together baking mix, ¾ cup milk, sugar, vanilla, and the egg. If the batter is too thick add an additional ¼ cup of milk. Stir in the chocolate chips and nuts.
2. Grease a heavy-bottomed skillet or griddle pan with butter, oil, or nonstick cooking spray. Heat over medium-high heat until a few drops of water flicked onto the pan sizzle immediately. Pour about 2 tablespoons of batter per pancake onto skillet. Continue to cook on medium-high heat until bubbles form and pop on top of the pancakes, or until the edges appear dry. Flip and cook an additional 30 seconds to 1 minute, until pancake bottoms are golden-brown.
3. Serve piping hot with butter or coconut oil and syrup or jam.

Oatmeal Raisin Scones

Scones are perfect with hot tea. Top these with an easy and decadent lemon glaze.

INGREDIENTS | SERVES 12–16

1¾ cups gluten-free baking mix

½ cup gluten-free quick-cooking oats

¾ cup raisins

1⅓ cups full-fat coconut milk or whipping cream

½ teaspoon almond extract

2 tablespoons coarse sugar or turbinado sugar

Lemon Glaze

Mix 1 cup of confectioners' sugar with 2–3 tablespoons of fresh lemon juice and stir vigorously with a whisk or fork until the glaze is smooth and creamy. If the glaze is too thick, thin with additional lemon juice 1 teaspoon at a time, until desired consistency is achieved. Drizzle over cooled scones and serve.

1. Preheat oven to 350°F. Line a large baking sheet with parchment paper.
2. In a large bowl mix together baking mix, oats, and raisins. Stir until thoroughly combined and raisins are evenly distributed throughout the mix.
3. Stir in the coconut milk and almond extract until you have a thick, slightly sticky dough.
4. Divide the dough into two balls and place on baking sheet. Pat each ball into a 4"–5" round disk that's about an inch thick. Divide each disk into 6–8 slices with a sharp knife. Gently separate the slices about 1" apart on the baking sheet. Sprinkle coarse sugar over scones and bake for 11–15 minutes until golden-brown.
5. Allow scones to cool completely on a wire rack and then drizzle with lemon glaze, if desired. Store leftover scones in an airtight container on the counter for up to 3 days. Scones can be frozen for up to 1 month.

Gluten-Free Drop Biscuits

*Do you miss "whack 'em on the counter" biscuits that come in refrigerated cans?
These gluten-free biscuits are just as quick and easy, and really tasty.*

INGREDIENTS | SERVES 6

1¼ cups gluten-free baking mix

3 tablespoons butter or Spectrum Palm Shortening

1 large egg

2–4 tablespoons cold water, as needed

1. Preheat oven to 350°F. Line a small baking sheet with parchment paper. In a medium bowl add gluten-free baking mix and cut in shortening with a fork and knife or a pastry blender until it's fully incorporated into the flour. Stir in the egg and 1 tablespoon of water at a time until you have a stiff but workable dough. You may not need all 4 tablespoons of water.
2. Drop 2–3 tablespoons of dough on baking sheet about 2" apart. Gently shape each biscuit into a circle. Bake for 12–15 minutes until biscuits are golden-brown. You can add a thin slice of butter on top of each biscuit and broil for about 1 minute to enhance browning. Serve hot with butter or coconut oil and jam.

Cheddar Garlic Biscuits

These cheesy morsels will remind you of the famous "Cheddar bay" biscuits served at a popular seafood chain restaurant. For your next special dinner make a double batch to serve to guests.

INGREDIENTS | SERVES 6

1¼ cups gluten-free baking mix

3 tablespoons butter or Spectrum Palm Shortening

1 large egg

2–4 tablespoons cold water, as needed

½ cup shredded Cheddar cheese

2 cloves garlic, crushed

1. Preheat oven to 350°F. Line a baking sheet with parchment paper.
2. In a medium bowl add gluten-free baking mix and cut in butter or shortening with a fork and knife or a pastry blender until it's fully incorporated into the flour. Stir in the egg and 1 tablespoon of water at a time until you have a stiff, but workable dough. You may not need all 4 tablespoons of water. Fold the cheese and garlic into the dough.
3. Drop 2–3 tablespoons of dough on baking sheet about 2" apart. Gently shape each biscuit into a circle. Bake for 12–15 minutes until golden-brown. You can add a thin slice of butter on top of each biscuit and broil for about 1 minute to enhance browning. Serve hot with butter or coconut oil.

Zesty Sausage Balls

A classic holiday appetizer or snack, these spicy little bites are super-easy to make and portable for family gatherings.

INGREDIENTS | YIELDS ABOUT 5 DOZEN

3 cups gluten-free baking mix

½ teaspoon ground pepper

¼ teaspoon red pepper flakes

¼ teaspoon smoked paprika

1 pound ground sausage

4 cups shredded Cheddar cheese

Gluten-Free Sausage

Make sure the sausage you use in this recipe is gluten-free. Most brands are naturally gluten-free, but some include fillers that could contain gluten. If in doubt, call the company listed on the package.

1. Preheat oven to 350°F. Line 2 large baking pans with parchment paper and set aside.
2. In a large bowl combine all ingredients. The mixture will be very crumbly.
3. Using your hands or a melon baller, form and press the mixture into 1" balls. Place the balls on the baking pans and bake for 18–20 minutes until golden-brown and sizzling.
4. Allow balls to cool for 15–20 minutes before serving. Store sausage balls in an airtight container in the refrigerator for up to 5 days. These also freeze well for up to 1 month.

Impossible Bacon Cheeseburger Pie

"Impossible" pies became popular in the 1970s when a popular biscuit mix shared recipes for them on their product packaging. Recipes have come and gone over the years, but are still wonderful, easy dinners.

INGREDIENTS | SERVES 8

1 pound ground beef

1 large onion, chopped

6 slices bacon, cooked and crumbled

1 cup shredded Cheddar cheese or dairy-free shredded cheese substitute

½ cup gluten-free baking mix

1 cup almond milk

2 large eggs

Salt and pepper, to taste

1. Preheat oven to 350°F. Grease a 9" pie pan or large baking dish. In heavy skillet over medium heat brown the ground beef and onions for 8–10 minutes until the onions are translucent and the beef is cooked through. Scoop the ground beef and onions onto a plate lined with paper towels to drain off grease.
2. Sprinkle drained beef mixture and crumbled bacon into pie pan. Sprinkle cheese evenly over the meat and onions.
3. In a medium bowl whisk together gluten-free baking mix, milk, eggs, salt, and pepper. Pour batter over the meat and cheese. Bake pie for 25–30 minutes until the top is golden-brown and a toothpick inserted in the middle comes out clean. Allow pie to cool for 10 minutes before slicing and serving.

Impossible Sausage Pizza Pie

This variation of "impossible pie" has all the flavors of a traditional sausage pizza.
Try different cheeses and toppings for your own unique recipe.

INGREDIENTS | SERVES 8

1 pound bulk Italian sausage, removed from casing

¼ cup chopped onion

½ cup chopped green pepper

½ teaspoon dried basil leaves

½ teaspoon dried oregano leaves

¼ teaspoon garlic salt

½ cup grated Parmesan cheese or dairy-free substitute

2 small Roma tomatoes, seeded and chopped

1 cup gluten-free baking mix

1½ cups almond milk

3 large eggs

1 cup shredded mozzarella cheese or dairy-free shredded cheese substitute

Instead of Parmesan Cheese . . .

Substitute the Parmesan cheese with ⅓ cup blanched almond flour mixed with 2 tablespoons nutritional yeast. You can use this mixture for vegan and vegetarian recipes, or anytime a recipe calls for Parmesan cheese. Blanched almond flour has a texture that is similar to Parmesan cheese and nutritional yeast has a wonderful "cheesy" flavor.

1. Preheat oven to 350°F. Grease a 9" pie pan or large baking dish.
2. In heavy skillet over medium heat brown sausage, onion, and green pepper for 8–10 minutes until the onions are translucent and the sausage is cooked through. Scoop the mixture onto a plate lined with paper towels to drain off grease.
3. Sprinkle drained sausage mixture, basil, oregano, garlic salt, Parmesan cheese, and tomatoes into pie pan.
4. In a medium bowl whisk together gluten-free baking mix, milk, and eggs. Pour batter over the pizza mixture. Sprinkle mozzarella cheese on top of the pie. Bake pie for 25–30 minutes until the top is golden-brown, the cheese is melted, and a toothpick inserted in the middle comes out clean. Allow pie to cool for 10 minutes before slicing and serving.

Impossible Barbecue Chicken Pie

*Use your favorite gluten-free barbecue sauce, such as Sticky Fingers,
Sweet Baby Ray's, or KC Masterpiece, on this chicken pie.*

INGREDIENTS | SERVES 8

2 cups chicken breast, cooked and cubed

1 cup canned sweet yellow corn, drained

¼ cup chopped fresh parsley or cilantro

½ cup gluten-free baking mix

¾ cup milk or dairy-free alternative

¼ cup plus 3 tablespoons gluten-free barbecue sauce

2 large eggs

2 teaspoons dried, minced onions

Quick Homemade Barbecue Sauce

Mix together 1 cup gluten-free ketchup, ¼ cup apple cider vinegar, 2 tablespoons brown sugar or molasses, 1 tablespoon Dijon mustard, 1 tablespoon water, ½ teaspoon salt, ½ teaspoon black pepper. Cook over medium heat for 3–5 minutes and use as you would any barbecue sauce.

1. Preheat oven to 350°F. Grease a 9" pie pan or large baking dish.
2. Put the chicken, corn, and parsley into pie pan.
3. In a medium bowl whisk together gluten-free baking mix, milk or alternative, ¼ cup barbecue sauce, and eggs. Pour batter over the chicken and corn mixture.
4. Bake pie for 25–30 minutes until the top is golden-brown. Drizzle remaining barbecue sauce over the top of the pie. Sprinkle dried onion evenly over barbecue sauce. Bake for an additional 5 minutes. Remove pie from oven and allow to cool for 10 minutes before slicing and serving.

Bacon Swiss Quiche

This quiche makes its own crust as it bakes. It's a delicious meal for breakfast, lunch, or dinner!

INGREDIENTS | SERVES 8

1 pound bacon, cooked and crumbled

1 cup shredded Swiss cheese

⅓ cup finely chopped onion

1 cup gluten-free baking mix

2 cups milk

4 large eggs

½ teaspoon salt

¼ teaspoon ground pepper

1. Preheat oven to 350°F. Grease a 9" pie pan or large baking dish.
2. Add bacon, cheese, and onion to pie pan.
3. In a medium bowl whisk together gluten-free baking mix, milk, eggs, salt, and pepper. Pour batter over the bacon, cheese, and onions.
4. Bake pie for 35–40 minutes until the top is golden-brown. Remove pie from oven and allow to cool for 10 minutes before slicing and serving.

Tex-Mex Calzones

This is a fun way to create a gluten-free pastry pocket for dinner. These pockets are sturdy enough to be a quick portable meal, yet special enough for company.

INGREDIENTS | SERVES 4

½ pound ground beef

½ cup chopped onion

½ packet gluten-free taco seasoning

2 cups gluten-free baking mix

1 cup boiling water

⅓ cup shredded Cheddar cheese

Make Your Own Taco Seasoning

You can easily make your own gluten-free taco seasoning by mixing together 1 tablespoon chili powder, 2 teaspoons cumin, ½ teaspoon paprika, and ¼ teaspoon each of garlic powder, onion powder, salt, and black pepper. Two tablespoons of this homemade seasoning can replace the gluten-free taco seasoning in this recipe.

1. Preheat oven to 375°F. Line a baking sheet with parchment paper.
2. In a heavy skillet brown ground beef and onions for 5–6 minutes over medium heat until the onions are softened and beef is cooked through. Add the taco seasoning to the mixture. Remove from heat and set aside.
3. In a medium bowl vigorously stir together the baking mix and boiling water until you have a stiff dough. Divide the dough into 4 even pieces. Dust a flat surface with additional gluten-free baking mix and roll each piece of dough into a 6" circle. Add ¼ cup of ground beef mixture on one side of each circle of dough and top with 1–2 tablespoons of shredded cheese. Fold the rest of the dough over the filling and press together the edges of the calzones with a fork to seal them. Place calzones on baking sheet.
4. Bake for 15–20 minutes until the calzones are golden-brown. Allow to cool for 5 minutes before serving.

Easy Pepperoni Pizza

Here is an easy, yeast-free pizza crust that you can put together in just a few minutes.
Feel free to use your favorite toppings instead of the ones listed below.

INGREDIENTS | SERVES 8

1½ cups gluten-free baking mix
¾ cup boiling water
1 (8-ounce) can pizza sauce
1 cup shredded mozzarella cheese
1 (3½-ounce) package sliced pepperoni
½ cup sliced mushrooms
½ cup chopped green peppers

1. Preheat oven to 400°F. Line a 12" round pizza pan with parchment paper.
2. In a medium bowl mix together gluten-free baking mix and boiling water and mix with a fork until you have a stiff dough. Sprinkle a little additional baking mix on the parchment paper and spread dough out into a 12" crust. It may be easier to spread using a rolling pin, rather than your hands.
3. Spread pizza sauce over the crust, leaving ½" bare around the edges. Top with cheese, pepperoni, mushrooms, and peppers. Bake for 15–18 minutes until cheese is melted and crust is golden-brown. Allow pizza to cool for 10 minutes before slicing and serving.

Pigs-in-a-Blanket

Who needs "whack-'em-on-the-counter" crescent rolls for pigs-in-a-blanket?
With this easy dough you can create a meal in no time.

INGREDIENTS | SERVES 8

2 cups gluten-free baking mix
1 cup boiling water
8 gluten-free hot dogs (a few generally safe brands are Oscar Mayer, Nathan's, Sabrett's, and Applegate)
4 slices American cheese, cut in half

1. Preheat oven to 375°F. Line a baking sheet with parchment paper.
2. In a medium bowl stir together baking mix and boiling water until you have a soft dough. Divide dough into 8 even pieces. Roll or pat out dough into 4" × 4" squares. Place a hot dog and half a slice of cheese in the middle of each square and roll dough around hot dog.
3. Place wrapped hot dogs on baking sheet and bake for 10–15 minutes until the "blankets" are golden-brown and the hot dogs are sizzling.
4. Allow to cool for several minutes before serving.

Broccoli and Chicken Casserole

You can never have too many one-pot recipes to choose from when planning gluten-free meals. Feel free to substitute turkey for the chicken.

INGREDIENTS | SERVES 6

2 cups fresh or frozen broccoli florets

1½ cups shredded Cheddar cheese (or nondairy alternative), divided

1 cup cooked and chopped chicken

1 medium onion, chopped

½ cup gluten-free baking mix

1 cup milk or nondairy alternative

2 large eggs

½ teaspoon salt

¼ teaspoon pepper

1. Preheat oven to 400°F. Grease a 9" pie pan with non-stick cooking spray or olive oil.
2. Add broccoli, ¾ cup cheese, chicken, and onion to the bottom of the baking dish.
3. In a medium bowl whisk together baking mix, milk, eggs, salt, and pepper. Pour over chicken and broccoli mixture. Bake for 30–35 minutes until golden-brown. Add remaining cheese and bake an additional 5–6 minutes until cheese has melted.
4. Allow to cool for several minutes and serve.

Ground Beef Tamale Pie

This is a fun Mexican twist on a meal-in-one. Round it out with a fresh green salad and you're ready for dinner.

INGREDIENTS | SERVES 6

Filling

1 pound ground beef

1 cup canned or frozen sweet yellow corn, drained

1 (14½-ounce) can of petite diced tomatoes

1 (2¼-ounce) can sliced black olives

2 tablespoons gluten-free baking mix

1 tablespoon chili powder

2 teaspoons cumin

½ teaspoon sea salt

Crust

1 cup gluten-free baking mix

½ cup gluten-free cornmeal

¾ cup milk (or nondairy alternative)

1 large egg

1. Preheat oven to 400°F. Grease a 9" pie pan with non-stick cooking spray or olive oil and set aside.
2. Brown ground beef in a skillet over medium heat for 6–8 minutes until beef is cooked through. Drain excess grease from beef.
3. In a medium bowl mix together beef and remaining filling ingredients. Stir together well and pour mixture into pie pan.
4. In another medium bowl whisk together the crust ingredients and pour over the ground beef mixture. Bake for 25–30 minutes until crust is light golden-brown. Allow casserole to cool for 5 minutes before serving.

Tuna Melt Casserole

As old-fashioned as this recipe seems it's still a hit with kids and adults,
and it's easy enough to prepare for a fast weeknight meal. Serve with steamed broccoli.

INGREDIENTS | SERVES 4–6

2 tablespoons butter or coconut oil

1 medium onion, chopped

1 (6¼-ounce) can tuna, drained

1½ cups shredded Cheddar cheese (or nondairy alternative), divided

1 cup frozen peas and carrots

1 cup gluten-free baking mix

1 cup milk (or nondairy alternative)

1 large egg

½ teaspoon salt

¼ teaspoon ground pepper

Make It a Traditional Pasta Casserole

Instead of using the baking mix, add 1 cup dry gluten-free pasta instead. Increase milk to 1½ cups and bake casserole for 30–35 minutes until pasta is al dente.

1. Preheat oven to 400°F. Grease a 9" pie pan or 2-quart baking dish with nonstick cooking spray or olive oil.
2. In a medium skillet heat butter over medium heat to sizzling. Add onions and continue to cook for 6–8 minutes until onions are softened and translucent.
3. In a medium bowl mix together cooked onions, tuna, ¾ cup cheese, and frozen vegetables and pour into baking dish.
4. In a medium bowl whisk together baking mix, milk, egg, salt, and pepper. Pour batter over the casserole. Bake for 25–30 minutes until crust is golden-brown.
5. Gently remove from oven and add remaining cheese to casserole. Return to oven and bake for an additional 5–8 minutes until cheese is melted. Allow casserole to cool for at least 5 minutes before serving.

Chocolate Chip Cookies

These soft, chewy, cakelike chocolate chip cookies can be made in a snap! For a chocolate chip brownie add the dough to a 9" × 13" greased baking pan and bake for 15–18 minutes until golden-brown.

INGREDIENTS | YIELDS 2–3 DOZEN COOKIES

½ cup Spectrum Palm Shortening or vegetable shortening

½ cup brown sugar

¼ cup sugar

2 large eggs

1 tablespoon vanilla

2¾ cups gluten-free baking mix

2–4 tablespoons cold water

1 cup chocolate chips

Dairy-Free Chocolate Chips?

Many brands of chocolate chips are naturally dairy-free, including Ghirardelli semi-sweet chocolate chips, Enjoy Life chocolate nuggets, and Trader Joe's chocolate chips. Just make sure to read labels and call the manufacturers if you have questions.

1. Preheat oven to 350°F. Line 2 baking sheets with parchment paper and set aside.
2. In a large bowl cream together the shortening, brown sugar, and sugar. Mix until creamy. Add the eggs and vanilla and stir together until fully incorporated. Stir in the baking mix ¼ cup at a time, until you have a stiff dough. If the dough seems too stiff (crumbly), add 2–4 tablespoons of water until you have a workable dough. Stir in the chocolate chips.
3. Drop dough by tablespoons, 1 inch apart, onto baking sheets. Flatten cookies slightly with the bottom of a glass or the palm of your hand.
4. Bake for 8–10 minutes until cookies are golden-brown. These cookies do not spread much; they are cakelike and soft. Move to a wire rack to cool completely. Store in an airtight container on the counter for up to 1 week.

Snickerdoodles

A childhood favorite, these soft cakelike cookies are coated in cinnamon and sugar. These are a wonderful treat for young children because they are the perfect size for little hands.

INGREDIENTS | YIELDS 2–3 DOZEN COOKIES

½ cup Spectrum Palm Shortening or vegetable shortening

¾ cup plus 3 tablespoons sugar

2 large eggs

2 tablespoons vanilla extract

2¾ cups gluten-free baking mix

2–4 tablespoons cold water

½ teaspoon cinnamon

1. Preheat oven to 350°F. Line 2 baking sheets with parchment paper and set aside.
2. In a large bowl cream together the shortening and ¾ cup sugar. Mix until creamy. Add the eggs and vanilla and stir together until fully incorporated. Stir in the baking mix ¼ cup at a time, until you have a stiff dough. If the dough seems too stiff (crumbly), add 2–4 tablespoons of water until you have a workable dough. Roll the dough into 1" balls.
3. In a small bowl mix together cinnamon and 3 tablespoons of sugar. Roll each cookie ball in the cinnamon-sugar mixture until fully coated. Place the cookies on baking sheets 1" apart. Flatten cookies slightly with the bottom of a glass or the palm of your hand.
4. Bake for 8–10 minutes until cookies are golden-brown. These cookies do not spread much, they are cakelike and soft. Move to a wire rack to cool completely. Store in an airtight container on the counter for up to 1 week.

Oatmeal Snack Cookies

Hearty and healthy, these oatmeal cookies contain little sugar and extra fiber.
They are perfect for an after-school snack or even as a grab-and-go breakfast cookie.

INGREDIENTS | YIELDS ABOUT 3 DOZEN COOKIES

1¼ cups gluten-free baking mix

2 teaspoons apple pie spice

¼ cup Spectrum Palm Shortening, vegetable shortening, or butter

¾ cup brown sugar, packed

2 large eggs

1 teaspoon vanilla extract

3 cups gluten-free quick oats or rolled oats

⅓ cup chopped pecans

¾ cup dried apples, finely chopped

1. Preheat oven to 350°F. Line 2 baking sheets with parchment paper and set aside.
2. In a small bowl whisk together baking mix and apple pie spice.
3. In a medium bowl cream together shortening and brown sugar until soft and creamy. Add the eggs and vanilla and stir until fully incorporated. Using a fork, stir in the baking mix and apple pie spice. Stir in oats about 1 cup at a time until you have a thick batter. Fold in pecans and apples.
4. Drop batter, 1 tablespoon at a time, onto the cookie sheets. Gently shape cookies into circles and flatten slightly with the bottom of a glass. Bake for 12–15 minutes until golden-brown. Allow cookies to cool on the baking sheets for about 5 minutes then transfer to a wire rack. These cookies freeze well and can be kept on the counter in an airtight container for up to 5 days.

Baking Mix Yellow Cupcakes

These cupcakes are perfect for a small birthday party, to share with someone special, or just because. Ice with gluten-free prepared frosting—call the manufacturer if you have questions.

INGREDIENTS | YIELDS 10–12 CUPCAKES

1½ cups gluten-free baking mix

¾ cup sugar

½ cup almond milk

¼ cup light-tasting olive oil

1 tablespoon vanilla extract

2 large eggs

Gluten-free vanilla frosting, such as Pillsbury

1. Preheat oven to 350°F. Line a muffin pan with paper liners. Lightly spritz nonstick cooking spray into each liner and set aside.
2. In a medium bowl whisk together baking mix and sugar. Make a well in the center of the dry ingredients and add milk, olive oil, vanilla, and eggs. Whisk wet ingredients into dry ingredients until you have a lump-free cake batter.
3. Fill each paper liner ¾ full with cake batter. Bake cupcakes for 12–15 minutes until light golden-brown on top and a toothpick inserted in the middle comes out clean. Allow cupcakes to cool completely on a wire rack before frosting.
4. Frost cupcakes with gluten-free frosting.

Baking Mix Chocolate Cupcakes

These gluten-free cupcakes take just a few minutes to whip up. Eat them as is, dusted with confectioners' sugar, or frosted with your favorite gluten-free frosting.

INGREDIENTS | YIELDS 10–12 CUPCAKES

1¼ cups gluten-free baking mix

¼ cup cocoa

¾ cup sugar

½ cup almond milk

¼ cup light-tasting olive oil

1 tablespoon pure vanilla extract

2 large eggs

¼ cup gluten-free mini chocolate chips (optional)

1. Preheat oven to 350°F. Line a muffin pan with paper liners. Lightly spritz nonstick cooking spray into each liner and set aside.
2. In a medium bowl whisk together baking mix, cocoa, and sugar. Make a well in the center of the dry ingredients and add milk, olive oil, vanilla, and eggs. Whisk wet ingredients into dry ingredients until you have a lump-free cake batter. Fold in mini chocolate chips, if using.
3. Fill each paper liner ¾ full with cake batter. Bake cupcakes for 12–15 minutes until the edges look dry and a toothpick inserted in the middle comes out clean. Allow cupcakes to cool completely on a wire rack.

Baking Mix Carrot Cupcakes

Hearty and delicious, carrot cupcakes are easy enough for dessert on the weeknights, but special enough to serve on holidays. You can add ½ cup raisins and/or ½ cup chopped walnuts to the batter as well.

INGREDIENTS | SERVES 16–18

1 cup gluten-free baking mix

1 teaspoon ground cinnamon

¾ cup brown sugar

2 large eggs

1 teaspoon vanilla extract

⅓ cup plus 2 tablespoons almond milk

¼ cup light-tasting olive oil

¼ cup unsweetened applesauce

1½ cups grated carrots

Easy Cream Cheese Icing

In a medium bowl cream together 4 ounces cream cheese with ¼ cup Spectrum Palm Shortening, butter, or vegetable shortening, and 1 teaspoon of vanilla. Stir in 2 cups of confectioners' sugar. If the frosting is too thick, add cold water 1 teaspoon at a time, until the frosting is the right consistency to easily spread on the cupcakes.

1. Preheat oven to 350°F. Line a muffin pan with paper liners. Lightly spritz nonstick cooking spray into each liner and set aside.

2. In a medium bowl whisk together baking mix, cinnamon, and brown sugar. Make a well in the center of the dry ingredients and add eggs, vanilla, almond milk, olive oil, and applesauce. Whisk wet ingredients into dry ingredients until you have a lump-free cake batter. Fold in grated carrots.

3. Fill each paper liner ¾ full with cake batter. Bake cupcakes for 12–15 minutes until the edges look dry and a toothpick inserted in the middle comes out clean. Allow cupcakes to cool completely on a wire rack before frosting.

4. Frost cupcakes with cream cheese frosting or your favorite gluten-free white frosting.

Baking Mix Strawberry Shortcake

Make this dessert as soon as fresh, local strawberries are available in your area.
That's when you'll appreciate the dessert most!

INGREDIENTS | SERVES 12

2 pints fresh strawberries

⅔ cup sugar

¾ cup whipping cream

1 double recipe prepared Gluten-Free Drop Biscuits (see recipe in this chapter)

Try Coconut Cream Instead

If you are dairy intolerant, try using coconut cream, which is also the top layer of coconut milk if you buy it in a can. Scrape off the thick coconut cream and whip it as you would whipping cream. It won't get quite as thick as whipping cream does, but it's delicious and tastes great in shortcake.

1. Remove stems from strawberries, rinse in cool water, and pat dry. Slice strawberries and place them in a medium bowl. Sprinkle sugar over the strawberries and allow them to chill in the refrigerator for at least 30 minutes.
2. In another bowl, beat whipping cream until stiff peaks form.
3. To assemble, slice each biscuit in half. Fill each biscuit with 2 tablespoons of sliced strawberries. Place the top on each biscuit and add another tablespoon of strawberries on top. Generously dollop whipping cream on top of each strawberry-covered biscuit. Serve immediately. Only assemble as many shortcakes as you need, as they don't keep well (the strawberry mixture will make the biscuits soggy if stored in the refrigerator).

Blueberry Streusel Coffee Cake

*Coffee cakes are a lost art. Popular in the 1960s, these crumbly cakes deserve a comeback!
Coffee cakes generally aren't super-sweet and can be enjoyed as a light dessert, as breakfast,
or as a treat with your mid-morning coffee!*

INGREDIENTS | SERVES 9

Streusel

⅓ cup gluten-free baking mix

⅓ cup brown sugar

½ teaspoon cinnamon

2 tablespoons butter or coconut oil

Cake

2 cups gluten-free baking mix

⅔ cup water, milk, or dairy-free alternative

2 large eggs

3 tablespoons sugar

2 teaspoons vanilla extract

½ cup fresh or frozen blueberries

1. Preheat oven to 375°F. Line a 9" round cake pan or an 8" × 8" square baking pan with parchment paper or grease with nonstick cooking spray or olive oil.
2. In a small bowl make the streusel topping by mixing together baking mix, brown sugar, and cinnamon. Cut in the butter or coconut oil with a fork, until it's mixed evenly throughout the dry ingredients. Set streusel aside.
3. In a medium bowl mix together all cake ingredients and pour batter into the lined or greased baking dish. Sprinkle streusel topping evenly over the top of the cake. Top the cake with blueberries.
4. Bake for 18–22 minutes until the top of the cake is golden-brown and a toothpick inserted in the middle comes out clean. Allow cake to cool for 10 minutes before serving. Store any leftovers in an airtight container in the refrigerator for up to 5 days.

Cinnamon Nut Coffee Cake

If you're a fan of cinnamon this cake is for you.
It's almost "cinnamon roll" in taste, but super-quick and easy to make.

INGREDIENTS | SERVES 9

Streusel

⅓ cup gluten-free baking mix

⅓ cup brown sugar

1½ teaspoons ground cinnamon

2 tablespoons butter or coconut oil

½ cup chopped pecans

Cake

2 cups gluten-free baking mix

½ teaspoon ground cinnamon

⅔ cup water, milk, or dairy-free alternative

2 large eggs

3 tablespoons brown sugar

1 tablespoon vanilla extract

Pure Almond Extract

If you get tired of using vanilla in most baked goods, try using pure almond extract instead. It has a strong, fruity, almost "cherry" like flavor and enhances the sweetness of most baked goods. Because it is such a strong extract, you generally need to use only half the amount called for. For example, this recipe calls for 1 tablespoon vanilla extract, so only use 1½ teaspoons almond extract instead.

1. Preheat oven to 375°F. Line a 9" round cake pan or an 8" × 8" square baking pan with parchment paper or grease with nonstick cooking spray or olive oil.
2. In a small bowl make the streusel topping by mixing together baking mix, brown sugar, and cinnamon. Cut in the butter or coconut oil with a fork, until it's mixed evenly throughout the dry ingredients. Stir in the chopped pecans. Set streusel aside.
3. In a medium bowl mix together all cake ingredients and pour batter into baking dish. Sprinkle streusel topping evenly over the top of the cake.
4. Bake for 18–22 minutes until the top of the cake is golden-brown and a toothpick inserted in the middle comes out clean. Allow cake to cool for 10 minutes before serving. Store any leftovers in an airtight container in the refrigerator for up to 5 days.

Baking Mix Walnut Brownies

Mix up a batch of brownies in one bowl with this gluten-free baking mix recipe.

INGREDIENTS | SERVES 12

1½ cups sugar

½ cup butter or Spectrum Palm Shortening

2 large eggs

2 teaspoons vanilla extract

1 cup gluten-free baking mix

½ cup cocoa

½ cup chopped walnuts

1. Preheat oven to 350°F. Line an 8" × 8" baking pan with parchment paper.
2. In a medium bowl cream together sugar and butter or shortening. Stir in eggs and vanilla until you have a creamy batter. Add baking mix and cocoa to the batter and whisk to combine. Pour batter in baking dish. Sprinkle walnuts on top of the brownies.
3. Bake for 18–25 minutes, until edges of brownies look dry and the center is set. Allow brownies to cool for 10–15 minutes before slicing and serving.

Baking Mix Butterscotch Brownies

If you're one to lick the bowl when making cookies, these brownies are for you.
Brown sugar and vanilla create that signature "cookie dough" taste in the form of a brownie.

INGREDIENTS | SERVES 12

1 cup plus 2 tablespoons brown sugar

⅓ cup butter or Spectrum Palm Shortening

2 large eggs

2 teaspoons vanilla extract

1 cup gluten-free baking mix

1 cup butterscotch morsels

1. Preheat oven to 350°F. Line an 8" × 8" baking pan with parchment paper.
2. In a medium bowl cream together brown sugar and butter. Stir in eggs and vanilla, until you have a creamy batter. Add baking mix to the batter and whisk to combine. Fold in butterscotch morsels. Pour batter in baking dish.
3. Bake for 18–25 minutes, until edges of brownies are golden-brown. Allow brownies to cool for 10–15 minutes before slicing and serving.

Baking Mix Lemon Bars

*This buttery shortbread crust made from gluten-free baking mix has
a cool lemon custard on top—the perfect combination of tangy and sweet.*

INGREDIENTS | SERVES 12

Crust

1 cup gluten-free baking mix

2 tablespoons sugar

3 tablespoons butter or Spectrum Palm Shortening

Lemon Custard Filling

¾ cup sugar

1 tablespoon gluten-free baking mix

2 large eggs, lightly beaten

3 tablespoons lemon juice

1 tablespoon freshly grated lemon zest

1. Preheat oven to 350°F. Line an 8" × 8" baking pan with parchment paper.
2. In a small bowl mix together the crust ingredients until you have a crumbly mixture. Press mixture into baking pan. Bake for 10 minutes until golden-brown and remove from oven.
3. In a medium bowl whisk together lemon custard filling ingredients. Pour filling on top of the prebaked crust. Return to oven and bake for 25 minutes until the filling is set.
4. Allow lemon bars to cool for 20 minutes on a wire rack, then place in refrigerator to chill for 2 hours. Right before serving, slice bars and dust with confectioners' sugar, if desired.

Easy Gluten-Free Pie Crust

*You can use this easy "pat-in-the-pan" pie crust for nearly any pie in this cookbook. For pies that
need a prebaked crust or if you just want to ensure that your pie crust does not get soggy,
place prepared pie crust in a preheated 400°F oven and bake 8–10 minutes until golden-brown.*

INGREDIENTS | YIELDS 1 (8" OR 9") PIE CRUST

¼ cup plus 1 tablespoon Spectrum Palm Shortening or vegetable shortening

1 cup gluten-free baking mix

1 large egg yolk

2–4 tablespoons ice-cold water

1. In a medium bowl cut shortening into baking mix with a pastry blender or a knife and fork, until it resembles very small peas throughout the dry mixture.
2. Make a well in the center of the mix and add the egg yolk and water. Stir together until you have a crumbly mix.
3. Pour crumbly mixture into a greased 8" or 9" pie pan. Press dough over the bottom of the pan and up the sides to create a crust. The crust is now ready to be used.

Easy Apple Pie

If you can find presliced apples at your grocery store, this really is the easiest apple pie you could make! However, it only takes a few minutes to slice the apples for this traditional favorite dessert.

INGREDIENTS | SERVES 8

6 cups cored, peeled, and sliced apples

2 tablespoons lemon juice

¾ cup sugar

3 tablespoons gluten-free baking mix

½ teaspoon ground cinnamon

½ teaspoon ground nutmeg

¼ teaspoon sea salt

1 prepared Easy Gluten-Free Pie Crust (see recipe in this chapter), unbaked

1. Preheat oven to 400°F.
2. In a large bowl mix together apples, lemon juice, sugar, baking mix, cinnamon, nutmeg, and salt. Stir until all apples have been coated with mixture.
3. Pour apple mixture evenly into the prepared gluten-free pie crust. Bake for 40–50 minutes until apples are soft and bubbly.
4. Allow pie to cool for 30 minutes before slicing. Store any leftovers in an airtight container in the refrigerator for up to 3–4 days.

Make an Oatmeal Crumble Topping

For an extra-special pie create a crumble topping by mixing the following together in a medium bowl: ½ cup gluten-free quick oats, ⅓ cup brown sugar, 2 tablespoons butter or Spectrum Palm Shortening, and ½ teaspoon cinnamon. Once thoroughly mixed, sprinkle over the top of the pie right before baking.

Easy Chocolate Pudding Pie

Enjoy this creamy chocolate pudding in a prebaked gluten-free pie crust. Top with whipped cream and shaved chocolate for a gourmet touch.

INGREDIENTS | SERVES 8

¼ cup sugar

3 tablespoons cornstarch

1¼ cups milk

1 cup plus 1 tablespoon chocolate chips, divided

1 teaspoon vanilla extract

1¼ cups whipping cream

1 tablespoon confectioners' sugar

1 prebaked Easy Gluten-Free Pie Crust (see recipe in this chapter)

1. In a saucepan over medium heat stir together sugar, cornstarch, milk, and 1 cup chocolate chips. Stir constantly for 6–8 minutes until chocolate melts and pudding thickens enough to coat the back of a spoon. Remove from heat and stir in vanilla.
2. Pour pudding in a glass bowl and place a thin layer of plastic wrap directly onto the top of the pudding to prevent a "skin" from forming while it cools. Place pudding in the refrigerator for at least 30 minutes.
3. When pudding is chilled, in a medium bowl beat whipping cream and confectioners' sugar until stiff peaks form. Fold whipped cream into the pudding and pour into the baked pie crust. Top with 1 tablespoon chocolate chips.
4. Chill pie for several hours before slicing. Store any leftovers in an airtight container in the refrigerator for up to 5 days.

Chocolate Almond Coconut Pie

This pie is reminiscent of a popular candy bar with a coconut center coated in dark chocolate. It's incredibly easy to put together and is great for people who don't consider themselves "bakers."

INGREDIENTS | SERVES 8

¼ cup sugar

¼ cup gluten-free baking mix

½ cup blanched almond flour

½ cup shredded unsweetened coconut

¾ teaspoon baking powder

⅛ teaspoon salt

2 large eggs

3 tablespoons coconut oil or butter, melted

1 (12-ounce) can coconut milk

½ teaspoon vanilla extract

½ cup chocolate chips

1. Preheat oven to 350°F. Grease a 9" or 10" pie pan or 2-quart baking dish.
2. In a large bowl whisk together sugar, baking mix, almond flour, coconut, baking powder, and salt. Make a well in the center of the dry ingredients and add eggs, melted oil or butter, coconut milk, and vanilla extract. Whisk wet ingredients into dry ingredients to create a wet batter. Stir in chocolate chips.
3. Pour batter into the pie pan. Bake for 45 minutes or until a knife inserted in the middle comes out clean. Chill pie for 8 hours before slicing and serving.

Try a Natural Sugar Substitute

If you are watching your sugar intake, try a natural sugar substitute in this recipe. Instead of sugar you can use ¼ cup coconut palm sugar, ¼ cup date sugar, ¼ cup stevia blend for baking, or even ¼ cup maple sugar. Because so little sugar is used in this recipe, it works well with different types of substitutes.

CHAPTER 4

Savory Baked Main Dishes

Ricotta Torte with Serrano Ham and Parmesan

If you can't find serrano ham, substitute prosciutto. Do not, however, use low-fat ricotta—it just doesn't do the trick.

INGREDIENTS | SERVES 6

2 shallots, peeled and minced

2 tablespoons butter

3 large eggs

1 pound ricotta cheese

½ cup grated Parmesan cheese

¼ cup finely chopped serrano ham or prosciutto

4 tablespoons butter, melted

1 teaspoon dried oregano

⅛ teaspoon nutmeg

Salt and pepper, to taste

1. Preheat the oven to 325°F.
2. In a skillet over medium heat, sauté the shallots in butter for 3–5 minutes, until they are softened. Place contents of skillet into a pie pan you have prepared with nonstick spray. Set aside.
3. In a medium bowl, beat the eggs and then add the rest of the ingredients, beating continuously. Pour mixture into pie pan and bake for 35 minutes, or until set and golden. Cut into wedges and serve.

"Crustless" Quiche Lorraine

Ham is often quite salty, so take that into consideration when deciding how much salt you add to the egg mixture in this recipe. The gluten-free bread "crust" is optional, as the quiche is just as delicious without it.

INGREDIENTS | SERVES 4

4 slices gluten-free bread, toasted

4 teaspoons butter

2 cups grated Swiss cheese

½ pound cooked ham, cut into cubes

6 large eggs

1 tablespoon mayonnaise

½ teaspoon Dijon mustard

1 cup heavy cream

Salt and freshly ground pepper, to taste (optional)

Dash of cayenne pepper (optional)

1. Preheat oven to 350°F. Grease a 2- or 3-quart baking dish with nonstick cooking spray or olive oil.
2. Butter each slice of toast with 1 teaspoon butter. Tear the toast into pieces and arrange the pieces butter-side down in the baking dish to form a "crust."
3. Spread half of the cheese over the toast pieces, and then spread the ham over the cheese, and top the ham layer with the remaining cheese.
4. In a medium bowl, beat the eggs together with the mayonnaise, mustard, cream, salt, pepper, and cayenne pepper, if using. Pour the egg mixture on top of the ingredients in the baking dish. Cover with foil and bake for 30–35 minutes until the egg mixture is cooked through. Remove the foil and bake another 5–6 minutes to melt and toast the cheese.

Biscuit-Topped Chicken Pie

This creamy chicken-and-vegetable pie topped with homemade gluten-free buttermilk drop biscuits is pure comfort food! To make the pie extra rich, drizzle a few tablespoons of melted butter over the biscuit topping right before cooking.

INGREDIENTS | SERVES 4–6

4 tablespoons brown rice flour

4 tablespoons butter

1 cup milk

1 cup gluten-free chicken broth

1 teaspoon salt

½ teaspoon pepper

2 cups cooked chicken, cut or torn into bite-sized pieces

1 (12-ounce) can mixed vegetables, drained

½ recipe prepared Fluffy Buttermilk Biscuits dough (see Chapter 2)

Gluten-Free Baking Mixes

Instead of the biscuit dough recipe, you can use your favorite homemade baking mix. It must be an all-purpose mix that includes xanthan gum and a leavening ingredient such as baking powder or baking soda. Use a recipe on the package that will make 8–10 gluten-free biscuits as a topping for chicken pie.

1. Preheat oven to 350°F. Grease a 3- or 4-quart baking dish with nonstick cooking spray or olive oil.
2. In a small saucepan whisk together brown rice flour and butter. When butter has melted slowly stir in milk, chicken broth, salt, and pepper. Cook on medium heat for 5–10 minutes, whisking constantly until mixture is the consistency of cream soup or gravy.
3. Add cooked chicken and drained vegetables to baking dish. Pour cream soup mixture into the baking dish and mix with chicken and vegetables.
4. Using an ice cream scoop, drop biscuit dough over chicken, vegetables, and sauce.
5. Cover dish with foil and bake for 35–40 minutes, until sauce is bubbling up around the biscuits, and the biscuits are cooked through. Remove foil in the last 10 minutes of baking to allow the biscuits to brown.

Baked Gluten-Free Mac and Cheese

*This is a popular dish for a carry-in supper or buffet. This recipe does not use eggs,
as they create a stiff custard dish instead of a creamy mac and cheese.*

INGREDIENTS | SERVES 8

½ pound gluten-free elbow macaroni,
cooked according to package directions

2½ cups milk

¼ cup brown rice flour

1 teaspoon sea salt

¼ teaspoon freshly grated nutmeg

¼ teaspoon freshly grated black pepper

¼ teaspoon cayenne pepper

2½ cups grated sharp white Cheddar
cheese

1 cup grated Gruyère or grated pecorino
Romano

½ cup crushed gluten-free tortilla chips
or gluten-free bread crumbs

3 tablespoons butter, melted

Who Needs Fancy Cheese?

You can also make a super delicious and
easy baked macaroni and cheese with
good old Velveeta. Add 2 cups cubed
Velveeta to a medium saucepan with 1½
cups milk and cook over medium heat,
whisking constantly until melted into a
creamy sauce. Mix cheese sauce with
cooked pasta and bake as directed in this
recipe.

1. Preheat oven to 375°F. Grease a 3-quart casserole dish with nonstick cooking spray or olive oil.

2. Cook the macaroni according to the package directions. Drain and add to greased casserole dish.

3. In a medium saucepan whisk together milk and brown rice flour. Add salt, nutmeg, black pepper, and cayenne. Turn heat to medium and cook mixture, whisking constantly for 6–8 minutes until the sauce has thickened. Add sharp Cheddar and Gruyère and whisk until melted thoroughly into sauce.

4. Pour cheese sauce over the cooked pasta. In a small bowl mix together the tortilla chips or bread crumbs and melted butter. Sprinkle mixture over the macaroni and cheese.

5. Cover dish with foil and bake for 25 minutes until sauce is bubbling around the edges of the casserole. Remove the foil and bake another 10–15 minutes to brown the topping. Allow casserole to cool for a few minutes before serving.

Homemade Baked Chicken Nuggets

Every kid's favorite, these easy baked chicken nuggets are coated either with gluten-free bread crumbs or blanched almond flour. Both options make crispy, dippable nuggets!

INGREDIENTS | SERVES 4

1½ cups gluten-free bread crumbs or 1½ cups blanched almond flour

1 teaspoon dried basil

1 teaspoon paprika

½ teaspoon salt

½ teaspoon pepper

½ teaspoon dried parsley

3–4 large boneless, skinless chicken breasts, cut into small strips

3 large eggs, beaten

1. Preheat oven to 350°F. Line a baking sheet with foil and grease foil with nonstick cooking spray or olive oil.
2. In a medium bowl whisk together bread crumbs or almond flour, basil, paprika, salt, pepper, and parsley. Dip chicken strips into the beaten eggs and dredge through the bread-crumb mixture.
3. Place dredged chicken strips onto baking sheet.
4. Bake for 25–30 minutes until strips are crispy and chicken is cooked through. (Pierce several chicken nuggets with a sharp knife, and the juices should run clear. If they are red or pink, the chicken is not done cooking.) Serve nuggets with a tray of dipping sauces and steamed carrots or broccoli.

Chicken Mushroom Marinara Bake

Combine chicken, marinara sauce, and mushrooms with your favorite gluten-free pasta for an easy one-pot meal.

INGREDIENTS | SERVES 4

1 pound fresh button mushrooms, sliced

2 tablespoons butter or olive oil

1 (16- or 18-ounce) jar marinara sauce

1 cup cooked and diced chicken breast

8 ounces gluten-free pasta, cooked according to package directions

1 teaspoon dried basil

½ teaspoon garlic salt

1 cup shredded mozzarella cheese

1. Preheat oven to 350°F. Grease a medium-sized casserole baking dish; set aside.
2. In a medium-sized sauté pan, cook mushroom slices in butter or olive oil for 4–5 minutes over medium heat until tender.
3. In a medium bowl, mix together marinara sauce, chicken, sautéed mushrooms, and cooked pasta. Pour into casserole dish. Sprinkle basil and garlic salt evenly over casserole. Top with mozzarella cheese.
4. Bake for 30–35 minutes until cheese is slightly browned and sauce is bubbly. Allow to cool for 5 minutes before serving.

Easy Vegetarian Lasagna with Spinach

You don't need to precook the noodles in this dish. This recipe feeds a crowd, so make it for a family gathering or potluck dinner. Serve with green salad and Crusty French Bread (see Chapter 5).

INGREDIENTS | SERVES 10

28 ounces fat-free ricotta cheese

10 ounces frozen cut spinach, defrosted and drained

1 large egg

½ cup shredded part-skim mozzarella cheese

8 cups (about 2 jars) marinara sauce

½ pound uncooked gluten-free lasagna noodles

1. Preheat oven to 350°F. Grease a 9" × 13" baking dish or large casserole dish with nonstick cooking spray or olive oil.
2. In a medium bowl, stir the ricotta, spinach, egg, and mozzarella together and then set aside.
3. Ladle a quarter of the marinara sauce along the bottom of the casserole dish. Bottom should be thoroughly covered in sauce. Add a single layer of lasagna noodles on top of the sauce, breaking noodles to fit if necessary.
4. Ladle an additional quarter of sauce over the noodles, covering all of the noodles. Top with half of the cheese mixture, pressing firmly with the back of a spoon to smooth. Add a single layer of lasagna noodles on top of the cheese, breaking noodles if necessary.
5. Ladle another quarter of the sauce on top of the noodles, and top with the remaining cheese. Press another layer of noodles onto the cheese and top with the remaining sauce. Make sure the noodles are entirely covered in sauce.
6. Place a large sheet of foil over the lasagna and bake for 40–50 minutes until the sauce is bubbly and the noodles are cooked through. Remove casserole from the oven and allow to cool for 10–15 minutes before serving.

Baked Spaghetti

*It doesn't get any easier than this. Because this meal cooks so quickly,
you can put it together as soon as you get home from work.
Serve with steamed asparagus and gluten-free Crusty French Bread (see Chapter 5).*

INGREDIENTS | SERVES 4

8 ounces gluten-free spaghetti noodles, uncooked

1 (15- or 16-ounce) jar marinara sauce

1 cup water

1 pound ground beef, browned

½ cup grated Parmesan cheese

Try a Different Jar!

There are so many different types of spaghetti and marinara sauces available, try a different kind each time you make this dish. Most brands are naturally gluten-free so they're a great shortcut to use for this recipe. The sauce will instantly change the flavor and give you a brand-new recipe. Try sausage and cheese sauce, roasted garlic sauce, or chopped tomato, olive oil, and garlic sauce.

1. Preheat oven to 350°F. Grease a 2- or 3-quart casserole dish with nonstick cooking spray or olive oil.
2. Break spaghetti noodles into 1–2" sticks and place in a medium bowl with marinara sauce, water, and ground beef. Stir together well and pour mixture into casserole dish.
3. Top casserole with Parmesan cheese. Bake for 30–35 minutes until sauce is bubbly and noodles are cooked through.

Chicken Pesto Polenta

This recipe uses precooked polenta cut and layered in a casserole lasagna-style.
Most prepared polenta comes in tube form and is naturally gluten-free.
Make sure to read the ingredients and call the manufacturer if you have any questions.

INGREDIENTS | SERVES 4–6

1½ pounds chicken (boneless breasts or thighs), cut into bite-sized pieces

1 cup pesto, divided

1 medium onion, finely diced

4 cloves garlic, minced

1½ teaspoons dried Italian seasoning

1 (16-ounce) tube prepared polenta cut into ½" slices

2 cups chopped fresh spinach

1 (14½-ounce) can petite diced tomatoes

1 (8-ounce) bag shredded low-fat Italian cheese blend

1. Preheat oven to 350°F. Grease a 2- or 3-quart casserole dish with nonstick cooking spray or olive oil.
2. In large bowl, combine chicken pieces with ½ cup pesto, onion, garlic, and Italian seasoning.
3. In the casserole dish, layer half of chicken mixture, half of polenta, half of spinach, and half of tomatoes. Continue to layer, ending with remaining tomatoes. Cover with foil and bake for 30–35 minutes until chicken is cooked through.
4. Remove foil and top casserole with shredded cheese. Bake an additional 10–15 minutes until cheese is melted and slightly browned.

Make Your Own Pesto

Instead of using prepared pesto you can easily make your own. In a high-powered blender or food processor add 2 cups fresh basil leaves, ½ cup extra-virgin olive oil, ½ cup pine nuts, 3 garlic cloves, and salt and pepper to taste. Blend on high for a few minutes until mixture is creamy. You can use blanched almond flour in place of Parmesan cheese, if you are dairy intolerant.

Corn Tortilla Casserole

Serve this casserole with a tossed salad. Have some additional taco or enchilada sauce at the table along with an assortment of optional condiments: chopped jalapeño peppers, diced green onions, sour cream, and guacamole.

INGREDIENTS | SERVES 8

2 pounds ground beef

2 tablespoons olive oil

1 small onion, peeled and diced

1 clove garlic, minced

1 envelope gluten-free taco seasoning

½ teaspoon salt

½ teaspoon freshly ground pepper

1 (15-ounce) can diced tomatoes

1 (6-ounce) can tomato paste

2 cups refried beans

9 corn tortillas

2 cups gluten-free enchilada sauce

2 cups (8 ounces) Cheddar cheese, grated

1. Preheat oven to 350°F. Grease a large casserole dish with nonstick cooking spray or olive oil and set aside.
2. In a large skillet, brown ground beef in olive oil and set aside in a large bowl. In the same skillet sauté onions, until softened, about 3–5 minutes. Add sautéed onions to ground beef.
3. Stir the garlic, taco seasoning, salt, pepper, tomatoes, tomato paste, and refried beans into the ground beef and onions.
4. Cover bottom of casserole dish with ⅓ of the beef mixture. Layer 3 corn tortillas on top of beef mixture and cover with ⅓ of the enchilada sauce, and then ⅓ of the shredded cheese. Repeat layers. Cover with foil and bake for 30–35 minutes until casserole is cooked through and cheese is melted. Remove foil and bake for an additional 5 minutes. Slice casserole into squares and serve.

Cheddar Baked Hominy

Hominy is a wonderful, naturally gluten-free alternative to wheat pasta.
Try it in this variation on macaroni and cheese.

INGREDIENTS | SERVES 4–6

1½ cups milk

2 tablespoons cornstarch

1½ tablespoons butter

2 cups shredded Cheddar cheese, divided

1 (29-ounce) can white or yellow hominy, drained

1 large egg, beaten

½ teaspoon sea salt

1 teaspoon freshly ground pepper

1 teaspoon garlic

¼ cup gluten-free bread crumbs or crushed tortilla chips

1. Preheat oven to 350°F. Grease a 2- or 3-quart casserole dish with nonstick cooking spray or olive oil.
2. In a small bowl whisk together milk and cornstarch.
3. Melt butter in a medium-sized saucepan and heat until sizzling. Add milk and cornstarch mixture. Whisk constantly for about 5–6 minutes until mixture thickens.
4. When thickened, add 1¼ cups cheese. Stir together until you have a thick, cheesy sauce. Add hominy and mix thoroughly into sauce. Add beaten egg. Stir in salt, pepper, and garlic.
5. Pour mixture into casserole dish and sprinkle bread crumbs or crushed tortilla chips on top. Bake for 30–35 minutes until casserole is golden-brown and cheese sauce is bubbling along the edges.
6. During the last 10 minutes of baking sprinkle remaining cheese on top of casserole. Serve with steamed mixed vegetables.

Spanish Chicken and Rice

*Have Spanish extra virgin olive oil at the table to drizzle a little over the rice.
For more heat, sprinkle some additional dried red pepper flakes on top of each serving.*

INGREDIENTS | SERVES 4

1 tablespoon olive or vegetable oil
4 chicken thighs
4 split chicken breasts
2 tablespoons lemon juice
4 ounces smoked ham, cubed
1 medium onion, peeled and diced
1 red bell pepper, seeded and diced
4 cloves garlic, peeled and minced
2½ cups water
1¾ cups chicken broth
1 teaspoon oregano
½ teaspoon salt
¼ teaspoon saffron threads, crushed
⅛ teaspoon dried red pepper flakes, crushed
2 cups converted long-grain rice

Baby Greens Salad with Fresh Lemon Dressing

Serve this dish with a fresh baby greens salad with added chopped herbs (such as basil and aromatic lemon thyme). In a large wooden bowl gently mix together washed baby greens, baby spinach leaves, and chopped herbs. In a small bowl whisk together 3–4 tablespoons fresh lemon juice, 1 teaspoon honey, 1 teaspoon white wine vinegar, ½ teaspoon freshly ground pepper, and ¼ teaspoon sea salt. Drizzle dressing over salad and serve!

1. Preheat oven to 350°F. Grease a large baking dish with nonstick cooking spray or olive oil.
2. Add oil to a large nonstick skillet over medium-high heat. When oil is sizzling put the chicken in the skillet skin side down and fry for 5 minutes or until the skin is browned. Transfer the chicken to a plate and sprinkle the lemon juice over the chicken.
3. Pour off and discard all but 2 tablespoons of the fat in the skillet. Reduce the heat to medium. Add the ham, onion, and bell pepper; sauté for 5 minutes or until the onion is transparent. Stir in the garlic and sauté for 30 seconds.
4. Pour the cooked ham and vegetables into the casserole dish. Add the water, broth, oregano, salt, saffron, red pepper flakes, and rice. Stir to combine.
5. Place the chicken thighs skin-side up in the rice and broth mixture and add the breast pieces on top of the thighs. Cover casserole dish and bake for 50 minutes to an hour, until the juices in the chicken run clear when pierced with a sharp knife. Serve chicken pieces over rice.

Cottage Pie with Carrots, Parsnips, and Celery

Cottage pie is similar to the more familiar shepherd's pie, but it uses beef instead of lamb. This version includes lots of vegetables and lean meat.

INGREDIENTS | SERVES 6

1 large onion, diced
3 cloves garlic, minced
1 carrot, diced
1 parsnip, diced
1 stalk celery, diced
1 pound 94% lean ground beef
1½ cups beef stock
½ teaspoon hot paprika
½ teaspoon crushed rosemary
1 tablespoon Worcestershire sauce
½ teaspoon dried savory
⅛ teaspoon salt
¼ teaspoon freshly ground black pepper
1 tablespoon cornstarch and 1 tablespoon water, mixed (if necessary)
¼ cup minced fresh parsley
2¾ cups cooked and mashed potatoes

1. Preheat oven to 350°F. Grease a large casserole dish with nonstick cooking spray or olive oil.
2. Sauté the onion, garlic, carrot, parsnip, celery, and beef in a large nonstick skillet until beef is browned. Drain off any excess fat and discard it. Place the mixture into casserole dish. Add the stock, paprika, rosemary, Worcestershire sauce, savory, salt, and pepper. Stir.
3. Place in oven and bake for 1 hour. If the meat mixture still looks very wet after an hour create a slurry by mixing together 1 tablespoon cornstarch and 1 tablespoon water. Stir this into the meat mixture.
4. In a medium bowl, mash the parsley and potatoes using a potato masher. Spread on top of beef mixture in the casserole dish. Place back in oven and bake for 20 minutes until potatoes are heated through.

Save Time in the Morning

Take a few minutes the night before cooking to cut up the vegetables you need for a recipe. Place them in an airtight container or plastic bag and refrigerate until morning. Measure dried spices and place them in a small container on the counter until needed.

French Fry Casserole

Here's another kid favorite that the whole family will love. Frozen French fries, ground beef, and a simple gluten-free cream soup make a tasty weeknight meal. Serve with a salad or streamed green beans.

INGREDIENTS | SERVES 6

1 pound ground beef

1 tablespoon butter

½ onion, finely diced

½ green pepper, diced

1 cup sliced mushrooms

2 tablespoons cornstarch

1⅓ cups milk

½ teaspoon salt

½ teaspoon pepper

3 cups frozen gluten-free shoestring French fries

¾ cup shredded Cheddar cheese

Gluten-Free Shortcuts

You can make several batches of gluten-free cream soup at the beginning of the week to make meals even easier to put together. Pour soup in a glass jar with an airtight lid, and store in the refrigerator for up to 1 week.

1. Preheat oven to 350°F. Grease a 3-quart casserole dish with nonstick cooking spray or olive oil.
2. Brown ground beef in a skillet over medium heat. Pour cooked beef into the casserole dish.
3. In a medium-sized saucepan, melt butter. Add onions, green pepper, and mushrooms. Cook for 3–5 minutes until softened. Mix cornstarch with milk and slowly add to cooked vegetables. Whisk together for 5–10 minutes over medium heat until thickened.
4. Pour soup over ground beef in casserole dish. Sprinkle salt and pepper over soup. Top casserole with French fries. Bake for 35–45 minutes until fries are crispy and golden-brown.
5. Sprinkle cheese on top and bake for an additional 10–15 minutes until cheese is melted.

Chicken Alfredo Pasta

Quartered artichokes add a tangy flavor to this easy pasta casserole.

INGREDIENTS | SERVES 4

1 pound boneless, skinless chicken thighs, cut into ¾" pieces

1 (14-ounce) can quartered artichokes, drained

1 (16-ounce) jar gluten-free Alfredo pasta sauce

1 cup water

½ cup drained and chopped sun-dried tomatoes

8 ounces gluten-free pasta, uncooked

2 tablespoons shredded Parmesan cheese

1. Preheat oven to 350°F. Grease a 2- or 3-quart casserole dish with nonstick cooking spray or olive oil.
2. Add chicken, artichokes, sauce, water, tomatoes, and uncooked pasta to the casserole dish. Cover with foil and bake for 35–40 minutes until the pasta is "al dente" and the sauce is bubbling up around the edges of the casserole dish.
3. Remove foil and bake an additional 10 minutes. Allow casserole to cool for 5 minutes and then sprinkle Parmesan cheese over individual servings, if desired.

Ham and Sweet Potato Casserole

Serve this dish with a tossed salad, applesauce, a steamed vegetable, and warm Gluten-Free Drop Biscuits (see Chapter 3).

INGREDIENTS | SERVES 6

1 (20-ounce) can pineapple tidbits

1 (2-pound) boneless ham steak

3 large sweet potatoes, peeled and diced

1 large sweet onion, peeled and diced

½ cup orange marmalade

2 cloves garlic, peeled and minced

¼ teaspoon freshly ground black pepper

½ teaspoon dried parsley

1 tablespoon brown sugar (optional)

1. Preheat oven to 350°F. Grease a large casserole dish with nonstick cooking spray or olive oil.
2. Drain the pineapple, reserving 2 tablespoons of the juice. Trim the ham and discard any fat. Cut ham into bite-sized pieces. Add the pineapple, 2 tablespoons pineapple juice, and ham to the casserole dish along with the sweet potatoes, onion, marmalade, garlic, black pepper, parsley, and brown sugar, if using. Stir to combine.
3. Cover dish with foil and bake for 50–60 minutes until sweet potatoes are fork tender. Allow dish to cool for 5 minutes before serving.

Cheesy Toast Casserole

This warm, hearty, cheese-filled casserole goes perfectly with homemade tomato soup.

INGREDIENTS | SERVES 4

5 cups gluten-free bread cubes, day old and toasted

4 large eggs, beaten

1½ cups milk

1 tablespoon Dijon mustard

2½ cups shredded Cheddar cheese, divided

½ teaspoon salt

½ teaspoon pepper

1. Preheat oven to 350°F. Grease a 3-quart casserole dish with nonstick cooking spray or olive oil.
2. In a large bowl mix together bread cubes, eggs, milk, mustard, and half of the cheese.
3. Pour the mixture into casserole dish. Top with remaining cheese, salt, and pepper.
4. Bake for 35–40 minutes until casserole is golden-brown. Cool for 5 minutes before serving with homemade tomato soup.

Homemade Tomato Soup

Serve Cheesy Toast Casserole with a side of comforting homemade tomato soup. Sauté 1 small, diced onion with 3 tablespoons butter in a Dutch oven. Add 3 (14½-ounce) cans of low-sodium diced tomatoes, 1 (15-ounce) can gluten-free chicken broth, and 1 tablespoon honey. Cook on medium heat for 20 minutes. Purée soup in small batches in a blender or use an immersion blender. Serve hot.

CHAPTER 5

Breads

Basic Gluten-Free Sandwich Bread

This easy and delicious gluten-free yeast bread recipe uses as few ingredients as possible.

To Proof or Not to Proof

In many bread recipes you need to "proof" the yeast by mixing it with warm water or milk and a little sugar. This activates the yeast, or helps it to start digesting the sugar to grow and create air bubbles that help the bread dough rise. Most of the yeast bread recipes in this book call for instant yeast (also called rapid-rise or bread-machine yeast), as opposed to active dry or fresh yeast—and instant yeast does not need to be proofed to start working. The yeast will start working as soon as it's mixed into the dry ingredients and introduced to warm water.

1. In a large bowl whisk together brown rice flour, arrowroot or tapioca starch, ground flaxseeds, oats, salt, xanthan gum, yeast, and sugar or honey. In a smaller bowl whisk together eggs, milk, and olive oil. Pour wet ingredients into dry ingredients. Stir with a wooden spoon or a fork for several minutes until batter resembles a thick cake batter. First it will look like biscuit dough, but after a few minutes it will appear thick and sticky.

2. Line an 8½" × 4½" metal or glass loaf pan with parchment paper or spritz generously with nonstick cooking spray. Pour bread dough into the pan. Using a spatula that's been dipped in water or spritzed with oil or nonstick cooking spray, spread the dough evenly in the pan. Continue to use the spatula to smooth out the top of the dough.

3. Cover the pan with a tea towel or cover loosely with plastic wrap that has been spritzed with nonstick spray or olive oil (so it will not stick to the dough). Allow dough to rise in a warm space for 1–2 hours until doubled in size. The top of the loaf should rise about 1" above the lip of the pan.

4. Once your dough has doubled, preheat the oven to 425°F. Remove the covering from the loaf and bake for 25–35 minutes. If the bread begins to brown more than desired, place a sheet of foil over the loaf and continue baking. The bread will be done when the internal temperature is between 190–200°F when tested with a food thermometer. Allow bread to cool completely on a wire rack for 2–3 hours before slicing. If you slice the bread when it is still hot, it may lose its shape and fall.

5. Bread will keep on the counter in a zip-top plastic bag for 2–3 days. After 3 days, slice and freeze the remaining loaf.

Dinner Rolls

This recipe proves how versatile gluten-free yeast dough can be. To create burger buns instead of dinner rolls, use English muffin rings or make your own 3½-inch diameter foil rings. Evenly divide dough between 6–8 greased foil rings and bake as directed below.

INGREDIENTS | YIELDS 12–14 ROLLS, DEPENDING ON SIZE

1 recipe Basic Gluten-Free Sandwich Bread dough (see recipe in this chapter)

½ teaspoon garlic powder (optional)

½ teaspoon toasted sesame seeds (optional)

½ teaspoon Italian seasoning (optional)

2–3 tablespoons olive oil or melted butter (optional)

Drop Rolls

Instead of using muffin pans you can make drop rolls. Line a baking sheet with parchment paper. Spritz paper with nonstick cooking spray and drop scoops of dough onto the paper. Bake as directed below.

1. Line a muffin pan with 12 paper liners and spritz liners with nonstick spray, or generously grease pan with oil or nonstick cooking spray.
2. Using an ice-cream scoop, scoop dough into 12 balls and place each ball into a greased paper liner. Sprinkle rolls with any of the optional toppings.
3. Cover the pan with a tea towel or cover loosely with plastic wrap that has been spritzed with nonstick spray or olive oil (so it will not stick to the dough). Allow the rolls to rise in a warm space for 30 minutes until they are about double in size.
4. Once the dough has doubled, preheat the oven to 425°F. Remove the covering from the loaf and bake for 20–25 minutes. If the rolls begin to brown more than desired, place a sheet of foil over the pan and continue baking.
5. Rolls will be done when the internal temperature is 190–200°F when tested with a food thermometer and the tops are golden-brown and crispy. Allow rolls to cool completely on a wire rack for about 30 minutes before eating.
6. Rolls will keep on the counter in a zip-top plastic bag for 2–3 days. After 3 days, freeze any remaining rolls.

Mock "Rye" Bread

Do you miss the distinct flavors of rye and caraway in a rich brown bread? This gluten-free loaf resembles rye bread in taste and texture. It is also rice-free, for those who need to avoid rice-based breads.

INGREDIENTS | YIELDS 1 (10" × 5") LOAF

1½ cups sorghum flour

1 cup arrowroot starch or tapioca starch

2 tablespoons unsweetened cocoa

2 teaspoons xanthan gum

1¼ teaspoons sea salt

2 teaspoons caraway seeds

1 teaspoon dried minced onion

½ teaspoon dill weed

2¼ teaspoons SAF-Instant Yeast, Red Star Quick-Rise or Bread Machine Yeast, or Fleischmann's Bread Machine Yeast

2 large eggs, room temperature

1¼ cups water, heated to 110°F

½ teaspoon apple cider vinegar

3 tablespoons molasses

4 tablespoons olive oil

Sesame seeds (optional)

1. In a large bowl whisk together sorghum flour, arrowroot starch or tapioca starch, cocoa, xanthan gum, salt, caraway seeds, dried onion, dill weed, and yeast. In a smaller bowl whisk together the eggs, water, vinegar, molasses, and olive oil. Pour wet ingredients into dry ingredients. Stir with a wooden spoon or a fork for several minutes until batter resembles a thick cake batter. First it will look like biscuit dough, but after a few minutes it will appear thick and sticky.

2. Line a 1½-pound loaf pan (10" × 5") with parchment paper or spritz generously with nonstick cooking spray. Pour bread dough into the pan. Using a spatula that's been dipped in water or spritzed with oil or nonstick cooking spray, spread the dough evenly in the pan. Continue to use the spatula to smooth the top of the dough.

3. Cover the pan with a tea towel or cover loosely with plastic wrap that has been spritzed with nonstick spray or olive oil (so it will not stick to the dough). Allow dough to rise in a warm space for 1–2 hours until doubled in size. The top of the loaf should rise about 1" above the lip of the pan.

4. Once dough has doubled, preheat the oven to 425°F. Remove the covering from the loaf and, if desired, sprinkle dough with sesame seeds. Bake for 35–45 minutes. If the bread begins to brown more than desired, place a sheet of foil over the loaf and continue baking.

5. Bread will be done when the internal temperature is 190–200°F when tested with a food thermometer. Allow bread to cool completely on a wire rack for 2–3 hours before slicing. If the bread is sliced when it is still hot, it may lose its shape and fall.

6. Bread will keep on the counter in a zip-top plastic bag for 2–3 days. After 3 days, slice and freeze the remaining loaf.

Challah Bread

This challah is lightly sweetened and moist. Your family will never know it's gluten-free.

INGREDIENTS | YIELDS 1 (1½-POUND) LOAF

2 cups brown rice flour

1¾ cups arrowroot starch or tapioca starch

¼ cup sugar

1 teaspoon salt

2½ teaspoons xanthan gum

2½ teaspoons SAF-Instant Yeast, Red Star Quick-Rise or Bread Machine Yeast, or Fleischmann's Bread Machine Yeast

4 large eggs, room temperature

1⅔ cups water, heated to 110°F

1 teaspoon apple cider vinegar

4 tablespoons melted butter

Sesame seeds (optional)

1. In a large bowl whisk together brown rice flour, arrowroot starch or tapioca starch, sugar, salt, xanthan gum, and yeast. In a smaller bowl whisk together the eggs, water, vinegar, and butter. Pour wet ingredients into dry ingredients. Stir with a wooden spoon or a fork for several minutes until batter resembles a thick cake batter. First it will look like biscuit dough, but after a few minutes it will appear thick and sticky.

2. Line a 1½-pound loaf pan (10" × 5") with parchment paper or spritz generously with nonstick cooking spray. Pour bread dough into the pan. Using a spatula that's been dipped in water or spritzed with oil or nonstick cooking spray, spread the dough evenly in the pan. Continue to use the spatula to smooth the top of the dough.

3. Cover the pan with a tea towel or cover loosely with plastic wrap that has been spritzed with nonstick spray or olive oil (so it will not stick to the dough). Allow the dough to rise in a warm space for 1–2 hours until doubled in size. The top of the loaf should rise about 1" above the lip of the pan.

4. Once dough has doubled, preheat the oven to 425°F. Remove the covering from the loaf and, if desired, sprinkle dough with sesame seeds. Bake for 35–45 minutes. If the bread begins to brown more than desired, place a sheet of foil over the loaf and continue baking.

5. Bread will be done when the internal temperature is 190–200°F when tested with a food thermometer. Allow bread to cool completely on a wire rack for 2–3 hours before slicing. If the bread is sliced when it is still hot, it may lose its shape and fall.

6. Bread will keep on the counter in a zip-top plastic bag for 2–3 days. After 3 days, slice and freeze the remaining loaf.

Soft, Light Sandwich Bread

This bread is similar to Udi's gluten-free white bread in texture and taste. It combines yeast and baking powder for a superior rise and lightness—great for kids' peanut butter and jelly sandwiches.

INGREDIENTS | YIELDS 1 (8½" × 4½") LOAF

1 cup brown rice flour

1 cup arrowroot starch or tapioca starch

¼ teaspoon cream of tartar

2 teaspoons sugar

2½ teaspoons SAF-Instant Yeast, Red Star Quick-Rise or Bread Machine Yeast, or Fleischmann's Bread Machine Yeast

2 teaspoon xanthan gum

1 teaspoon salt

1 teaspoon baking powder

¾ cup water, heated to 110°F

3 large egg whites

2 tablespoons olive oil

½ teaspoon apple cider vinegar

Freezing Homemade Gluten-Free Bread

When freezing gluten-free bread, make sure it has cooled completely. Once completely cool, slice the loaf and wrap it in plastic wrap. Then place the loaf in an airtight zip-top plastic bag and freeze. If you've removed most of the air from the bag, you should be able to remove individual slices straight from the freezer without a problem. You can also freeze slices individually.

1. In a large bowl whisk together brown rice flour, arrowroot starch or tapioca starch, cream of tartar, sugar, yeast, xanthan gum, salt, and baking powder. In a smaller bowl whisk together the water, egg whites, olive oil, and vinegar. Pour wet ingredients into dry ingredients. Stir with a wooden spoon or a fork for several minutes until batter resembles a thick cake batter. First it will look like biscuit dough, but after a few minutes it will appear thick and sticky.

2. Line an 8½" × 4½" metal or glass loaf pan with parchment paper or spritz generously with nonstick cooking spray. Pour dough into the pan. Using a spatula that's been dipped in water or spritzed with oil or nonstick cooking spray, spread the dough evenly in the pan. Continue to use the spatula to smooth the top of the bread dough.

3. Cover the pan with a tea towel or cover loosely with plastic wrap that has been spritzed with nonstick spray or olive oil (so it will not stick to the dough). Allow the dough to rise in a warm space for 1–2 hours until doubled in size. The top of the loaf should rise about 1" above the lip of the pan.

4. Once dough has doubled, preheat the oven to 425°F. Remove the covering from the loaf and bake for 25–35 minutes. If the bread begins to brown more than desired, place a sheet of foil over the loaf and continue baking.

5. Bread will be done when the internal temperature is 190–200°F when tested with a food thermometer. Allow bread to cool completely on a wire rack for 2–3 hours before slicing. If the bread is sliced when it is still hot, it may lose its shape and fall.

6. Bread will keep on the counter in a zip-top plastic bag for 2–3 days. After 3 days, slice and freeze the remaining loaf.

Artisan Boule Loaves

Most gluten-free bread dough is actually more of a batter that turns into a dough-like texture as it rises and the chemistry changes in the bread. This lets you create gluten-free bread dough that is kneadable. It's a bit more dense than the other breads in this book, but it's fun to make!

INGREDIENTS | YIELDS 2 (1-POUND) BOULES

1 cup brown rice flour

¾ cup sorghum flour

1½ cups arrowroot starch or tapioca starch

1 tablespoon SAF-Instant Yeast, Red Star Quick-Rise or Bread Machine Yeast, or Fleischmann's Bread Machine Yeast

1½ teaspoons sea salt

2 teaspoons xanthan gum

1⅓ cups water, heated to 110°F

2 large eggs

2½ tablespoons olive oil

1 tablespoon honey

1. In a large bowl whisk together brown rice flour, sorghum flour, arrowroot starch or tapioca starch, yeast, salt, and xanthan gum. In another large bowl stir together water, eggs, olive oil, and honey. Pour wet mixture into the dry ingredients.
2. Stir for several minutes until the dough is like a very thick cake batter and you can form it into a loose ball. Oil a large glass, ceramic, or plastic bowl and set aside.
3. Pour about a tablespoon of olive oil over dough. Using your hands, coat the dough with the oil. Place the ball of dough into the oiled bowl to rise. Cover the bowl loosely with plastic wrap or a tea towel and set in a warm place.
4. Allow the dough to rise for 2 hours, or until it's doubled in size. Place a large piece of parchment paper or a Silpat mat onto a cookie sheet. Dust it with sorghum flour or brown rice flour. Gently pour the risen dough onto the dusted surface. Using a sharp knife, cut the dough into two pieces. Shape each piece into a "boule," or a rustic oval shape. Place loaves several inches apart on the dusted surface. Using a sharp knife, make three ¼" slits on the top of each loaf.
5. Preheat the oven to 400°F. If using a pizza stone, place it in the oven now to get very hot. While the oven is heating, cover the dough with plastic wrap or a tea towel and allow it to rest and rise for an additional 30 minutes. This is your second rise.
6. After the dough has risen it's time to put it in the oven. If you're using a pizza stone, use the cookie sheet to slide the parchment paper with the bread loaves onto the hot stone. If you're just using the cookie sheet, place it carefully in the oven. Bake the bread for 30–45 minutes. When finished the bread should be golden-brown,

should sound a bit hollow if tapped, and should reach an internal temperature of 180–190°F if tested with a thermometer.

7. Place the bread loaves on a wire rack and allow to cool at least 2 hours. The longer you let the bread cool, the better the texture will be when you slice it. To store, place in a zip-top plastic bag. The bread will keep on the counter for about 3 days. After that slice it and freeze any remaining bread.

Italian Focaccia

This chewy and crunchy bread would also make an outstanding deep-dish pizza crust.

INGREDIENTS | YIELDS 12–16 SLICES, DEPENDING ON SIZE

1½ cups brown rice flour

½ cup sorghum flour

2 cups arrowroot starch or tapioca starch

⅔ cup blanched almond flour or nonfat dry milk powder

1 tablespoon xanthan gum

2 teaspoons SAF-Instant Yeast, Red Star Quick-Rise or Bread Machine Yeast, or Fleischmann's Bread Machine Yeast

1 teaspoon salt

1½ cups water, heated to 110°F

3 tablespoons olive oil

4 large egg whites, room temperature

Olive oil for spreading dough

1 clove garlic, finely minced

Fresh herbs, finely chopped (optional, such as rosemary, oregano, or thyme)

Chopped and seeded kalamata olives and Roma tomatoes (optional)

1. Line a 9" × 14" baking dish with parchment paper and grease with nonstick cooking spray or olive oil.
2. In a large bowl whisk together brown rice flour, sorghum flour, arrowroot starch or tapioca starch, almond flour or milk powder, xanthan gum, yeast, and salt. In another bowl whisk together water, olive oil, and egg whites. Pour wet ingredients into dry ingredients and stir together thoroughly into a stiff dough. Continue to mix as much as you can (it is a *very* stiff dough) for an additional 3–4 minutes.
3. Transfer the dough to baking dish. Drizzle the dough with a little olive oil and then evenly spread dough over the entire baking dish. Cover the dough lightly with plastic wrap and allow to rise in a warm place for about 35 minutes.
4. When ready to bake, preheat oven to 400°F. Gently poke the dough all over with your fingers so small wells appear in the dough. Drizzle with additional olive oil and sprinkle on the minced garlic and any of the additional toppings you like.
5. Bake for 15–20 minutes until focaccia is golden-brown and crispy. Allow to cool for 10 minutes, then slice into squares and serve.

Pizza Crust

This crusty, thick, and chewy pizza dough is very similar to the focaccia and French bread recipes and relies on egg whites for that chewy, bready mouth-feel of an awesome pizza.

INGREDIENTS | YIELDS 2 (12") PIZZA CRUSTS

2 cups brown rice flour

2 cups arrowroot starch or tapioca starch

⅔ cup blanched almond flour or nonfat dry milk powder

1 tablespoon sugar

1 teaspoon salt

3 teaspoons xanthan gum

2 teaspoons SAF-Instant Yeast, Red Star Quick-Rise or Bread Machine Yeast, or Fleischmann's Bread Machine Yeast

1 teaspoon Italian seasoning (optional)

1½ cups water, warmed to 110°F

4 large egg whites, room temperature

3 tablespoons olive oil

½ teaspoon apple cider vinegar

Coarse-ground gluten-free cornmeal (optional)

1. In a large bowl whisk together brown rice flour, arrowroot starch or tapioca starch, blanched almond flour or milk powder, sugar, salt, xanthan gum, and yeast. If desired, add Italian seasoning to mixture. In a smaller bowl whisk together the water, egg whites, olive oil, and vinegar.

2. Pour wet ingredients into dry ingredients. Stir with a wooden spoon or a fork for several minutes until batter resembles a thick cake batter. First it will look like biscuit dough, but after a few minutes it will appear thick and sticky.

3. Line 2 (12-inch) pizza pans with parchment paper or spritz pan generously with nonstick cooking spray. If desired, generously sprinkle coarsely ground cornmeal over each pan. Divide pizza dough in half and place dough in the center of each pan. Place a piece of plastic wrap over the dough and gently pat out into an 11" or 12" pizza crust. Leave the crust edges a little bit higher than the center of the dough, so they can contain the sauce and fillings.

4. Cover dough loosely with plastic wrap that has been spritzed with nonstick spray or olive oil (so it will not stick to the dough). Allow dough to rise in a warm space for 10–20 minutes. Preheat oven to 400°F.

5. Remove the plastic wrap from the dough. Prebake dough for 10–15 minutes before adding toppings, fillings, and cheese. Finish baking pizza for an additional 15–20 minutes until cheese is melted and fillings are heated through.

6. Allow pizza to cool for 10–15 minutes before slicing and serving.

White "Snowflake" Rolls

Soft, light rolls dusted generously with brown rice flour are perfect for holiday meals or family dinners.

INGREDIENTS | YIELDS 12–14 ROLLS

1 recipe Basic Gluten-Free Sandwich Bread dough (see recipe in this chapter)

2–3 tablespoons olive oil or melted butter (optional)

⅓ cup brown rice flour

¼ teaspoon sea salt

Try a Muffin Pan Instead

If the rolls don't turn out as round as you'd like on a baking sheet, try placing the dough in a heavily greased muffin pan instead. You could also roll the dough into little balls and place three balls in each greased muffin cup to form homemade "cloverleaf" rolls.

1. Line a baking sheet with parchment paper. Spitz paper with nonstick spray.
2. Using an ice-cream scoop, scoop dough into 12 balls and place each ball onto parchment paper, about 2" apart. Gently brush rolls with oil or butter.
3. Cover the rolls loosely with plastic wrap that has been spritzed with nonstick spray or olive oil (so it will not stick to the dough). Allow the rolls to rise in a warm space for 30 minutes until they are about double in size.
4. Once the rolls have doubled, preheat the oven to 425°F. Remove the plastic wrap. Add the brown rice flour to a wire mesh sifter or small wire mesh colander. Sift the flour generously over the rolls, until the tops are covered and it looks like snow has fallen on them. Dust rolls with sea salt. Bake for 20–22 minutes until rolls are a very light golden-brown with a white topping. You don't want the rolls to brown too much.
5. Allow rolls to cool completely on a wire rack for about 30 minutes before eating.
6. Rolls will keep on the counter in a zip-top plastic bag for 2–3 days. After 3 days, freeze any that remain.

Sourdough Starter

Traditional sourdough starter does not use processed yeast in the preparation, but this type of starter can be hard to develop. Leaving the starter out for several weeks can also invite bad or unhealthy bacteria and yeast organisms. This recipe eliminates those problems.

INGREDIENTS | YIELDS 1–1½ CUPS

1 cup leftover water from cooking potatoes, or 1 cup water mixed with 1 teaspoon potato flakes, heated to 90–100°F

2¼ teaspoons SAF-Instant Yeast, Red Star Quick-Rise or Bread Machine Yeast, or Fleischmann's Bread Machine Yeast

1 teaspoon sugar

1 cup brown rice flour

The Traditional Way to Make Bread

Before baking powder and baking soda became commercially available to the public in the mid-nineteenth century, most breads were created with a homemade sourdough starter made from wheat flour and water. The mixture was allowed to ferment for a period of several days to several weeks, during which it picked up wild yeast in the air from the surrounding environment. Everything from biscuits to loaf bread to crackers were made with the natural starter. The taste of the bread differed depending on where you lived and the strain of wild yeast in your area.

1. In a clean 1–1½ quart glass jar, add potato water and yeast. Stir to combine.
2. Add sugar and brown rice flour and stir again. Cover the jar with a piece of cloth secured with a string or a rubber band around the jar.
3. Place jar in a warm area for 2–3 days until the mixture is bubbly and has fermented and smells yeasty. A thin layer of clear liquid may appear on top of the starter. This is called "hooch" and you can either discard it or stir it back into the starter.
4. To replenish the starter after using it to make bread, add ½ cup of lukewarm water and ¾ cup of brown rice flour; stir to combine. Allow to sit for another 2–3 days to ferment the new mixture.
5. If at *any* time the mixture seems to smell "off," toss it and start a new batch.

Gluten-Free Sourdough Bread

This delicious loaf is quite a bit different than its wheat counterpart, but provides the same great tangy taste as that San Francisco sourdough you know and love.

INGREDIENTS | YIELDS 1 (8½" × 4½") LOAF

1 cup sorghum flour

1 cup arrowroot starch or tapioca starch

1½ teaspoons xanthan gum

½ teaspoon sea salt

⅓ cup blanched almond flour or nonfat dry milk powder

2 tablespoons sugar

2 teaspoons SAF-Instant Yeast, Red Star Quick-Rise or Bread Machine Yeast, or Fleischmann's Bread Machine Yeast

1 large egg

1 large egg white

½ teaspoon apple cider vinegar

½ cup Sourdough Starter (see recipe in this chapter)

3 tablespoons olive oil

1 cup water, heated to 110°F

1. In a large bowl whisk together sorghum flour, arrowroot starch or tapioca starch, xanthan gum, salt, almond milk or milk powder, sugar, and yeast. In a smaller bowl whisk together the egg, egg white, vinegar, sourdough starter, olive oil, and water.

2. Pour wet ingredients into dry ingredients. Stir with a wooden spoon or a fork for several minutes until batter resembles a thick cake batter. First it will look like biscuit dough, but after a few minutes it will appear thick and sticky.

3. Line an 8½" × 4½" metal or glass loaf pan with parchment paper or spritz generously with nonstick cooking spray. Pour dough into the pan. Using a spatula that's been dipped in water or spritzed with oil or nonstick cooking spray, spread the dough evenly in the pan. Continue to use the spatula to smooth the top of the dough.

4. Cover the pan with a tea towel or cover loosely with plastic wrap that has been spritzed with nonstick spray or olive oil (so it will not stick to the dough). Allow the dough to rise in a warm space for 1–2 hours until doubled in size. The top of the loaf should rise about 1" above the lip of the pan.

5. Once dough has doubled, preheat the oven to 425°F. Remove the covering from the loaf and bake for 25–35 minutes. To get a very crispy crust, place a metal pan on the bottom shelf of the oven while it's preheating. When you put bread in to cook, also add 5–6 ice cubes in the metal pan and close the oven door quickly. If the bread begins to brown more than desired while baking, place a sheet of foil over the loaf and continue baking. Bread will be done when the internal temperature is 190–200°F when tested with a food thermometer. Allow bread to cool completely on a wire rack for 2–3 hours

before slicing. If the bread is sliced when it is still hot, it may lose its shape and fall.

6. Bread will keep on the counter in a zip-top plastic bag for 2–3 days. After 3 days, slice and freeze the remaining loaf. Make sure to replenish the sourdough starter if you plan on using it again for another loaf of bread.

Boston Brown Bread

This hearty, amber-colored bread is made in recycled vegetable cans.

INGREDIENTS | YIELDS 3 (15-OUNCE) CANS OF BROWN BREAD

¾ cup gluten-free cornmeal

¾ cup sorghum flour

¾ cup brown rice flour

1 tablespoon cocoa powder

½ teaspoon baking soda

½ teaspoon baking powder

½ teaspoon sea salt

½ teaspoon xanthan gum

1 cup buttermilk or nondairy milk mixed with 1 teaspoon apple cider vinegar or lemon juice

½ cup molasses

1 large egg

½ cup raisins or currants (optional)

Safely Using Recycled Vegetable Cans

When using recycled aluminum cans for baking, make sure to carefully cut away sharp edges with wire cutters so that you do not cut your fingers when filling or emptying the cans. Use cans that do not have plastic inner liners, which can melt when you are baking with them. Use only pure aluminum cans. Clean cans carefully between each use with a baby bottle cleaner.

1. Preheat oven to 325°F. Grease 3 emptied and cleaned 15-ounce aluminum cans and set aside.
2. In a large bowl whisk together cornmeal, sorghum flour, brown rice flour, cocoa, baking soda, baking powder, salt, and xanthan gum.
3. In a smaller bowl mix together buttermilk, molasses, and egg.
4. Mix wet ingredients into dry ingredients with a fork until you have a thick batter. Fold in raisins or currants if desired. Pour ⅓ of the batter into each can. The cans will be about ½ full. Alternately, you can use 2 larger (28-ounce) cans, or a 9" × 5" greased loaf pan.
5. Heat 3–4 cups of water in the microwave on high for 3 minutes. Place cans in a Dutch oven and pour the water around the cans. Cover the Dutch oven with the lid. (If using larger cans or a loaf pan, place in a 9" × 13" baking dish and pour water around the cans or loaf pan. Cover with foil.) Bake for 90 minutes until a toothpick inserted in the middle of the loaf comes out clean.
6. Remove the cans or loaf pan from the water and allow to cool for 5 minutes. Turn out the bread from the baking containers and cool completely on a wire rack. Slice and serve. Leftover bread can be stored in the refrigerator for 2–3 days. Freeze after the third day.

Crusty French Bread

This recipe makes two loaves of tasty French bread. Eat one with your meal and freeze the extra loaf and voilà, you have instant French bread that can be heated in 15–20 minutes in a preheated oven.

INGREDIENTS | YIELDS 2 LOAVES

1 cup arrowroot starch or tapioca starch

2 cups brown rice flour

½ teaspoon sea salt

1 tablespoon xanthan gum

1½ tablespoons SAF-Instant Yeast, Red Star Quick-Rise or Bread Machine Yeast, or Fleischmann's Bread Machine Yeast

2 tablespoons sugar

3 large egg whites

1½ cups water, heated to 110°F

2 tablespoons olive oil

1 teaspoon apple cider vinegar

1 large egg white, lightly beaten with 1 tablespoon water

1. In a large bowl whisk together arrowroot or tapioca starch, brown rice flour, salt, xanthan gum, yeast, and sugar. In a smaller bowl whisk together the egg whites, water, olive oil, and vinegar.

2. Pour wet ingredients into dry ingredients. Stir with a wooden spoon or a fork for several minutes until batter resembles a thick cake batter. First it will look like biscuit dough, but after a few minutes it will appear thick and sticky.

3. Line a French bread pan or baguette pan with parchment paper or spritz generously with nonstick cooking spray. Divide the dough in half and pour into the pan. Shape two long loaves using a spatula that's been dipped in water or spritzed with oil or nonstick cooking spray. Spread the dough evenly in the pan. Continue to use the spatula to smooth the top and sides of the dough. Using a sharp knife, make 3–4 cuts about ¼" deep across the top of each loaf.

4. Cover the pan with a tea towel or cover loosely with plastic wrap that has been spritzed with nonstick spray or olive oil (so it will not stick to the dough). Allow the dough to rise in a warm space for 1–2 hours until it's doubled in size.

5. Once dough has doubled, preheat the oven to 350°F. Remove the covering from the loaf, brush each loaf gently with the egg white and water mixture, and bake for 35 minutes. After 35 minutes, place a sheet of foil over the loaf and continue baking for an additional 20 minutes. Allow bread to cool completely on a wire rack for 30 minutes to 1 hour before slicing.

6. Bread will keep on the counter in a zip-top plastic bag for 2–3 days. After 3 days, slice and freeze the remaining loaf.

Irish Soda Bread

Serve this biscuit-like bread on St. Patrick's Day or any cool day with a big bowl of hot soup or stew.

INGREDIENTS | YIELDS 1 (8" OR 9")
ROUND LOAF

1½ cups sorghum flour

½ cup arrowroot or tapioca starch

2 tablespoons sugar

1 teaspoon baking soda

1½ teaspoons baking powder

1 teaspoon sea salt

1½ teaspoons xanthan gum

6 tablespoons cold butter or Spectrum Palm Shortening

¾ cup buttermilk or nondairy milk mixed with 1 teaspoon apple cider vinegar or lemon juice

2 large eggs

1 cup currants or raisins

1. Preheat oven to 375°F. Line a baking sheet with parchment paper, and sprinkle with brown rice flour. Set aside.
2. In the bowl of a food processor, combine sorghum flour, arrowroot starch or tapioca starch, sugar, baking soda, baking powder, salt, and xanthan gum. Pulse to combine ingredients. (If you don't have a food processor, combine all dry ingredients in a medium-sized mixing bowl and whisk together well.)
3. Add the butter or shortening and pulse until the butter is the size of peas. Or, use a pastry blender to cut the butter into the dry ingredients, working quickly because you want the butter to stay cold.
4. Add the buttermilk or nondairy milk and eggs, and run the food processor until the dough comes together in a sticky ball. (Alternately, you can use a wooden spoon and stir until the dough comes together.) Stir in the raisins or currants.
5. Turn dough out onto baking sheet and flour your hands with more brown rice flour. Working quickly, pat the dough down into a large 8" or 9" circle. With a sharp knife, cut an "X" about ¼-inch deep into the center of the loaf. Gently brush the top of the loaf with additional buttermilk or nondairy milk.
6. Bake for 30 minutes, or until the loaf is golden-brown and crispy on top. Allow to cool for 25–30 minutes on a cooling rack before slicing into 8 triangles and serving. Store any remaining bread in an airtight container on the counter for 2–3 days.

Sweet Corn Bread

*This sweet corn bread is a great accompaniment to a hearty pot of chili.
For extra texture and flavor add ½ cup cooked and drained sweet corn kernels
and 4 slices cooked and crumbled bacon to the batter before baking.*

INGREDIENTS | YIELDS 12 SLICES

⅓ cup brown rice flour

⅔ cup arrowroot starch

⅔ cup gluten-free cornmeal

1 teaspoon xanthan gum

2 teaspoons baking powder

½ teaspoon salt

3 tablespoons sugar

¼ cup oil

2 large eggs

1 cup milk

1. Preheat oven to 425°F.
2. In a large bowl whisk together brown rice flour, arrowroot starch, and cornmeal. Add xanthan gum, baking powder, salt, and sugar. Mix thoroughly. In a smaller bowl mix together the oil, eggs, and milk.
3. Mix wet ingredients into dry ingredients with a fork, until you have a thick batter. Grease a 9" cake pan or iron skillet and pour batter into the pan. Spread the batter evenly over the whole pan.
4. Bake corn bread for 18–20 minutes until golden-brown and crispy around the edges. Cool for 5–10 minutes before slicing and serving.

Gluten-Free Corn Bread Stuffing

Crumble 1 recipe of day-old gluten-free corn bread. Combine in a large bowl with 1½ teaspoons poultry seasoning, 1 cup each sautéed celery and onions, and ½ teaspoon each salt and pepper. Stir in 1–2 cups gluten-free chicken broth and ¼ cup melted butter. Bake in a large casserole dish at 350°F for 20–30 minutes until the top of the stuffing is as crispy as you like it. Cool for 5 minutes before serving.

Cheddar Dill Bread

This savory, cheesy bread is delicious with any easy weeknight meal. For variety, try a different type of cheese and add additional or different seasonings, such as herbes de Provence or Greek seasoning.

INGREDIENTS | YIELDS 1 (8" OR 9") ROUND LOAF

1 cup brown rice flour

1 cup arrowroot starch or tapioca starch

2 teaspoons baking powder

1 teaspoon xanthan gum

½ teaspoon sea salt

1 tablespoon sugar

2 teaspoons dill weed

¼ cup butter or Spectrum Palm Shortening

1 cup shredded Cheddar cheese, or nondairy cheddar substitute

1 large egg

1 cup milk or nondairy substitute

1. Preheat oven to 350°F.
2. In a large bowl whisk together brown rice flour and arrowroot starch or tapioca starch. Add baking powder, xanthan gum, salt, sugar, and dill weed. Mix thoroughly. Cut in butter or shortening until mixture is crumbly. In a smaller bowl mix together the cheese, egg, and milk.
3. Mix wet ingredients into dry ingredients with a fork, until you have a thick batter. Heavily grease an 8" or 9" cake pan and pour batter into the pan. Spread the batter evenly over the whole pan.
4. Bake bread for 35–40 minutes until golden-brown and crispy around the edges. Cool for 10–15 minutes before slicing and serving.

Crescent Rolls

These rolls take a bit of work to make, but they're worth it. For a fun meal, wrap individual crescent rolls around hot dogs and bake as directed for meal-size Pigs-in-a-Blanket (see Chapter 3).

INGREDIENTS | YIELDS 10–12 ROLLS

½ cup sorghum flour, plus more for the baking sheet

½ cup arrowroot starch or tapioca starch

1 teaspoon xanthan gum

⅛ teaspoon sea salt

¾ teaspoon baking powder

1 teaspoon sugar

4 tablespoons butter, frozen and grated

¾ cup full-fat, small-curd cottage cheese

1. Preheat oven to 350°F. Sprinkle sorghum flour on a parchment paper-lined baking sheet and set aside.
2. In a large bowl whisk together sorghum flour, arrowroot starch or tapioca starch, xanthan gum, salt, baking powder, and sugar. In another large bowl mix together butter and cottage cheese.
3. Add the dry ingredients to the butter mixture and mix thoroughly until a ball of dough forms. Roll out the dough onto the parchment paper in a large 8–10" circle to ¼" thickness.
4. Using a pizza cutter, slice the circle into 8 triangles. Roll each triangle up starting with the wide end and continuing to the tip. Place the crescent rolls about 2" apart on baking sheet.
5. Bake 18–20 minutes until rolls are golden-brown. Serve hot. Store any leftover rolls in the refrigerator for 2–3 days. Baked rolls can also be frozen for up to 3 months and reheated to serve.

Hot Cross Buns

Traditionally Christians serve these buns on Good Friday. They are slightly sweetened yeast-risen buns seasoned with different types of fruit and spices. But these buns are way too good to only serve once a year!

INGREDIENTS | YIELDS 12 BUNS

1½ cups sorghum flour

1½ cups arrowroot starch or tapioca starch

2 teaspoons xanthan gum

½ teaspoon sea salt

1 teaspoon cinnamon

¼ teaspoon allspice

1 teaspoon baking powder

1 teaspoon lemon zest

1 teaspoon orange zest

2¼ teaspoons SAF-Instant Yeast, Red Star Quick-Rise or Bread Machine Yeast, or Fleischmann's Bread Machine Yeast

¼ cup brown sugar

2 large eggs, room temperature

3 tablespoons olive oil

1 teaspoon apple cider vinegar

1 cup water, heated to 110°F

¾ cup raisins or currants

1 large egg white, lightly beaten with 1 tablespoon water

Citrus Glaze for Hot Cross Buns

In a small bowl whisk together 1 cup of confectioners' sugar with 1 teaspoon finely grated orange zest and 1–2 teaspoons of lemon juice. Mix until glaze is thick, but pourable. If needed, add 1 more teaspoon lemon juice. Pour glaze into a sandwich-sized plastic bag and snip one corner off the bag. Use the plastic bag as a piping bag and place an icing "cross" over each bun after it has cooled.

1. In a large bowl whisk together sorghum flour, arrowroot starch or tapioca starch, xanthan gum, salt, cinnamon, allspice, baking powder, lemon zest, orange zest, yeast, and brown sugar. In a smaller bowl whisk together the eggs, oil, vinegar, and water.

2. Pour wet ingredients into dry ingredients. Stir in the raisins or currants. Stir with a wooden spoon or a fork for several minutes until batter resembles a thick cake batter. First it will look like biscuit dough, but after a few minutes it will appear thick and sticky.

3. Using an ice-cream scoop, scoop dough into 12 balls and place each ball onto the greased parchment paper, about 2" apart.

4. Cover the rolls loosely with plastic wrap that has been spritzed with nonstick spray or olive oil (so it will not stick to the dough). Allow the rolls to rise in a warm space for 30 minutes until they are about double in size.

5. Once the rolls have doubled, preheat the oven to 375°F. Remove the plastic wrap and brush each roll gently with the egg white and water mixture, and then bake for 30–35 minutes until rolls are a very light golden-brown.

6. Allow rolls to cool completely on a wire rack for about 30 minutes. Add citrus glaze as directed in the sidebar.

7. Rolls will keep on the counter in a zip-top plastic bag for 2–3 days. After 3 days, freeze any remaining rolls.

CHAPTER 6

Cobblers and Crisps

Grandma's Blueberry Cobbler

This old-fashioned cobbler has sweetened fruit on the bottom
and a crunchy, biscuit topping. Serve it plain or with vanilla ice cream.

INGREDIENTS | SERVES 4–6

¾ cup water

⅔ cup, plus 2 tablespoons, sugar, divided

2 tablespoons cornstarch or arrowroot starch

3 cups fresh or frozen blueberries

½ cup brown rice flour

½ cup arrowroot starch or tapioca starch

1 teaspoon baking powder

¼ teaspoon xanthan gum

⅓ cup milk or nondairy substitute

1 tablespoon melted butter or canola oil

½ teaspoon cinnamon, mixed with 2 teaspoons sugar

2 tablespoons cold butter or nondairy margarine

Make It Easier

If you don't want to go to the trouble of making your own fruit filling, use a can of cherry or apple pie filling, or even a can of whole cranberry jelly. Make the cobbler even easier by replacing the brown rice flour, arrowroot starch, baking powder, and xanthan gum with 1 cup Bisquick Gluten Free.

1. Preheat oven to 425°F. Grease a 2-quart baking dish, pie pan, or casserole dish and set aside.
2. In a small saucepan add water, ⅔ cup sugar, and cornstarch or arrowroot starch. Mix or whisk together and cook over high heat, stirring constantly until boiling. Allow to boil for 1 minute. The cornstarch-water mixture will turn translucent and thicken. Remove from heat and add blueberries. Pour blueberry filling into baking dish.
3. In a small bowl whisk together brown rice flour, arrowroot or tapioca starch, baking powder, remaining sugar, and xanthan gum. Make a well in the center of the dry ingredients and add milk and melted butter. Mix until you have a thick batter. Drop batter by tablespoons on top of the blueberry filling and use a fork to spread evenly over the casserole. It doesn't have to be perfectly covered.
4. Sprinkle cinnamon-sugar mixture over the top of the casserole. Dot with the cold butter. Place the casserole dish on a cookie sheet to prevent filling spills in the oven while baking. Bake for 25–30 minutes until fruit filling is bubbling on the sides of the dish and the biscuit topping is cooked through and crispy. Allow cobbler to cool for 30 minutes before serving.

Cranberry Apple Cobbler

*Tart cranberries with sweet, yet tart Granny Smith apples make
a perfect filling for this simple gluten-free cobbler.*

INGREDIENTS | SERVES 6–8

Filling

5 Granny Smith apples, peeled, cored,
and chopped

1 cup raw cranberries

¼ cup sugar

¼ cup brown sugar

½ teaspoon ground cinnamon

¼ teaspoon ground nutmeg

2 teaspoons cornstarch

1 medium lemon, juiced and strained
(about 3 tablespoons lemon juice)

⅛ teaspoon sea salt

Batter

½ cup sorghum flour

½ cup arrowroot starch or tapioca starch

½ cup sugar

2 teaspoons baking soda

¼ teaspoon sea salt

¾ cup milk or nondairy substitute

6 tablespoons cubed cold butter

1. Preheat oven to 350°F. Grease a 2-quart baking dish, pie pan, or casserole dish and set aside.
2. In a large bowl mix together all filling ingredients. Pour the filling into the baking dish.
3. In a small bowl whisk together sorghum flour, arrowroot starch, sugar, baking soda, and sea salt. Make a well in the center of the dry ingredients and add milk. Mix until you have a thick batter. Drop batter by tablespoons on top of cranberry-apple filling and use a fork to spread evenly over the casserole. It doesn't have to be perfectly covered.
4. Dot the cobbler with butter. Place the casserole dish on a cookie sheet to prevent any filling from spilling over in the oven while baking. Bake for 25–30 minutes until fruit filling is bubbling on the sides of the topping and the soft topping is golden-brown. Allow cobbler to cool for 30 minutes before serving. Serve plain or with ice cream.

Maple Walnut Apple Crisp

This is the perfect dish to make with that big jug of maple syrup you brought back from New England (or your local grocery store). Try this crisp with sliced almonds, if you prefer.

INGREDIENTS | SERVES 6–8

Filling

5 medium apples, cored, peeled, and diced

¼ cup sugar

¼ cup maple syrup

Topping

1¼ cups gluten-free rolled oats

¾ cup brown rice flour

⅓ cup walnuts, chopped

2 tablespoons packed brown sugar

2 teaspoons ground cinnamon

¼ teaspoon ground nutmeg

½ teaspoon sea salt

¼ cup maple syrup

½ cup butter, softened

1. Preheat oven to 350°F. Grease a 2-quart baking dish, pie pan, or casserole dish and set aside.
2. In a large bowl mix together apples, sugar, and maple syrup. Pour the apple filling into the baking dish.
3. In a small bowl whisk together oats, brown rice flour, chopped walnuts, brown sugar, spices, and salt. Make a well in the center of the dry ingredients and stir in maple syrup. Cut in butter with a fork, until you have a crumbly topping mixture. Sprinkle crumb topping evenly over apple filling. It doesn't have to be perfectly covered.
4. Place the casserole dish on a cookie sheet to prevent spills in the oven while baking. Bake for 35–40 minutes until the top is crisp and lightly browned. Allow crisp to cool for 30 minutes before serving. Serve plain or with ice cream.

Try It with Molasses

For a truly unique crisp, replace the maple syrup in this recipe with molasses for just a slightly sweet filling and topping. The molasses will create a darker topping and give a rich flavor and color to this dish. Blackstrap molasses is a bit darker than "regular" molasses and is more concentrated. It also contains more vitamins and minerals than the regular variety.

Blueberry Buckle

A "buckle" is an old-fashioned one-layer moist cake that often has lots of fruit or berries. It has a crumbly topping, but the "filling" is a solid cake, not a thickened fruit filling. Substitute different fruits or berries to create your very own buckle.

INGREDIENTS | SERVES 6–8

Cake

½ cup sorghum flour

½ cup arrowroot starch or tapioca starch

½ teaspoon xanthan gum

1 teaspoon baking powder

½ teaspoon sea salt

¼ cup (4 tablespoons) butter, softened

¾ cup sugar

1 large egg

½ cup milk or nondairy substitute

1 pint blueberries, washed and patted dry

Topping

½ cup sugar

½ cup sorghum flour

½ cup arrowroot starch or tapioca starch

½ teaspoon ground cinnamon

¼ cup (4 tablespoons) butter, softened

1. Preheat oven to 350°F. Heavily grease an 8" cake pan or springform pan and set aside.
2. Make the cake: In a medium bowl whisk together ½ cup sorghum flour, ½ cup arrowroot starch, xanthan gum, baking powder, and salt. In a large bowl cream together the butter and ¾ cup sugar. Stir in the egg and milk. Slowly stir in the flour mixture a little at a time, until you have a thick batter. Fold in the blueberries. (If you use frozen blueberries, don't defrost them or your batter will turn blue.) Pour the batter into the greased pan.
3. Make the topping: In a small bowl whisk together sugar, ½ cup sorghum flour, ½ cup arrowroot or tapioca starch, and cinnamon. Cut in butter with a fork, until you have a crumbly topping mixture. Sprinkle crumb topping evenly over the cake batter.
4. Bake for 35–40 minutes until the top is crisp and lightly browned and a toothpick inserted in the middle comes out clean. Allow to cool for 30 minutes before serving. Serve plain or with ice cream.

Peach Cobbler

This is a popular dessert in barbecue restaurants all over eastern North Carolina. The best peach cobblers have simple ingredients and are super buttery and crispy around the edges.

INGREDIENTS | SERVES 6–8

½ cup butter

1 cup brown rice flour

½ teaspoon ground cinnamon

¼ teaspoon xanthan gum

1 cup milk or nondairy substitute

1 large egg

1 tablespoon vanilla extract

3–4 cups fresh or frozen peeled, sliced, and seeded peaches

Try It with Canned Peaches

If you don't have fresh peaches available try using a 29-ounce can of sliced peaches. Make sure to drain the peaches thoroughly before adding to the baking dish. Too much liquid will make a very watery cobbler.

1. Preheat oven to 350°F. Grease a 9" × 13" baking pan. Put butter in the pan and place in the oven to melt.
2. In a small bowl whisk together brown rice flour, cinnamon, and xanthan gum. Make a well in the center of the dry ingredients and add milk, egg, and vanilla. The batter should have the texture of pancake batter.
3. Using potholders, remove the baking dish from oven. Pour the batter into baking dish and then drop peaches evenly throughout the batter. Don't mix them in, just gently drop them over the top of the batter.
4. Bake for 25–30 minutes until the topping is golden-brown and butter is bubbling around the edges of the pan. Allow cobbler to cool for 30 minutes before serving. Serve plain or with ice cream.

Cherry Oat Crisp

This crisp is special because it has a rich bottom crust, so it's almost like a pie with a crispy topping.

INGREDIENTS | SERVES 6–8

Crust

1 cup brown rice flour

¼ teaspoon sea salt

¼ cup packed brown sugar

½ cup softened butter or Spectrum Palm Shortening

Filling

¾ cup sugar

¼ cup cornstarch

1 cup cherry juice blend or apple juice

4 cups pitted dark-red plain cherries, not cherry pie filling (frozen or canned; if canned, drain before using)

Crisp Topping

1½ cups gluten-free rolled oats

¼ cup packed brown sugar

¼ cup brown rice flour

5 tablespoons butter, softened

1. Preheat oven to 350°F. Grease a 2-quart baking dish, pie pan, or casserole dish and set aside.
2. In a medium bowl mix together 1 cup brown rice flour, salt, and ¼ cup brown sugar. Cut in ½ cup butter with a pastry blender, until mixture is crumbly. Press crust mixture into the bottom of the baking dish. Bake for 15 minutes and remove from oven.
3. Make the filling: In a small saucepan add sugar, cornstarch, and juice. Mix or whisk together and cook over high heat, stirring constantly until boiling. Allow to boil for 1 minute. The cornstarch/juice mixture will turn translucent and thicken. Remove from heat and add cherries. Pour cherry filling over the baked crust.
4. In another small bowl whisk together oats, ¼ cup brown sugar, and ¼ cup brown rice flour. Cut in 5 tablespoons of butter with a pastry blender, until the mixture is crumbly. Sprinkle the topping evenly over the cherry filling.
5. Place crisp on a cookie sheet to prevent spills in the oven while baking. Bake for 25–30 minutes until crispy topping is golden-brown and cherry filling is bubbling around the edges. Allow the crisp to cool for 30 minutes before serving. Serve plain or with ice cream.

Apple Cobbler with Cheddar Biscuit Crust

This cobbler is very easy to prepare in advance—bake it just before serving.

INGREDIENTS | SERVES 8–10

1 cup brown rice flour

1 cup arrowroot starch or tapioca starch

½ teaspoon xanthan gum

½ teaspoon salt

4 teaspoons baking powder

½ teaspoon cayenne pepper

¼ cup butter, softened

¾ cup buttermilk

¾ cup grated sharp Cheddar cheese

8 large tart apples such as Granny Smiths, peeled, cored, and sliced

⅓ cup lemon juice

2 teaspoons cinnamon

¼ teaspoon nutmeg

1½ tablespoons cornstarch

¼ cup dark brown sugar

¼ cup sugar

Pinch salt

4 tablespoons butter

1. Preheat the oven to 325°F.
2. In a large bowl, mix the brown rice flour, arrowroot starch or tapioca starch, xanthan gum, salt, baking powder, and pepper. Cut in the butter with a fork until it looks like oatmeal. Add the buttermilk and stir. Stir in the cheese and set aside.
3. Place the apples in a 9" × 13" baking dish or a 2-quart casserole. Sprinkle them with lemon juice.
4. In a small bowl, mix together cinnamon, nutmeg, cornstarch, sugars, and salt. Pour over the apples and toss together. Dot with butter. Drop the cheese mixture by the tablespoonful over the top.
5. Bake for 50 minutes, or until crust is browned and the apples are bubbling. Serve with extra slices of cheese or vanilla ice cream.

Blueberry Peach Cobbler

This cobbler smells and tastes like August; however, if you blanch and freeze your peaches and buy frozen blueberries, you can reminisce over a past August in January.

INGREDIENTS | SERVES 10

6 ripe peaches, blanched in boiling water, peeled, pitted, and sliced

½ cup fresh lemon juice

1 cup sugar, divided

1 pint blueberries, rinsed and picked over, stems removed

½ cup unsalted butter, melted

½ teaspoon salt

1½ cups brown rice flour or sorghum flour

1 tablespoon baking powder

1 cup buttermilk

1. Preheat the oven to 375°F.
2. Place peaches in a large bowl and sprinkle with lemon juice and ½ cup sugar. Add the blueberries and mix well.
3. Prepare a 9" × 13" baking dish with nonstick spray. Spread the peaches and blueberries on the bottom.
4. Pour the butter into a large bowl. Add the remaining ½ cup sugar and salt and whisk in the flour and baking powder. Add the buttermilk and stir; don't worry about lumps.
5. Drop the batter by tablespoons over the fruit. Bake for 35–40 minutes. Cool for 25 minutes. Serve with vanilla ice cream or whipped cream.

Instead of Buttermilk

If you prefer, you can use plain yogurt instead of buttermilk. If you are dairy-intolerant you can use your favorite non-dairy milk, such as almond milk, and mix 1 cup with 2 tablespoons apple cider vinegar or lemon juice. If you allow the mixture to sit, it will separate, but that's okay. Just stir it back together and use as directed for the buttermilk.

Apple Brown Betty

This simple dessert will please the pickiest of palates. The lemon zest and freshly grated nutmeg really make this dessert—don't leave them out!

INGREDIENTS | SERVES 6–8

2 teaspoons freshly grated nutmeg

½ cup sugar

3 cups (¼") bread cubes from about 4–5 slices gluten-free bread

4 tablespoons melted butter

2 tablespoons freshly grated lemon zest (from 2 medium lemons)

2 pounds large apples, such as Gala or Pink Lady

2–4 tablespoons cold water

1. Preheat oven to 375°F.
2. In a small bowl combine the nutmeg and sugar. Set aside 2 tablespoons of this mixture for later. Add the bread cubes to a large bowl and toss together with the remaining sugar mixture, melted butter, and lemon zest.
3. Peel, core, and slice the apples into thick wedges. Line the bottom of a 3- or 4-quart casserole dish with 1 cup bread cubes. Add a layer of apples. Repeat layers until you have no more apples or bread cubes. Drizzle the water over the casserole and then evenly sprinkle the 2 tablespoons of sugar and nutmeg over the apple mixture. Place the lid on the casserole dish or cover with foil.
4. Bake covered for 40 minutes. Then remove lid or foil and bake an additional 10–15 minutes until the top of the casserole is golden-brown and crusty.
5. Allow to cool for 10 minutes before serving in bowls with a scoop of ice cream or whipped cream.

Blackberry Almond Crisp

This is a lighter crisp with less sugar and butter than most of the recipes in this chapter. It's delicious served with nonfat frozen yogurt.

INGREDIENTS | SERVES 6

Filling

1½ pints fresh blackberries, rinsed, and excess water shaken off (do not pat dry)

¼ cup plus 2 tablespoons brown sugar

½ teaspoon ground cinnamon

Topping

½ cup gluten-free rolled oats

2 tablespoons brown rice flour

¼ teaspoon sea salt

2 tablespoons butter, softened

¼ cup sliced almonds

1. Preheat oven to 350°F. Grease a 2-quart baking dish, pie pan, or casserole dish and set aside.
2. In a large bowl mix together the blackberries, brown sugar, and cinnamon. Pour the blackberry filling into the baking dish.
3. In a small bowl whisk together the oats, brown rice flour, and salt. Cut in the butter with a pastry blender, until you have a crumbly mixture. Evenly sprinkle topping over the blackberry filling, then sprinkle with sliced almonds.
4. Place the baking dish on a cookie sheet to prevent spills in the oven while baking. Bake for 35 minutes until berries are bubbling on the sides of the topping and the crisp is golden-brown. Allow to cool for 20 minutes before serving.

Strawberry Cobbler

This cobbler recipe uses a pancake-like batter to surround the fruit in the dish. It's similar to the peach cobbler in this book, though strawberries lend a different flavor and texture to this dish.

INGREDIENTS | SERVES 6

½ cup butter

½ cup sorghum flour

½ cup arrowroot starch

¼ teaspoon baking powder

¼ teaspoon xanthan gum

¼ teaspoon cinnamon

1 cup sugar

1 cup milk or nondairy substitute

1 teaspoon vanilla extract

2–3 cups fresh or frozen sliced strawberries (if you use frozen, don't defrost them)

Use a Different Extract

You can use other extracts to vary the flavors in recipes like this. Instead of vanilla extract, try using strawberry or lemon extract instead. It will enhance the sweetness of the dish and give the cobbler a stronger fruit flavor.

1. Preheat oven to 350°F. Place the butter into a 2- to 3-quart casserole dish and place in the hot oven to melt.
2. In a small bowl whisk together brown rice flour, arrowroot starch, baking powder, xanthan gum, cinnamon, and sugar. Make a well in the center of the dry ingredients and add milk and vanilla. The batter should have the texture of pancake batter.
3. Using potholders, remove baking dish from the oven. Pour batter into the dish and then drop strawberries evenly throughout the batter. Don't mix them in, just gently drop them over the top of the batter.
4. Bake for 25–30 minutes until the topping is golden-brown and butter is bubbling around the edges of the pan. Allow cobbler to cool for 30 minutes before serving. Serve plain or with ice cream.

Old-Fashioned Chocolate Cobbler

This rich and delicious gluten-free chocolate dessert creates its own chocolate sauce underneath the cake. Don't be alarmed if it doesn't look like a normal cake. It's meant to be served with ice cream or whipped cream on top.

INGREDIENTS | SERVES 6–8

4 tablespoons butter, melted

1 cup brown rice flour

½ teaspoon baking powder

¼ teaspoon salt

½ cup plus ⅓ cup sugar, divided

2 tablespoons plus ¼ cup cocoa powder, divided

1 teaspoon vanilla

¾ cup milk

1 large egg

1¼ cups boiling water

1. Preheat oven to 350°F. Place the butter into a 2- to 3-quart casserole dish and place in the hot oven to melt.

2. In a small bowl whisk together the brown rice flour, baking powder, salt, ½ cup sugar, and 2 tablespoons cocoa powder. Stir in the vanilla, milk, and egg. Using potholders, remove the dish from the oven. Pour the batter into the dish and spread it evenly over the butter. It's okay if the butter comes up around the batter. Sprinkle the additional ⅓ cup of sugar and ¼ cup cocoa powder over the cake batter. Then pour the boiling water over the entire cake.

3. Bake for 35 minutes until the topping is deep brown and chocolate sauce is bubbling around the edges of the pan. The actual "cake" part of the cobbler will *not* be pretty—it may seem too dark and it may not crisp up. That's okay. Allow cobbler to cool for at least 40 minutes before serving. This is crucial to allow the chocolate sauce to set up underneath the cobbler top.

4. Serve warm with vanilla ice cream or whipped cream.

Apple Oatmeal Crisp

You may need to adjust the cooking time depending on the type of apples you use. A Golden Delicious apple should be cooked through and soft in the recommended cooking time, but a crisper Granny Smith, Roma, or Gala apple may take 10–15 minutes longer.

INGREDIENTS | SERVES 8

Filling

8 medium apples, cored and sliced
3 tablespoons orange juice
½ cup sugar
3 tablespoons gluten-free quick-cooking oats
½ teaspoon apple pie spice (or ¼ teaspoon each ground cinnamon and ground nutmeg)
3 tablespoons water

Topping

1 cup gluten-free quick-cooking oats
½ cup pecans, chopped
⅓ cup brown sugar
½ teaspoon cinnamon
¼ cup butter, softened

1. Preheat oven to 350°F. Grease a 2-quart baking dish, pie pan, or casserole dish and set aside.
2. In a large bowl mix together all the filling ingredients. Pour the apple filling into the baking dish.
3. Make the topping: In a small bowl whisk together the oats, chopped pecans, brown sugar, and cinnamon. Cut in the softened butter with a pastry blender, until you have a crumbly mixture. Evenly sprinkle topping over filling.
4. Place the baking dish on a cookie sheet to prevent spills in the oven while baking. Bake for 35 minutes until filling is bubbling on the sides of the topping and the top of the crisp is golden-brown. Allow crisp to cool for 20 minutes before serving with whipped cream or ice cream.

Chai Latte Cupcakes with Nutmeg Cardamom Icing (Chapter 8)

Baked Chocolate Doughnuts (Chapter 2)

Chewy Gluten-Free Vegan Bagels (Chapter 13)

Almond Flour Irish Soda Bread (Chapter 12)

Mini Flourless Cupcakes (Chapter 10)

Favorite Lemon Squares (Chapter 7)

Homemade Toaster Pastries (Chapter 13)

Snickerdoodles (Chapter 3)

Cranberry Cobbler (Chapter 11)

Orange Crispy Cookies (Chapter 10)

Devil's Food Cake with Mocha Buttercream
(Chapter 8)

Italian Breadsticks (Chapter 13)

Soft, Light Sandwich Bread (Chapter 5)

Honey Pumpkin Pie (Chapter 12)

Mini Cherry Cheesecakes (Chapter 10)

Classic Coconut Cake (Chapter 8)

Grandma's Blueberry Cobbler (Chapter 6)

Cheddar Garlic Biscuits (Chapter 3)

Banana Walnut Bread (Chapter 12)

Corn Bread Muffins (Chapter 10)

Cream Cheese Raspberry Danish (Chapter 2)

Easy Vegetarian Lasagna with Spinach (Chapter 4)

Date Pinwheel Cookies (Chapter 7)

Lattice-Topped Cherry Pie (Chapter 9)

Peach Nutmeg Crisp

This crisp combines the bold flavors of nutmeg and cardamom.
If you enjoy chai tea, you'll love how these spices work with the peaches and crispy topping.
If you don't have cardamom, substitute the same amount of cinnamon.

INGREDIENTS | SERVES 6–8

6 whole peaches, pitted, peeled, and sliced

2 tablespoons lemon juice

½ cup sugar

1 cup brown rice flour

½ cup brown sugar

1 teaspoon freshly grated nutmeg

½ teaspoon ground cardamom

¼ teaspoon ground ginger

¼ teaspoon sea salt

½ cup butter, softened

A Leftover Dessert?

Crisps and cobblers were very popular during the Depression when food was scarce, and during the days before refrigeration because they used up fruits that otherwise would have spoiled.

1. Preheat oven to 350°F. Grease a 2- or 3-quart baking dish, pie pan, or casserole dish and set aside.
2. In a large bowl mix together the sliced peaches, lemon juice, and sugar. Pour the peach filling into baking dish.
3. In a small bowl whisk together the brown rice flour, brown sugar, nutmeg, cardamom, ginger, and sea salt. Cut in the softened butter with a pastry blender, until you have a crumbly mixture. Evenly sprinkle topping over the peach filling.
4. Place the baking dish on a cookie sheet to prevent spills in the oven while baking. Bake for 35 minutes until filling is bubbling on the sides of the topping and the top of the crisp is golden-brown. Allow crisp to cool for 20 minutes before serving with whipped cream or ice cream.

Zucchini Crisp

You could also call this a "Mock Apple Crisp" as zucchini will generally taste like anything you season them with. This recipe uses cinnamon and nutmeg to make it taste like an apple pie, but you get the added nutrition of zucchini.

INGREDIENTS | SERVES 12

Filling
8 cups cubed zucchini
½ cup apple juice or orange juice
2 tablespoons brown rice flour
2 teaspoons ground cinnamon
1 teaspoon freshly grated nutmeg
½ cup sugar

Topping
1⅓ cups gluten-free rolled oats
1 cup brown rice flour
1 cup brown sugar
¼ teaspoon sea salt
⅔ cup (about 11 tablespoons) butter, softened

1. Preheat oven to 375°F. Grease a 2- or 3-quart baking dish, pie pan, or large casserole dish and set aside.
2. In a large bowl mix together the zucchini, juice, brown rice flour, cinnamon, nutmeg, and sugar. Pour zucchini filling into the greased baking dish.
3. In a small bowl whisk together the oats, brown rice flour, brown sugar, and salt. Cut in the butter with a pastry blender, until you have a crumbly mixture. Evenly sprinkle the topping over filling.
4. Place the baking dish on a cookie sheet to prevent spills in the oven while baking. Bake for 45–50 minutes until filling is bubbling on the sides of the topping, the zucchini is tender, and the top of the crisp is golden-brown. Allow crisp to cool for 20 minutes before serving with whipped cream or ice cream.

Pumpkin Crisp

Did you think the only thing you could do with pumpkin was make a pie?
Pumpkin works well in a variety of gluten-free baked goods, including breads,
muffins, and cake—it is particularly good in this crisp recipe.

INGREDIENTS | SERVES 8

Filling

2 (15-ounce) cans plain pumpkin purée
⅓ cup brown sugar
½ cup sugar
3 tablespoons orange juice
1 tablespoon orange zest
3 large eggs, beaten
½ cup milk

Topping

¾ cup chopped pecans
½ cup gluten-free rolled oats
½ cup brown rice flour
½ cup brown sugar
1 teaspoon cinnamon
½ cup butter, softened

1. Preheat oven to 375°F. Grease a 2- or 3-quart baking dish, pie pan, or large casserole dish and set aside.
2. In a large bowl whisk together the filling ingredients. Pour the pumpkin filling into the baking dish.
3. In a small bowl whisk together the chopped pecans, oats, brown rice flour, brown sugar, and cinnamon. Cut in the butter with a pastry blender, until you have a crumbly mixture. Evenly sprinkle the topping over filling.
4. Place the baking dish on a cookie sheet to prevent spills in the oven while baking. Bake for 45–50 minutes until the top of the crisp is golden-brown and the pumpkin filling is set. A knife inserted into the middle of the crisp should come out clean. Allow crisp to cool for at least 20 minutes before serving with whipped cream or ice cream.

Triple Berry Cobbler

Berries work well in cobblers because they release their own juices as they bake, which thicken with the cornstarch and sugar added to the filling. If you can't find fresh berries, frozen will work (just don't defrost them before using).

INGREDIENTS | SERVES 4

Filling

¾ cup cranberry juice or water

½ cup sugar

¼ teaspoons ground cinnamon

3 tablespoons cornstarch

1 cup raspberries, fresh or frozen

1 cup blueberries, fresh or frozen

1 cup blackberries, fresh or frozen

Topping

¼ cup sugar

⅔ cup brown rice flour

½ teaspoon baking powder

¼ teaspoon sea salt

⅓ cup milk

½ teaspoon vanilla extract

2 tablespoons butter, melted

½ teaspoon cinnamon mixed with 2 teaspoons sugar

3 tablespoons cold butter

1. Preheat oven to 375°F. Grease a 2-quart baking dish, pie pan, or casserole dish and set aside.
2. Make the filling: In a small saucepan add cranberry juice or water, sugar, cinnamon, and cornstarch. Mix or whisk together and cook over high heat, stirring constantly until boiling. Allow to boil for 1 minute. The cornstarch and juice or water mixture will turn translucent and thicken. Remove from heat and add berries. Pour berry filling into the baking dish.
3. Make the topping: In a small bowl whisk together sugar, brown rice flour, baking powder, and salt. Make a well in the center of the dry ingredients and add milk, vanilla, and melted butter. Mix until you have a thick batter. Drop batter by tablespoons on top of the berry filling and use a fork to spread evenly over the casserole. It doesn't have to be perfectly covered.
4. Sprinkle cinnamon-sugar mixture over the top of the casserole. Dot with cold butter. Place the casserole dish on a cookie sheet to prevent spills in the oven while baking. Bake for 25–30 minutes until filling is bubbling on the sides of the topping and the biscuit topping is cooked through and crispy. Allow cobbler to cool for 30 minutes before serving. Serve plain or with ice cream.

Blueberry Mango Crisp

The topping on this crisp can be used on any kind of fresh fruit crisp.
If you cannot tolerate gluten-free oats, you can substitute quinoa flakes.

INGREDIENTS | SERVES 6

1 cup sugar

1 tablespoon cornstarch

1½ teaspoons ground cinnamon, divided

2 mangoes, peeled and diced to ½" pieces

4 cups blueberries

2 teaspoons vanilla

1 cup gluten-free oats

½ cup brown rice flour

½ cup packed brown sugar

Pinch nutmeg

½ cup cold butter

1. Preheat oven to 350°F.
2. In a large bowl, stir together the sugar, cornstarch, and 1 teaspoon cinnamon. Add the mangoes, blueberries, and vanilla. Stir to coat the fruit with the sugar mixture. Pour into a greased 8" × 8" baking dish and set aside.
3. To make the topping, stir together the oats, brown rice flour, brown sugar, ½ teaspoon cinnamon, and nutmeg. Using a pastry cutter or two knives, cut the cold butter into the oat-flour mixture until large crumbs, about the size of a pea, remain.
4. Sprinkle the topping over fruit in the baking dish, and spread to create an even layer.
5. Bake for 40–45 minutes, or until the fruit is hot and bubbly.
6. Remove from oven and allow to cool for at least 15 minutes before serving. This is delicious served warm with a scoop of vanilla ice cream.

CHAPTER 7

Cookies and Bars

Stovetop Oatmeal Fudge Cookies

You may know these cookies as "Preacher Cookies," "Stovetop Cookies," "Oatmeal Fudgies," or "No-Bake Cookies." If you need cookies fast, these are the way to go!

INGREDIENTS | SERVES 24–30

½ cup butter

2 cups sugar

½ cup milk

½ cup baking cocoa

1 teaspoon vanilla extract

½ cup peanut butter

2 cups gluten-free quick-cooking oats

Make Them Dairy-Free

You can make these cookies dairy-free by using ⅓ cup coconut oil or ⅓ cup Spectrum Palm Shortening in place of the butter (you use less because butter contains some milk/liquid) and your favorite nondairy milk such as almond or cashew milk.

1. Line 2–3 cookie sheets with parchment paper and set aside. Melt butter in a medium-sized saucepan over medium heat until fully melted. Add sugar, milk, and cocoa to the butter and whisk to remove any lumps.
2. Continue to cook over medium-high heat until mixture is simmering. Cook for an additional 6–7 minutes, stirring constantly to prevent the mixture from burning. Remove from heat.
3. Add vanilla extract and peanut butter and stir until peanut butter has dissolved into the hot mixture. Quickly stir in the oats.
4. Working quickly (as the mixture will harden as it sets), drop cookie mixture 1 tablespoon at a time onto the parchment paper. You should have enough batter to make 24–30 cookies.
5. Allow cookies to cool completely before serving or moving to a storage container. Cookies should be somewhat soft, but will harden enough so that they can be picked up and held. Store cookies at room temperature in an airtight container between sheets of parchment paper or plastic wrap. The cookies will stick to each other and be hard to pull apart if placed in a container without being separated.

Mint Chocolate Wafer Cookies

Do you miss Girl Scout Thin Mint cookies? These cookies are the gluten-free answer to that crunchy minty goodness! The dough can be made ahead of time and stored in the freezer.

INGREDIENTS | SERVES 28–36

1 cup sugar

12 tablespoons butter or Spectrum Palm Shortening

1 large egg

1 teaspoon vanilla extract

2 teaspoons pure peppermint extract or oil, divided

1 cup brown rice flour

½ cup arrowroot starch

¾ cup cocoa powder

¼ teaspoon sea salt

1 teaspoon xanthan gum

6 ounces semisweet chocolate morsels

Make Plain Chocolate Wafers for Instant Pie Crusts

To make plain chocolate wafers, leave out the peppermint extract. You can use vanilla extract instead or just omit it entirely. Otherwise, make the cookies as directed, but do not use the chocolate topping. You can use these plain chocolate cookies to make the Chocolate Wafer Pie Crust in Chapter 9.

1. In a large bowl cream together the sugar and butter until thoroughly combined. Add the egg, the vanilla extract, and 1½ teaspoons peppermint extract and stir to combine.

2. In a smaller bowl whisk together the brown rice flour, arrowroot starch, cocoa powder, salt, and xanthan gum. Stir the dry ingredients into the sugar-and-butter mixture. Combine until the batter is very thick and can be formed into a large ball of dough.

3. Divide the dough into two smaller balls and place each ball on a separate 12" sheet of plastic wrap. Using the plastic wrap to keep the dough from sticking to your hands, shape each ball of dough into a 9"–10" log. Cover each log completely with plastic wrap and place in the refrigerator for at least 1 hour.

4. Heat oven to 350°F. Place parchment paper on 2 large baking sheets. Slice each log of dough into 14–18 slices. Place cookie slices 1" apart in 4–5 rows on each cookie sheet. Bake for 15–18 minutes until the edges of the cookies appear to be dry. These cookies do not spread or change their shape.

5. Allow cookies to cool for at least 15 minutes on the baking sheets before moving to a cooling rack. The cookies will easily crumble if moved immediately from the baking sheets. After 15–20 minutes, place cookies on a cooling rack. Allow to cool completely.

6. Melt 6 ounces chocolate morsels in a glass bowl in the microwave for 20 seconds at a time until fully melted. Stir in ½ teaspoon peppermint extract and then drizzle decoratively over cooled cookies. Store cookies in an airtight container on the counter for up to 1 week or freeze for up to 2 months.

Best Chocolate Chip Cookies

One trick for perfectly "gooey-on-the-inside-but-crunchy-on-the-outside" chocolate chip cookies is to make sure not to over bake them. Seven to nine minutes is all they need.

INGREDIENTS | SERVES 24

¼ cup Spectrum Palm Shortening

¼ cup sugar

¾ cup brown sugar

1 large egg

1 tablespoon vanilla extract

½ cup arrowroot starch

¾ cup sorghum flour

½ teaspoon sea salt

¼ teaspoon xanthan gum

1 teaspoon baking powder

½ teaspoon baking soda

1 cup semisweet chocolate chips

Sorghum Flour

Sorghum is a cereal grain that has been used as a food source for thousands of years in various parts of the world, especially in developing nations. Sorghum flour is used in this recipe because some people feel that brown rice flour gives the cookies a grainy texture.

1. Preheat oven to 350°F. Line 2 baking sheets with parchment paper and set aside.
2. In a large bowl cream together shortening, sugar, and brown sugar. When thoroughly combined, stir in the egg and vanilla.
3. In a smaller bowl whisk together arrowroot starch, sorghum flour, salt, xanthan gum, baking powder, and baking soda. Slowly stir dry ingredients into the creamed sugar mixture. Stir chocolate chips into the thick batter.
4. Drop batter 1 teaspoon at a time about 2" apart onto the baking sheets. Bake for 7–9 minutes, just until the edges of the cookies are golden-brown and tops are slightly brown.
5. Remove from oven and allow to cool on the baking sheets for 15–20 minutes before removing to a cooling rack.
6. Store cookies in an airtight container on the counter for up to 2 days. These cookies are best the day they are made. They can also be frozen (either as raw dough or as baked cookies) for up to 2 months.

Easy Peanut Butter Cookies

Here's a gluten-free cookie made from three easy ingredients—it doesn't get any better than that! These cookies are a great project to make with young children as their small hands can easily roll the dough into balls.

INGREDIENTS | YIELDS 2 DOZEN COOKIES

1 cup peanut butter

1 cup sugar

1 large egg

Make "Other" Butter Cookies

People with peanut allergies can make these cookies with almond butter, cashew butter, walnut, or pecan butter, or even a seed butter like SunButter, made from sunflower seeds. These "other" butters are often available at specialty grocery stores, health food stores, and online.

1. Preheat oven to 350°F. Line a cookie sheet with parchment paper and set aside.
2. In a large bowl cream together the peanut butter and sugar. Once thoroughly mixed, stir in the egg.
3. The batter will be very thick and sticky. For small cookies, use a spoon to scoop out about 1 tablespoon of batter, roll it into a ball, and place on the cookie sheet about 1" apart. For large cookies, scoop out about 2 tablespoons of dough, roll into a larger ball, and place on the cookie sheet about 2" apart.
4. Using a fork, flatten cookies and make a crisscross pattern on them. Place in oven and bake for 8–10 minutes until golden-brown. Allow cookies to cool on baking sheet for about 10 minutes before placing them on a cooling rack.
5. Store cookies in an airtight container on the counter for 2–3 days. Cookies and cookie dough can also be frozen for up to 1 month.

White Chocolate Macadamia Nut Cookies

There's something about the combination of white chocolate and macadamia nuts that is divine. These cookies are perfect for sharing with neighbors and friends over the holidays.

INGREDIENTS | YIELDS 2 DOZEN COOKIES

¼ cup Spectrum Palm Shortening
¼ cup sugar
¾ cup brown sugar
1 large egg
1 tablespoon vanilla extract
¾ cup arrowroot starch
¾ cup sorghum flour
½ teaspoon sea salt
¼ teaspoon xanthan gum
1 teaspoon baking powder
½ teaspoon baking soda
½ cup white chocolate chips
½ cup macadamia nuts, chopped

Holiday Variations

To share these cookies over the holidays, add ½ cup dried cranberries into the batter with white chocolate chips and macadamia nuts. If you want to go all out, add a few drops of green food coloring to the basic cookie batter and then stir in the dried cranberries and white chocolate chips.

1. Preheat oven to 350°F. Line 2 baking sheets with parchment paper and set aside.
2. In a large bowl cream together shortening, sugar, and brown sugar. When thoroughly combined, stir in the egg and vanilla.
3. In a smaller bowl whisk together arrowroot starch, sorghum flour, salt, xanthan gum, baking powder, and baking soda. Slowly stir dry ingredients into the creamed sugar mixture. Stir chocolate chips and macadamia nuts into the batter.
4. Drop batter 1 tablespoon at a time about 2" apart onto baking sheets. Bake for 7–9 minutes, just until the edges of the cookies are golden-brown and the tops are slightly brown.
5. Remove from oven and allow to cool on the baking sheets for 15–20 minutes before removing to a cooling rack.
6. Store cookies in an airtight container on the counter for up to 2 days. These cookies are best the day they are made. They can also be frozen (either as raw dough or as baked cookies) for up to 2 months.

Coconut Honey Macaroons

A few simple ingredients make these naturally gluten-free coconut macaroons. These are a perfect treat for people who want something just a little sweet, but somewhat healthy as well.

INGREDIENTS | YIELDS ABOUT 22 COOKIES

3 cups shredded, unsweetened coconut

2 teaspoons vanilla or almond extract

⅛ teaspoon sea salt

¼ teaspoon cream of tartar

⅔ cup honey, heated just enough to be runny

4 large egg whites

1. Preheat oven to 350°F. Line 1 cookie sheet with parchment paper and set aside.
2. In a medium-sized bowl mix together the coconut, vanilla or almond extract, salt, and cream of tartar. Stir in honey until thoroughly combined.
3. In another bowl, beat egg whites until stiff peaks form. Slowly fold egg whites into the coconut and honey mixture.
4. Scoop batter firmly with a cookie scoop or a large spoon and press cookies onto the cookie sheet 1½" apart. Bake for 10–15 minutes until lightly browned. Allow cookies to cool for 20 minutes on baking sheet. Store in an airtight container on the counter for up to 1 week. Cookies can also be frozen for up to 1 month.

Cinnamon "Graham" Crackers

This versatile cookie can be used for s'mores, pie crusts, and of course for enjoying with a mug of hot chocolate or glass of milk. These cookies are not overly sweet and are a great snack for traveling.

INGREDIENTS | YIELDS 36–40 CRACKERS

½ cup plus 2 tablespoons sorghum flour

½ cup brown rice flour

⅔ cup arrowroot starch

1 teaspoon cinnamon

1 teaspoon baking powder

½ teaspoon xanthan gum

½ teaspoon sea salt

⅓ cup Spectrum Palm Shortening

1 large egg

¼ cup honey

3–4 tablespoons cold water

Extra Special Cinnamon Sugar "Graham" Crackers

To make these "graham" crackers extra special sprinkle a mixture of 2 tablespoons sugar and 1 teaspoon cinnamon evenly over the top of the rolled-out dough before baking. You can also use cookie cutters to make fun shapes with the cookies. Kids love these!

1. Preheat oven to 350°F.
2. In a large bowl whisk together sorghum flour, brown rice flour, arrowroot starch, cinnamon, baking powder, xanthan gum, and salt.
3. Cut shortening into the dry ingredients with a knife and fork or a pastry blender until the shortening resembles small peas throughout the dry ingredients. Make a well in the center of dry ingredients and add the egg and honey. Mix thoroughly (using a fork) into the dry ingredients. Add water 1 tablespoon at a time, mixing until you have a ball of thick batter. You may not need to use all of the water depending on how "wet" your dough is.
4. Place a sheet of parchment paper, long enough to fit a large baking sheet (17" × 11") on your countertop or a flat, dry surface. Sprinkle a little arrowroot starch over the parchment paper and place the ball of dough in the center. Place another piece of parchment paper (or plastic wrap) on top of the dough. Using a rolling pin, roll the dough out into a large rectangle until it is about ¼" thick. It should cover most of the parchment paper. Remove the top layer of paper or wrap and gently slide rolled-out dough on paper onto a large cookie/baking sheet.
5. Using a pizza cutter, gently score the dough into 36–40 rectangles. Then mark the dough 2–3 times per cracker with the tines of a fork to make them look like traditional graham crackers.
6. Bake the crackers for 15–18 minutes until golden-brown around the edges. Remove from oven and allow the cookies to cool for 20 minutes on the baking sheet, then gently break apart into individual graham crackers. Store in an airtight container on the counter for up to 1 week or freeze cookies for up to 1 month.

Classic Oatmeal Raisin Cookies

Who says you can't have oatmeal raisin cookies when you're gluten-free?
Make sure to purchase certified gluten-free quick oats for these recipes, as regular oats
processed in facilities that also process wheat products can be easily contaminated.

INGREDIENTS | YIELDS 28–30 LARGE COOKIES

⅔ cup Spectrum Palm Shortening

1½ cups brown sugar

½ cup unsweetened applesauce

2 teaspoons vanilla extract

2 tablespoons honey or molasses

1 cup sorghum flour

¾ cup arrowroot starch

1 teaspoon xanthan gum

½ teaspoon baking soda

1 teaspoon baking powder

1 teaspoon cinnamon

½ teaspoon allspice

½ teaspoon sea salt

2 cups gluten-free rolled oats, or gluten-free quick-cooking oats

½ cup raisins

Cookies without Eggs (and Oats?)

This delicious gluten-free recipe is surprisingly made without eggs. It's perfect for people with egg allergies. You can even make these cookies oat-free, if you are sensitive to gluten-free oats. Substitute 2 cups of quinoa flakes, which are rolled quinoa grains. These can be found at most specialty grocery stores.

1. Preheat oven to 350°F. Line 2 baking sheets with parchment paper and set aside.
2. In a large bowl cream together shortening and brown sugar. When thoroughly combined, stir in the applesauce, vanilla, and honey.
3. In a smaller bowl whisk together sorghum flour, arrowroot starch, xanthan gum, baking soda, baking powder, cinnamon, allspice, and salt. Slowly stir dry ingredients into the creamed sugar mixture. Stir gluten-free quick oats into the thick batter. Finally, fold in the raisins.
4. Drop batter 1–2 tablespoons at a time about 2" apart onto baking sheets. Bake for 12–15 minutes, just until the edges of the cookies are golden-brown and tops are slightly brown.
5. Remove from oven and allow to cool on the baking sheets for 15–20 minutes before removing to a cooling rack.
6. Store cookies in an airtight container on the counter for up to 2 days. These cookies are best the day they are made. They can also be frozen (either as raw dough or as baked cookies) for up to 2 months.

PB&J Cookies

This variation of "thumb-print" cookies uses a peanut butter cookie base and your favorite jam to recreate a sweet version of peanut butter sandwiches.

INGREDIENTS | YIELDS ABOUT 3 DOZEN COOKIES

½ cup Spectrum Palm Shortening
½ cup all-natural peanut butter
½ cup sugar
½ cup firmly packed brown sugar
1 large egg
¾ cup brown rice flour
¾ cup arrowroot starch
½ teaspoon xanthan gum
½ teaspoon baking powder
¾ teaspoon baking soda
¼ teaspoon sea salt
½ cup jelly or jam, any flavor

1. Preheat oven to 350°F. Line 2 baking sheets with parchment paper and set aside.
2. In a large bowl cream together shortening, peanut butter, sugar, and brown sugar. When thoroughly combined, stir in the egg.
3. In a smaller bowl whisk together brown rice flour, arrowroot starch, xanthan gum, baking powder, baking soda, and salt. Slowly stir dry ingredients into peanut butter mixture.
4. Shape dough by rolling into 1½" balls. Place 2" apart on baking sheets. Flatten each ball with the back of a teaspoon or your thumb, making an indentation in the center of each cookie. Add ½–1 teaspoon jelly or jam to the center of each cookie. Bake for 10–12 minutes, just until the edges of the cookies are golden-brown.
5. Remove from oven and allow to cool on the baking sheets for 15–20 minutes before removing to a cooling rack.
6. Store cookies in an airtight container on the counter for up to 2 days. These cookies are best the day they are made. They can also be frozen (either as raw dough or as baked cookies) for up to 2 months.

Date Pinwheel Cookies

These classic refrigerator cookies take more preparation time than most,
but they are well worth the effort! Serve them warm from the oven.

INGREDIENTS | YIELDS 3 DOZEN COOKIES

½ cup pitted, chopped dates

½ cup hot water

½ cup sugar

½ cup walnuts, finely chopped

½ cup Spectrum Palm Shortening

1 cup packed brown sugar

1 large egg

1 teaspoon vanilla

1 cup brown rice flour

¾ cup arrowroot starch

½ teaspoon xanthan gum

½ teaspoon baking soda

½ teaspoon cream of tartar

¼ teaspoon sea salt

Make Fig Walnut Pinwheels Instead

If you're not a fan of dates, but really miss Fig Newtons, try using ½ cup figs to make the filling in these cookies instead. You can buy fresh figs and cook them down, use premade fig jam, or use dried figs.

1. Combine dates, hot water, and sugar in a medium saucepan. Cook over medium heat about 6–8 minutes, stirring constantly until mixture thickens and creates a homemade jam. Remove from heat and stir in walnuts. Set aside and allow to cool completely.
2. In a large bowl cream together shortening and brown sugar. When thoroughly combined, stir in the egg and vanilla.
3. In a smaller bowl whisk together brown rice flour, arrowroot starch, xanthan gum, baking soda, cream of tartar, and sea salt. Slowly stir dry ingredients into the creamed sugar mixture.
4. Divide dough into thirds. Roll each portion into a 12" square on separate sheets of wax paper or parchment paper. Spread each square with ⅓ of the date-walnut mixture. Lifting up the edge of the wax paper or parchment paper, gently peel it off of dough and roll into a "jelly roll" beginning with the long end. Wrap the rolls in wax or parchment paper and refrigerate for at least 8 hours. (The dough can be frozen in logs at this point.)
5. To make cookies, remove roll from the refrigerator, remove wrapping, and slice dough into ¼" cookies. Place 2" apart on baking sheets. Bake in a 350°F oven for 8–10 minutes, just until the edges of the cookies are golden-brown.
6. Remove from oven and allow to cool on the baking sheets for 10 minutes before removing to a cooling rack.
7. Store cookies in an airtight container on the counter for up to 2 days. These cookies are best the day they are made. They can also be frozen (either as raw dough or as baked cookies) for up to 2 months.

New York Black-and-White Cookies

These New York deli–style cookies were once made with leftover cake batter. They have a cakelike consistency and a vanilla-lemon base with the classic glossy black-and-white frosting.

INGREDIENTS | YIELDS 14–15 LARGE COOKIES OR 30–40 SMALL COOKIES

2 cups brown rice flour

1 cup arrowroot starch

1½ teaspoons baking powder

¾ teaspoon xanthan gum

¾ teaspoon sea salt

¾ cup Spectrum Palm Shortening or softened butter (butter will give a more traditional cake flavor)

1½ cups sugar

2 large eggs

2 teaspoons vanilla extract

½ teaspoon lemon extract

¾ cup almond milk

Classic Black-and-White Frosting

Add 4 cups confectioners' sugar to a large bowl. Mix in ⅓–½ cup very hot water, just enough water to make an icing that is thick enough to coat the back of a spoon. Spread half of each round cookie with white frosting. Work quickly as icing will harden. Place remaining icing in the top of a double boiler. Add 3 ounces unsweetened chocolate and 1 teaspoon honey and stir into hot icing. Add 1 tablespoon cocoa if icing is not dark enough. Spread black icing on the other half of each cookie and serve immediately.

1. Preheat oven to 350°F. Line 2 large rimmed baking sheets with parchment paper and set aside.
2. In a medium-sized bowl whisk together the brown rice flour, arrowroot starch, baking powder, xanthan gum, and salt.
3. In a large bowl cream the shortening (or butter) and the sugar together until well incorporated. Add in the eggs, vanilla extract, and lemon extract. Stir in half of the dry ingredients into sugar mixture. Stir in half of the almond milk. Repeat process until all ingredients have created cookie batter, which will look like a thick cake batter.
4. To make large bakery-style cookies, scoop about ½ cup of batter onto the cookie sheet and separate each cookie by 3". Bake for 20–25 minutes until cookies are golden-brown and puffy.
5. To make smaller cookies, scoop 2 tablespoons batter onto cookie sheet and separate each cookie by 2". Bake for 15–16 minutes until cookies are golden-brown and puffy.
6. Frost cookies with Classic Black-and-White Frosting or use your favorite gluten-free store-bought icing.

Orange Pecan Refrigerator Cookies

This easy refrigerator cookie is rolled into a log and then sliced into cookies.
Change the flavors of these cookies by using lemon juice and zest or key lime juice and zest.

INGREDIENTS | YIELDS 4 DOZEN SMALL COOKIES

1 cup Spectrum Palm Shortening
½ cup sugar
½ cup packed brown sugar
1 large egg, beaten
2 tablespoons freshly grated orange zest
2 tablespoons orange juice concentrate
1 cup brown rice flour
1 cup arrowroot starch
1 teaspoon xanthan gum
¼ teaspoon baking soda
½ cup chopped pecans

1. Preheat oven to 350°F. Line 2 baking sheets with parchment paper and set aside.
2. In a large bowl cream together shortening, sugar, and brown sugar. When thoroughly combined, stir in the egg, orange zest, and orange juice concentrate.
3. In a smaller bowl whisk together brown rice flour, arrowroot starch, xanthan gum, and baking soda. Slowly stir dry ingredients into sugar mixture. Stir chopped pecans into the thick batter. Divide the dough into two smaller balls and place each ball on a separate 12" sheet of plastic wrap. Using the plastic wrap (to keep the dough from sticking to your hands) shape each ball of dough into a 9"–10" log. Cover each log completely with the plastic wrap and place in the refrigerator for at least 2 hours.
4. Heat oven to 350°F. Place parchment paper on 2 large baking sheets. Slice each log of dough into 20–24 slices. Place cookie slices 1" apart in 4–5 rows on each cookie sheet. Bake for 15–18 minutes until the edges of the cookies appear to be dry. These cookies do not spread very much.
5. Allow cookies to cool for at least 15 minutes on the baking sheets before moving to a cooling rack. The cookies will easily crumble if moved immediately from the baking sheets. After 15–20 minutes, place cookies on a cooling rack. Store cookies in an airtight container on the counter for up to 1 week or freeze for up to 2 months.

Big Soft Sugar Cookies

These pillowy sugar cookies will remind you of decorated deli cookies. They can be hard to replicate without gluten. The key ingredients here are milk (or a dairy-free replacement) and 2 eggs to help the cookies rise and give them a soft, cakelike texture.

INGREDIENTS | **YIELDS 14–15 LARGE COOKIES OR 30–40 SMALL COOKIES**

2 cups brown rice flour

1 cup arrowroot starch

1½ teaspoons baking powder

¾ teaspoon xanthan gum

¾ teaspoon sea salt

¾ cup Spectrum Palm Shortening

1½ cups sugar

2 large eggs

2 tablespoons vanilla extract or 2 teaspoons almond extract

1 teaspoon lemon extract

¾ cup almond milk

1. Preheat oven to 350°F. Line 2 large, rimmed baking sheets with parchment paper and set aside.
2. In a medium-sized bowl whisk together the brown rice flour, arrowroot starch, baking powder, xanthan gum, and salt.
3. In a large bowl cream the shortening and sugar together until well incorporated. Add in the eggs, vanilla extract, and lemon extract. Stir half of the dry ingredients into sugar mixture. Stir in half of the almond milk. Repeat process until all ingredients have created batter that will look like thick cake batter.
4. To make large bakery-style cookies, scoop about ½ cup of batter per cookie onto the cookie sheets and separate each cookie by 3". Bake for 20–25 minutes until cookies are golden-brown and puffy.
5. To make smaller cookies, scoop 2 tablespoons batter per cookie onto cookie sheets and separate each cookie by 2". Bake for 15–16 minutes until cookies are golden-brown and puffy.
6. Frost cookies using your favorite store-bought or home-made vanilla frosting or simply dust with confectioners' sugar. These cookies are best the day they are made, but can be stored up to five days in an airtight container on the counter. These cookies do not freeze well.

Gingersnaps

Crispy, crunchy gingersnaps are great for traveling or a quick snack.
Molasses, ginger, cinnamon, and cloves give them that classic spicy "snap."

INGREDIENTS | YIELDS 6 DOZEN COOKIES

¾ cup Spectrum Palm Shortening

1½ cups sugar, divided

1 large egg

¼ cup molasses

1 cup sorghum flour

1 cup arrowroot starch

1 teaspoon xanthan gum

1½ teaspoons ground ginger

1 teaspoon ground cinnamon

1 teaspoon ground cloves

Make Cookies That "Snap" a Little Bit More

You can make crisper cookies by lowering the oven temperature to about 250°F and baking the cookies an additional 20–30 minutes. This will dry out the cookies more and give them a bigger crunch factor.

1. In a large bowl cream together shortening and 1 cup sugar until light and fluffy. Add egg and molasses and beat well.
2. In a smaller bowl whisk together sorghum flour, arrowroot starch, xanthan gum, ginger, cinnamon, and cloves. Slowly stir dry ingredients into the creamed sugar mixture. Cover dough and refrigerate for at least 2 hours.
3. When ready to bake, heat oven to 350°F. Place parchment paper on 2 large baking sheets. Shape dough into 1" balls and coat with remaining sugar. Place balls 2" apart on baking sheets and flatten slightly with the bottom of a glass. Bake for 15–18 minutes until the edges of the cookies appear dry.
4. Allow cookies to cool for at least 15 minutes on the baking sheets before moving to a cooling rack—they will easily crumble if moved immediately from the baking sheets. After 15–20 minutes, place cookies on a cooling rack. Store cookies in an airtight container on the counter for up to 1 week or freeze for up to 2 months.

Pecan Sandies

Rich and buttery with a wonderful crumb and the flavor of toasted pecans, these cookies contain both sugar and confectioners' sugar, which create their distinctive sandy texture.

INGREDIENTS | YIELDS 3 DOZEN COOKIES

½ cup Spectrum Palm Shortening
½ cup light-tasting olive oil or canola oil
1 cup sugar, divided
½ cup confectioners' sugar
1 large egg
1 cup brown rice flour
1 cup arrowroot starch
1 teaspoon xanthan gum
½ teaspoon baking soda
½ teaspoon cream of tartar
½ teaspoon sea salt
1 cup chopped pecans

1. Preheat oven to 350°F. Line 2 baking sheets with parchment paper and set aside.
2. Cream shortening, oil, ½ cup sugar, and confectioners' sugar. Add the egg and stir thoroughly.
3. In a medium bowl whisk together brown rice flour, arrowroot starch, xanthan gum, baking soda, cream of tartar, and salt. Stir dry ingredients into the creamed sugar mixture. Stir in chopped pecans.
4. Scoop batter and shape into 1" balls and then roll in remaining sugar before placing 2" apart on the baking sheets. Slightly flatten cookies with the bottom of a glass.
5. Bake 10–12 minutes until edges of cookies are golden-brown. Cool for 10–15 minutes on the baking sheets, then cool completely on wire racks. Store cookies in an airtight container on the counter for up to 1 week. Cookies and dough can also be stored in the freezer for up to 2 months.

Butter Shortbread

Shortbread is a traditional Scottish cookie, or "biscuit" as it's called in its native land. It was originally made with only three ingredients: 1 part sugar, 2 parts butter, and 3 parts flour.

INGREDIENTS | YIELDS 24 COOKIES

1 cup confectioners' sugar
1½ cups butter, softened
1 cup arrowroot starch
1 cup sorghum flour

1. In a medium-sized bowl cream together sugar and butter. In a small bowl whisk together arrowroot starch and sorghum flour.
2. Stir flour mixture into the creamed butter and sugar. Place dough on a piece of plastic wrap and shape into a 12" log. Wrap the dough completely with the plastic wrap and refrigerate for at least 2 hours.
3. When ready to bake, heat oven to 350°F. Remove the plastic wrap and slice dough into 24 shortbread cookies. Prick cookies all over with a fork. Place cookies 1" apart on a baking sheet lined with parchment paper. Bake for 18–20 minutes until cookies are golden-brown on the edges.

Benne Seed Wafers

These unique cookies hail from Charleston, South Carolina, and are thought to have been brought to the United States from Africa in early colonial times. Toasted sesame seeds and butter give these cookies their rich, buttery flavor.

INGREDIENTS | YIELDS 2–4 DOZEN COOKIES

1 cup packed brown sugar

¼ cup butter, room temperature

1 large egg

1 teaspoon lemon juice

½ teaspoon vanilla extract

½ cup brown rice flour

¼ teaspoon salt

⅛ teaspoon baking powder

1 cup toasted sesame seeds

How to Toast Sesame Seeds

Toasting seeds and nuts on your stovetop is super easy. You just need to watch them very carefully as most seeds and nuts will burn in a matter of seconds if you don't keep an eye on them. Add 1 cup of sesame seeds to a very lightly greased cast-iron skillet and cook at medium heat for 2–3 minutes, stirring constantly, just until you begin to smell the aroma of toasted sesame. Remove the seeds from the pan and cool them on a paper towel. You can store the toasted seeds in an airtight container in the pantry for up to 3 months.

1. Preheat oven to 325°F. Line 2 large, rimmed baking sheets with parchment paper and set aside.
2. In a medium bowl cream together brown sugar and butter. Beat in the egg, lemon juice, and vanilla extract.
3. In a smaller bowl whisk together brown rice flour, salt, and baking powder. Stir dry ingredients into sugar-and-butter mixture. Stir in toasted sesame seeds. Cover bowl of batter with plastic wrap and chill for 30 minutes.
4. Drop batter by teaspoons 2" apart on lined baking sheets. Bake for 15–17 minutes until cookies have spread and are golden-brown. Do not over bake, as these cookies can burn quickly. Allow cookies to cool completely on the baking sheet for 30–40 minutes. Store cookies in an airtight container on the counter for up to 1 week. They can also be frozen for up to 1 month.

Oatmeal Lace Cookies

Crispy, sweet oatmeal lace cookies are named for the lacelike patterns they form while baking.
It's important to use butter in these cookies to help them spread correctly, so don't substitute shortening.

INGREDIENTS | YIELDS 3 DOZEN COOKIES

1 cup sugar

½ cup butter, room temperature

1 large egg

1 teaspoon vanilla extract

¼ teaspoon sea salt

¼ teaspoon baking soda

1 cup gluten-free quick oats

2 tablespoons sorghum flour

¼ teaspoon cinnamon

1. Preheat oven to 325°F. Line 2 large, rimmed baking sheets with parchment paper and set aside.
2. In a medium bowl cream together sugar and butter. Beat in the egg and vanilla extract.
3. In a smaller bowl whisk together salt, baking soda, oats, sorghum flour, and cinnamon. Stir dry ingredients into sugar-and-butter mixture. Allow batter to rest for 10 minutes to activate the baking soda.
4. Drop batter by teaspoons 3" apart on baking sheets. Bake for 8–10 minutes until cookies have spread, and are bubbly and golden-brown. Do not over bake, as these cookies can burn quickly. Allow cookies to cool completely on the baking sheet for 20–30 minutes. Store cookies in an airtight container on the counter for up to 1 week. These cookies do not freeze well as they are quite fragile.

Southern Tea Cakes

In some European countries, tea cakes are little, light, yeast-risen buns with raisins and other dried fruits. In some parts of the United States, they are akin to fruitcake, but in the South, they are simple, buttery sugar cookies that can either be thin and crispy or thick and cakelike.

INGREDIENTS | YIELDS 2–3 DOZEN COOKIES

1½ cups sugar

1 cup butter, room temperature

2 large eggs, room temperature

1 teaspoon vanilla extract

2 cups brown rice flour

2 cups arrowroot starch

2 teaspoons xanthan gum

¼ teaspoon ground nutmeg

1¼ teaspoons baking soda

¼ teaspoon salt

1. Preheat oven to 350°F. Line 2 large baking sheets with parchment paper and set aside.
2. In a medium bowl cream together sugar and butter until light and fluffy. Beat in the eggs and vanilla extract.
3. In a smaller bowl whisk together brown rice flour, arrowroot starch, xanthan gum, nutmeg, baking soda, and salt. Stir dry ingredients, ½ cup at a time, into the sugar-and-butter mixture. You will have a thick cookie dough.
4. Lightly flour (with arrowroot starch) a dry surface to roll out cookies to ¼"–½" thick. Cut cookies into 2" rounds and carefully place on the baking sheets. Gather scraps and roll out remaining dough to create the rest of the cookies.
5. Bake 10–12 minutes until cookies are light golden-brown around the edges. Allow cookies to cool completely on the baking sheet for 15–20 minutes. Store cookies in an airtight container on the counter for up to 1 week. Cookies and dough can be frozen for up to 2 months.

Banana Bread Cookies

These soft, cakelike cookies are the perfect way to use up those ripe, leftover bananas.

INGREDIENTS | YIELDS ABOUT 30 COOKIES

1 cup sugar

½ cup butter or Spectrum Palm Shortening

1 large egg

1 cup mashed bananas (about 2½ medium-sized bananas)

1 cup brown rice flour

1 cup arrowroot starch

1 teaspoon xanthan gum

1 teaspoon baking soda

½ teaspoon ground cinnamon

½ teaspoon ground nutmeg

½ teaspoon ground cloves

½ cup chopped pecans (optional)

1. Preheat oven to 350°F. Line 2 large, rimmed baking sheets with parchment paper and set aside.
2. In a medium bowl cream together sugar and butter. Beat in the egg and bananas.
3. In a smaller bowl whisk together brown rice flour, arrowroot starch, xanthan gum, baking soda, cinnamon, nutmeg, and cloves. Stir dry ingredients into sugar-and-butter mixture. If desired, fold in chopped pecans.
4. Drop batter by tablespoons 2" apart on lined baking sheets. Bake for 12–15 minutes until cookies are golden-brown. Allow cookies to cool completely on the baking sheet for 15–20 minutes. Store cookies in an airtight container on the counter for up to 1 week. These cookies can be frozen for up to 2 months.

Walnut Butterscotch Cookies

Butterscotch is an unforgettable flavor in cookies. These are a favorite for people who aren't fans of chocolate chip cookies. Allergy note: This recipe may be a bit difficult to make casein-free, as most store-bought butterscotch morsels contain milk.

INGREDIENTS | SERVES 24

¼ cup Spectrum Palm Shortening

¼ cup sugar

¾ cup brown sugar

1 large egg

1 tablespoon vanilla extract

½ cup arrowroot starch

¾ cup sorghum flour

½ teaspoon sea salt

¼ teaspoon xanthan gum

1 teaspoon baking powder

½ teaspoon baking soda

1 cup butterscotch morsels

½ cup chopped walnuts

Delicious Variations

You can add many different ingredients to these cookies, such as ½ cup of gluten-free quick oats. Raisins can also be used. Instead of walnuts, substitute toasted pine nuts for a lighter tasting, uniquely flavored cookie.

1. Preheat oven to 350°F. Line 2 baking sheets with parchment paper and set aside.
2. In a large bowl cream together shortening, sugar, and brown sugar. When thoroughly combined, stir in the egg and vanilla.
3. In a smaller bowl whisk together arrowroot starch, sorghum flour, salt, xanthan gum, baking powder, and baking soda. Slowly stir dry ingredients into sugar mixture. Stir butterscotch morsels and chopped walnuts into the thick batter.
4. Drop batter 1–2 teaspoons at a time about 2" apart onto baking sheets. Bake for 7–9 minutes, just until the edges of the cookies are golden-brown and the top is slightly brown.
5. Remove from oven and allow to cool on the baking sheets for 15–20 minutes before removing to a cooling rack.
6. Store cookies in an airtight container on the counter for up to 2 days. These cookies are best the day they are made. They can also be frozen (either as raw dough or as baked cookies) for up to 2 months.

Molasses Spice Cookies

Molasses is a wonderful ingredient to add to cookies. It can act as a "humectant," meaning that it helps baked goods stay moist for several days, so it's a natural preservative.

INGREDIENTS | YIELDS 2–3 DOZEN COOKIES

¾ cup Spectrum Palm Shortening

1½ cups sugar, divided

1 large egg

¼ cup molasses

1 cup brown rice flour

1 cup arrowroot starch

1 teaspoon baking powder

1 teaspoon baking soda

1 teaspoon xanthan gum

1 teaspoon ground ginger

1 teaspoon ground cinnamon

½ teaspoon ground nutmeg

¼ teaspoon ground cloves

¼ teaspoon ground allspice

1. Preheat oven to 350°F. Line 2 baking sheets with parchment paper and set aside.
2. In a large bowl cream together shortening and 1 cup sugar. When thoroughly combined, stir in the egg and molasses.
3. In a smaller bowl whisk together brown rice flour, arrowroot starch, baking powder, baking soda, xanthan gum, and all spices. Slowly stir dry ingredients into the creamed sugar mixture. Chill the dough for at least 1 hour.
4. Roll chilled dough into 1" balls, then roll balls in the remaining sugar and place about 2" apart on baking sheets. Bake for 9–11 minutes, just until the edges of the cookies are golden-brown and starting to crackle on top.
5. Remove from oven and allow to cool on the baking sheets for 15–20 minutes before removing to a cooling rack.
6. Store cookies in an airtight container on the counter for up to 5 days. They can also be frozen (either as raw dough or as baked cookies) for up to 2 months.

Salted Caramel Pecan Bars

This recipe uses Honeyville blanched almond flour as the base for these sweet bars. Versatile almond flour is ideal for people on a gluten-free diet who can tolerate nuts.

INGREDIENTS | YIELDS 16–20 BARS

1 cup chopped pecans

¾ cup blanched almond flour

1 cup packed brown sugar, divided

¾ cup butter or Spectrum Palm Shortening

2 tablespoons whipping cream or full-fat coconut milk

1 teaspoon vanilla

¼ teaspoon coarse sea salt

Don't Want to Use Almond Flour?

If you have store-bought or homemade gluten-free graham crackers, you can crumble them, then add 2 tablespoons butter or Spectrum Palm Shortening and ¼ cup brown sugar. Press into the baking dish instead of using almond flour. Make the remainder of the recipe as directed.

1. Preheat oven to 350°F. When oven is warm, place pecans on a baking sheet and toast for 8–10 minutes. Remove from oven and set aside. Line an 8" × 8" baking dish with parchment paper.
2. In a small bowl mix together almond flour and ¼ cup of brown sugar. Press mixture into the bottom of the baking pan.
3. Combine butter, remaining ¾ cup brown sugar, and cream in a medium saucepan. Bring to a boil over medium heat and cook for an additional 2–3 minutes, stirring constantly. Remove from heat and add vanilla and pecans. Pour mixture over crust in the baking pan.
4. Bake for 10–12 minutes until the bars are golden-brown. Remove from oven and evenly sprinkle sea salt over them. Allow to cook completely in the pan, and then cut into 16–20 bars. Store in an airtight container on the counter for 2–3 days. Bars can be frozen for up to 1 month.

Chocolate Chip Toffee Bars

In this recipe, you can use either Cinnamon "Graham" Crackers (see recipe in this chapter) or a store-bought version. A popular gluten-free brand is Kinnikinnick S'moreables Graham Style Crackers.

INGREDIENTS | YIELDS ABOUT 2 DOZEN BARS

11 whole gluten-free graham crackers (4½" × 2¼"), broken into squares

1 cup butter

1 cup sugar

1 teaspoon ground cinnamon

½ cup finely chopped pecans or walnuts

⅓ cup semisweet mini chocolate chips

1. Preheat oven to 350°F. Line a 9" × 13" baking dish with parchment paper and then arrange graham crackers on paper. Set aside.
2. Combine butter and sugar in a medium saucepan and cook over medium heat, stirring until the mixture begins to boil. Boil for 2 minutes. Remove from heat and stir in cinnamon and nuts. Pour the mixture evenly over the graham crackers, spreading to the edges of the pan.
3. Bake for 10–12 minutes and remove from oven. Sprinkle chocolate chips evenly over the top. Allow to cool completely in the refrigerator and then cut into bars. The chocolate should melt slightly over the bars as they are cooling.
4. Store bars between sheets of parchment paper or wax paper in a container in the refrigerator for up to 1 week or freeze for up to 2 months.

Raspberry Oat Bars

These bars could just as easily be served for a special breakfast as for dessert.
You can substitute your favorite type of jam for raspberry.

INGREDIENTS | YIELDS 2 DOZEN BARS

¾ cup butter, room temperature, or Spectrum Palm Shortening

1 cup packed brown sugar

1½ cups gluten-free rolled oats

¾ cup brown rice flour

¾ cup arrowroot starch

1 teaspoon salt

½ teaspoon baking powder

1 (10-ounce) jar raspberry preserves

A Less-Crumbly Variation

If you prefer a firmer, less-crumbly bar, add an egg after creaming the brown sugar and butter. The bars will have a more cakelike texture.

1. Preheat oven to 400°F. Line a 9" × 13" baking dish with parchment paper.
2. In a large bowl cream butter and brown sugar; set aside briefly. In a smaller bowl whisk together oats, brown rice flour, arrowroot starch, salt, and baking powder. Pour oat mixture into the creamed sugar and stir with a fork to combine into a crumbly mixture.
3. Press half of the crumbly mixture into the bottom of the lined baking dish to create a crust. Spread all the raspberry preserves evenly over the crust. Then sprinkle the remainder of the crumbly oat mixture over the top of the preserves.
4. Bake for 20–25 minutes until the bars are golden-brown and jam is just a bit bubbly. Cool completely before cutting.
5. Store bars layered between wax paper or parchment paper in an airtight container in the refrigerator for up to 5 days. Bars can be frozen for up to 1 month.

Favorite Lemon Squares

Some people claim the lemon bar was invented by the Betty Crocker company in the early 1960s. However, as the bars are basically a classic shortbread topped with a simple lemon curd, they've likely been around a lot longer.

INGREDIENTS | YIELDS ABOUT 3 DOZEN SQUARES

1¼ cups brown rice flour, divided

1 cup arrowroot starch

2 cups sugar, divided

1 cup butter or Spectrum Palm Shortening

4 large eggs

2 lemons, juiced and zested

Confectioners' sugar, for dusting the bars

Lemon Curd

Citrus curd is a delicious thick jam made from eggs and sugar, and lemons, limes, tangerines, or oranges. It's an old English dessert ingredient used to spoon over scones, on toast, or as a filling in cakes. You can buy citrus curds or make them yourself. The lemon curd in this recipe is baked onto the shortbread, but for other recipes you can mix together 1½ cups sugar, 4 eggs, the juice and zest of 2 lemons, and ¼ cup brown rice flour or 2 tablespoons cornstarch. Add to a saucepan and cook on medium heat, whisking constantly until the mixture thickens. Store in a jar in the refrigerator for up to 1 month.

1. Preheat oven to 350°F. Line a 9" × 13" baking dish with parchment paper and set aside.
2. In a medium mixing bowl whisk together 1 cup brown rice flour, arrowroot starch, and ½ cup of sugar. Cut in softened butter or shortening with a fork and knife or a pastry blender, until you have a crumbly mixture. Press into the bottom of the baking dish.
3. Bake the crust for 15–20 minutes until it is firm and golden-brown.
4. In another medium mixing bowl whisk together remaining 1½ cups sugar, remaining ¼ cup brown rice flour, eggs, lemon juice, and lemon zest. Pour mixture over crust and bake an additional 20 minutes. Cool completely in the refrigerator for 1–2 hours to allow bars to firm up.
5. When ready to serve, cut into small squares and sprinkle lightly with confectioners' sugar, if desired.

Basic Cocoa Brownies

This easy brownie recipe can be adapted in a million different ways. Enjoy nuts? Add ½ cup chopped to the batter or on the top. Want more chocolate? Stir ½ cup mini chocolate chips into the batter.

INGREDIENTS | YIELDS 16 BROWNIES

½ cup brown rice flour

¼ cup arrowroot starch

½ teaspoon xanthan gum

½ cup butter or ⅓ cup Spectrum Palm Shortening

3–4 tablespoons cocoa (depending on how chocolaty you want the brownies)

1 tablespoon light-tasting olive oil or canola oil

1 cup sugar

2 large eggs

1 teaspoon vanilla

½ cup chopped walnuts, chopped pecans, white chocolate chips, mini chocolate chips, or candy-coated chocolate (optional)

1. Preheat oven to 350°F. Line an 8" × 8" baking pan with parchment paper.
2. In a medium bowl, whisk together brown rice flour, arrowroot starch, and xanthan gum. Set aside.
3. Melt butter in a small saucepan over medium heat. Stir in cocoa, oil, and sugar and mix until simmering. Remove from heat, allow to cool for 5 minutes, and then stir in eggs and vanilla. Mix to combine. Slowly stir flours into the warm sugar-and-cocoa mixture. If desired, add ½ cup of one or more optional ingredients.
4. Pour batter into baking pan. Bake for 25–30 minutes. Be careful not to over bake as brownies can dry out. Allow to cool for 20 minutes before cutting into bars and serving. These brownies are pretty dusted with confectioners' sugar when cool.

Chunky Candy Bar Brownies

For a truly decadent treat you can chop 1 or 2 (2-ounce) candy bars, such as Snickers or Milky Way, and stir into the batter instead of nuts or chocolate chips. The candy will melt while baking, but set again when cooling. These candy bar brownies are best eaten when still slightly warm from the oven.

Classic Blondies

These caramel-colored bars will remind you of chocolate chip cookie batter. As with the basic cocoa brownies, you can mix in different ingredients just before baking to create your own signature blondie.

INGREDIENTS | YIELDS 32 BARS

1½ cups butter, softened, or 1 cup Spectrum Palm Shortening

1⅔ cups sugar

1 cup brown sugar

4 large eggs

2 tablespoons vanilla extract

1½ cups brown rice flour

1½ cups arrowroot starch

1 teaspoon xanthan gum

2 teaspoons baking powder

½ teaspoon sea salt

½ cup chocolate chips, chopped walnuts, chopped macadamia nuts, chopped pecans, or butterscotch morsels (optional)

1. Preheat oven to 350°F. Line a 9" × 13" baking dish with parchment paper and set aside.
2. In a large bowl cream butter and sugars until light and fluffy. Stir in eggs and vanilla until well incorporated.
3. In a medium bowl whisk together brown rice flour, arrowroot starch, xanthan gum, baking powder, and salt. Slowly stir the flour mixture into sugar mixture, until fully incorporated. If desired, add ½ cup of one or more optional ingredients.
4. Pour batter into baking dish. Bake for 40–45 minutes until golden-brown. Allow to cool completely before cutting. Store in an airtight container in the refrigerator for up to 5 days. Batter and bars will freeze well for up to 1 month.

Chunky Double Chocolate Brownies

This recipe uses melted and whole chocolate chunks along with cocoa powder for a super-rich, decadent chocolate treat. Many chocolate chunks brands, such as Enjoy Life, are free of both gluten and dairy.

INGREDIENTS | YIELDS 16 BROWNIES

2 tablespoons water

¾ cup sugar

⅓ cup butter or Spectrum Palm Shortening

1 (11½-ounce) bag chocolate chunks, divided

2 large eggs

1 teaspoon vanilla extract

½ cup plus 2 tablespoons sorghum flour

2 tablespoons cocoa powder

¼ teaspoon salt

½ cup chopped hazelnuts, walnuts, or pecans (optional)

1. Preheat oven to 325°F. Line an 8" × 8" baking dish with parchment paper and set aside.
2. Combine water, sugar, and butter in a medium saucepan over medium heat until melted. Add half of the chocolate chunks and stir until fully melted into the mixture. Remove from heat. Allow to cool for 5 minutes and then stir in eggs and vanilla extract.
3. In a small bowl whisk together sorghum flour, cocoa, and salt. Slowly stir into the warm chocolate mixture. Stir in remaining chocolate chunks and nuts, if desired. Pour batter into baking dish. Bake for 25–30 minutes until brownies are firm. Allow to cool for 30–40 minutes before cutting into bars. Brownies should be slightly gooey.
4. Store cut brownies separated by wax paper or parchment paper in an airtight container in the fridge. Brownies and batter will freeze for up to 1 month.

CHAPTER 8

Cakes and Cupcakes

Basic Yellow Cake

Yellow cake gets its color from the egg yolks in the ingredients. This will become your go-to recipe for basic cupcakes or sheet cakes—decorate with any type of gluten-free frosting.

INGREDIENTS | SERVES 12

½ cup butter, softened, or Spectrum Palm Shortening

1½ cups sugar

3 large eggs

2 teaspoons vanilla extract

1 cup brown rice flour

1⅓ cups arrowroot starch or tapioca starch

1 teaspoon xanthan gum

1 teaspoon baking powder

1 teaspoon baking soda

½ teaspoon sea salt

1 cup milk or nondairy alternative

1. Preheat oven to 350°F. Line a 9" × 13" baking pan or 2 (8" or 9") cake pans with parchment paper and then grease with oil or nonstick cooking spray.
2. In a large bowl cream together the butter and sugar thoroughly until light and fluffy. Add the eggs and vanilla and mix well.
3. In a smaller bowl whisk together brown rice flour, arrowroot starch or tapioca starch, xanthan gum, baking powder, baking soda, and salt.
4. Add the dry ingredients to the wet alternately in thirds with the milk, beginning and ending with the flour mixture.
5. Pour batter evenly into the cake pan(s) and bake for 25–35 minutes until a toothpick inserted in the center comes out clean and the top of the cake is golden-brown.
6. Allow cake to cool in the pans for 5 minutes, then transfer to a wire rack to cool completely before frosting.

Devil's Food Cake with Mocha Buttercream

You can make this recipe into a fancy two-layer cake or cupcakes, depending on the occasion.

INGREDIENTS | SERVES 16

Cake

½ cup Dutch-processed cocoa powder

½ cup hot coffee (or water)

1¼ cups brown rice flour

¾ cup plus 1 tablespoon arrowroot starch or tapioca starch

1 teaspoon xanthan gum

2 teaspoons baking powder

1 teaspoon baking soda

¼ teaspoon salt

¾ cup unsalted butter, softened or Spectrum Palm Shortening

1 cup sugar

¾ cup brown sugar

3 large eggs

2 teaspoons vanilla extract

1 cup milk or nondairy substitute

Frosting

1 cup unsalted butter, softened

1 cup Dutch-processed cocoa powder

1 teaspoon vanilla extract

½ teaspoon instant espresso powder

4 cups sifted confectioners' sugar

4–6 tablespoons water

1. Preheat the oven to 350°F. Line two 9" round baking pans with parchment paper.
2. In a small bowl, mix together ½ cup cocoa powder and coffee. Let sit for a few minutes while you prepare the other ingredients.
3. In a medium bowl, sift together the brown rice flour, arrowroot starch or tapioca starch, xanthan gum, baking powder, baking soda, and salt. Set aside.
4. In the bowl of a stand mixer, beat the butter, sugar, and brown sugar until light and fluffy, scraping down the bowl when necessary. Add in the eggs one at a time, and 2 teaspoons vanilla extract. Mix until well blended.
5. Add the milk to the cocoa-coffee mixture.
6. With the stand mixer running on low, add half of the sifted dry ingredients to the mixer. Mix until nearly blended. Add the cocoa mixture, and when that is incorporated, add the rest of the dry ingredients. Once it all is incorporated, divide the batter between the two pans. Place on middle rack in preheated oven and bake for 35–40 minutes, or until a toothpick inserted into the middle of the cake comes out clean.
7. Remove cakes from oven and allow to sit for 5 minutes before running a knife around the outside of each cake, and inverting the cakes onto a wire cooling rack. Cool completely before frosting.
8. Make the frosting: With a hand mixer, beat together butter, cocoa powder, vanilla, espresso powder, and confectioners' sugar. Slowly add enough water to reach desired consistency. You want the frosting to be stiff enough to hold its shape, but soft enough to easily spread over the cake.
9. Use an offset spatula to frost the cake as desired.

White Cake

Every well-stocked recipe collection should have a recipe for white cake. Frost this cake with your favorite store-bought gluten-free white frosting.

INGREDIENTS | SERVES 15

1½ cups white or brown rice flour

¾ cup arrowroot starch or tapioca starch

1 teaspoon xanthan gum

1½ cups sugar

2 teaspoons baking powder

1 teaspoon baking soda

½ teaspoon salt

½ cup unsalted butter, softened

¾ cup milk

2 teaspoons vanilla

4 large egg whites

White Rice Flour

If you want the cake to be white, you will need to use white rice flour. Brown rice flour will cause the cake to be more of a tan color.

1. Preheat oven to 350°F. Spray a 13" × 9" pan with nonstick cooking spray and set aside.
2. In a large bowl, combine rice flour, arrowroot starch or tapioca starch, xanthan gum, sugar, baking powder, baking soda, and salt and mix well with a wire whisk.
3. In a stand mixer fitted with a paddle attachment, beat the butter until fluffy. Add the flour mixture, along with the milk and vanilla. Beat until blended, and then beat on medium speed for 2 minutes.
4. Add the unbeaten egg whites, all at once, and beat 2 minutes longer. Pour batter into prepared pan. Bake 35–40 minutes, or until cake begins to pull away from edges and is light golden-brown. Cool completely on wire rack.

Moist Banana Cake

This moist cake stays fresh in an airtight container for days on the counter. Although it doesn't require a frosting to be enjoyed, it is tasty topped with sweetened whipped cream or chocolate frosting.

INGREDIENTS | SERVES 15

½ cup brown rice flour

1¾ cups sorghum flour

¼ cup arrowroot starch or tapioca starch

1 teaspoon xanthan gum

2 teaspoons baking soda

1 teaspoon baking powder

1 teaspoon espresso powder (optional)

½ teaspoon ground cinnamon

½ teaspoon salt

½ cup unsalted butter, softened

1 cup sugar

¾ cup brown sugar

3 large eggs

1 teaspoon vanilla extract

3 large overripe bananas, mashed (about 2 cups total)

⅔ cup sour cream

½ cup chopped walnuts (optional)

1. Preheat the oven to 350°F, and lightly grease one 9" × 13" pan. Set aside.
2. In a large mixing bowl, whisk together the brown rice flour, sorghum flour, arrowroot starch or tapioca starch, xanthan gum, baking soda, baking powder, espresso powder, ground cinnamon, and salt. Set aside.
3. In a separate large mixing bowl, or the bowl of a stand mixer, beat the softened butter with the sugar and brown sugar until light and fluffy.
4. In another bowl, stir to combine the eggs, vanilla, mashed bananas, and sour cream.
5. Pour the banana mixture into the butter-sugar mixture, and beat until well blended.
6. With the mixer running on medium-low speed, add the dry ingredients to the wet ingredients. Stir to combine. Add the walnuts and stir again to incorporate them.
7. Pour cake batter into prepared pan, leveling the top with a rubber spatula. Bake for 45–50 minutes, or until a toothpick inserted into the middle comes out clean. The cake will also release from the edges of the pan, and the top may begin to crack slightly.
8. Remove from oven and cool completely before serving.

Chocolate Raspberry Cupcakes with Fluffy Raspberry Frosting

These cupcakes are lighter than air, but they are heavy on chocolate flavor with a hint of raspberry. The raspberry purée makes the frosting pink.

INGREDIENTS | SERVES 26

Cupcakes

1½ cups sugar
¾ cup sorghum flour
¾ cup arrowroot starch or tapioca starch
¾ cup unsweetened cocoa powder
1 teaspoon xanthan gum
2 teaspoons baking soda
2 teaspoons baking powder
½ teaspoon salt
1 cup milk
2 large eggs
½ cup oil
2 teaspoons raspberry extract
1 cup boiling water

Frosting

1 cup unsalted butter, softened
½ teaspoon salt
4 tablespoons raspberry purée
2 teaspoons raspberry extract
4 cups confectioners' sugar
1–2 tablespoons heavy cream or milk
26 fresh, plump raspberries (optional)

No Seeds, Please

To make the frosting free of seeds, push the mashed berries through a mesh strainer with the back of a spoon. This will leave you with seedless raspberry purée.

1. Preheat oven to 350°F. Line muffin tins with paper liners. In a large bowl, whisk together the sugar, sorghum flour, arrowroot starch or tapioca starch, cocoa powder, xanthan gum, baking soda, baking powder, and ½ teaspoon salt until evenly blended.

2. In a small bowl, whisk together the milk, eggs, oil, and 2 teaspoons raspberry extract. Pour the wet ingredients into the dry ingredients, and beat for 1 minute. Add the boiling water, and using a wooden spoon, stir until it is completely mixed into the batter. The batter will be thin.

3. Fill the muffin tins ⅔ full with the batter. Bake on the center rack of preheated oven for about 20–22 minutes. Test to see if cupcakes are completely baked by inserting a toothpick into the middle of the cupcake. If the toothpick comes out clean, the cupcakes are done. If there is still batter on the toothpick, bake for another 2 minutes and test again.

4. Remove from oven and let sit for 5 minutes before removing cupcakes to wire rack to cool completely. Do not frost cupcakes until they have cooled completely.

5. Make the frosting: In a stand mixer fitted with a paddle attachment, beat the butter until light colored. Add salt, raspberry purée, and raspberry extract. Beat until completely mixed. Add the confectioners' sugar and run the mixer until it all comes together. Scrape down the sides and mix again. Add the milk, 1 tablespoon at a time, until you get the frosting the consistency you want.

6. You can either spread the frosting on with a knife, or pipe it on with a piping bag with a large tip. Top each cupcake with a fresh raspberry, if desired. Store the cupcakes in an airtight container. They are best if eaten in the first 2 days.

Chocolate Mint Swirl Cheesecake
with Chocolate Nut Crust

This delicious special-occasion cake has layers of deep flavor. Cut the pieces small—it's very, very rich.

INGREDIENTS | SERVES 10–12

1½ cups ground walnuts (a food processor works well)

½ cup sugar

⅓ cup unsalted butter, melted

4 ounces semisweet chocolate, melted

4 large eggs, separated

4 ounces semisweet chocolate

2 tablespoons peppermint schnapps

3 (8-ounce) packages cream cheese (not low- or nonfat)

1 cup sour cream

¾ cup sugar

1½ teaspoons vanilla extract

2 tablespoons arrowroot starch or tapioca starch

1 teaspoon salt

4 cups whipped cream (optional)

Baking with Cream Cheese

It's best to use cream cheese that is not low- or nonfat. The lower the fat content, the more chemicals are in the cheese to make it spread easily. When baking, use the purest ingredients, as heat will change the consistency of anything artificial.

1. In a medium bowl, mix the first four ingredients together. Spray a 9-inch springform pan with nonstick spray and press the walnut mixture into the bottom to make a crust. Chill for at least 1 hour.

2. Preheat the oven to 350°F. In a small bowl, beat the egg whites until stiff. Set aside.

3. In a small glass (or microwave-safe) bowl, melt 4 ounces semisweet chocolate with the schnapps, heating for 10 seconds at a time until the chocolate is completely smooth when stirred with a fork. Set melted chocolate aside.

4. In a large bowl, using an electric mixer, beat the cream cheese, sour cream, sugar, vanilla, arrowroot starch, and salt.

5. With the motor running, add the egg yolks to the cream cheese mixture, one at a time, beating vigorously. Fold in the stiff egg whites. Using a knife, swirl the melted chocolate and schnapps into the bowl.

6. Pour into the springform pan and bake for 1 hour. Turn off the oven, and with the door cracked, let the cake cool for another hour. Chill before serving. You can add whipped cream to the top before serving.

Molten Lava Dark Chocolate Cake

For such an easy recipe, it comes off as an elegant dessert. This is a very rich chocolate cake, so feel free to make it in smaller portions if you have smaller containers.

INGREDIENTS | SERVES 8

¾ cup plus 8 teaspoons butter, divided

⅓ cup plus 8 tablespoons sugar, divided

8 ounces semisweet baking chocolate

6 ounces unsalted butter

3 large whole eggs

3 large egg yolks

⅓ cup sugar

1 tablespoon arrowroot starch or tapioca starch

1 teaspoon vanilla

1 quart raspberry sorbet

1. Butter the insides of 8 6-ounce custard cups, then coat with sugar, using 1 teaspoon butter and 1 tablespoon sugar for each. Preheat oven to 425°F. In a heavy saucepan over very low heat, melt the chocolate and remaining butter.

2. Beat the eggs, egg yolks, ⅓ cup sugar, arrowroot starch, and vanilla for about 10 minutes. Add the chocolate mixture by the tablespoonful until the eggs have digested some of the chocolate. Fold in the rest of the chocolate-butter mixture.

3. Divide the mixture between the custard cups. Place the cups on a cookie sheet and bake for 12–13 minutes. The sides should be puffed and the center very soft. Serve hot with raspberry sorbet spooned into the "craters."

Cherry Vanilla Cheesecake with Walnut Crust

If you can tolerate soy products, Tofutti cream cheese is an easy dairy-free substitute. It's the perfect consistency for baking and makes a delicious dairy-free cheesecake.

INGREDIENTS | SERVES 10–12

1½ cups ground walnuts

½ cup sugar

½ cup unsalted butter, melted

4 large eggs, separated

3 (8-ounce) packages cream cheese

1 cup sour cream

2 teaspoons vanilla extract

1 teaspoon salt

2 tablespoons brown rice flour

⅔ cup cherry preserves, melted

Nut Crusts for Cheesecake

Walnuts work well in these recipes because they are probably the least expensive shelled nuts and have a wonderful flavor. However, you can substitute hazelnuts, almonds, or pecans. Pecans add a Southern touch and are really good, but they are more expensive. Grinding nuts is simple—just use your food processor or add the nuts to a zip-top plastic bag and mash the bag against a hard counter with a wooden rolling pin until the nuts are as fine as you'd like them.

1. In a medium bowl, mix together the walnuts, sugar, and melted butter. Prepare a springform pan with nonstick spray and press the nut mixture into the bottom to form a crust. Chill for at least 1 hour.
2. Preheat oven to 350°F. In a small bowl, beat the egg whites and set aside.
3. In a large bowl, using an electric mixer, beat the cream cheese, sour cream, vanilla, salt, and brown rice flour together.
4. Add the egg yolks, one at a time, while beating. When smooth, fold in the egg whites and mix in the melted cherry preserves.
5. Pour into springform pan and bake for 1 hour. Turn off oven and crack the door. Let cake cool for another hour. Chill before serving.

Lemon Cheesecake with Nut Crust

This cheesecake has a light consistency with a complex and inviting lemon flavor.
It's a lovely summer cheesecake that will make your guests ask for more.

INGREDIENTS | SERVES 10–12

1¼ cups ground walnuts
½ cup sugar
½ cup unsalted butter, melted
5 large egg whites
3 (8-ounce) packages cream cheese
1 cup sour cream
⅔ cup sugar
2 tablespoons brown rice flour
1 teaspoon salt
3 large egg yolks
Juice of 1 lemon
Minced rind of 1 lemon
½ cup chopped walnuts
8 paper-thin lemon slices

1. In a medium bowl, mix together nuts, sugar, and butter. Grease a springform pan with nonstick spray. Press the nut mixture into the bottom to form a crust, and chill.
2. Preheat oven to 350°F. In a small bowl, beat the egg whites until stiff and set aside.
3. In a large bowl, using an electric mixer, beat the cheese, sour cream, sugar, brown rice flour, salt, and egg yolks, adding the yolks one at a time. Beat in the lemon juice and lemon rind.
4. Gently fold in the egg whites. Pour the cheese-lemon mixture into the springform pan. Bake for 1 hour. Turn off oven and crack the door, letting cool for another hour. Top with chopped walnuts and lemon slices. Chill before serving.

Stiffly Beaten Egg Whites

Be very careful not to get even a speck of egg yolk in the whites when beating. Even a drop of egg yolk will prevent the whites from stiffening. Always use clean beaters. Any fat or oil will prevent the whites from fluffing up. You can add a drop of vinegar or lemon juice to help them stiffen.

Orange Ginger Carrot Cake

Fresh lemon juice and grated orange rind give this delicious cake a nice zing.
The gingerroot adds an appealing sophistication and spiciness.

INGREDIENTS | SERVES 8–10

4 large eggs, separated

½ cup brown sugar

1½ cups grated carrots

1 tablespoon lemon juice

Grated zest of ½ fresh orange

½ cup brown rice flour

1 inch fresh gingerroot, peeled and minced

1½ teaspoons baking soda

½ teaspoon salt

1. Liberally butter a springform pan or line an 8" cake pan with parchment paper and heavily grease the paper. Preheat oven to 325°F.
2. In a small bowl, beat the egg whites until stiff and set aside.
3. In a large bowl, beat the egg yolks, sugar, and carrots together. Add lemon juice, orange zest, and brown rice flour. When smooth, add the gingerroot, baking soda, and salt. Gently fold in the egg whites.
4. Pour batter into the springform pan (or cake pan) and bake for 1 hour. Test by inserting a toothpick into the center of the cake—if it comes out clean, the cake is done.

German Chocolate Cake

This retro cake is made with a killer chocolate-coconut frosting.

INGREDIENTS | SERVES 8–10

1⅓ cups coconut milk

1¼ cups sugar

⅓ cup cornstarch mixed with ¼ cup water

1 tablespoon vanilla extract

2½ cups sweetened (or unsweetened) flaked coconut

1½ cups chopped pecans

1 recipe Devil's Food Cake (see recipe in this chapter), baked in 2 (8") cake pans and unfrosted

1. In a medium saucepan whisk together the coconut milk, sugar, and cornstarch-water mixture. Cook over medium-high heat stirring constantly until mixture boils and thickens, about 5–6 minutes. Cook for 1 minute more after it boils and then remove from heat.
2. Stir in vanilla extract, coconut, and pecans. Stir the mixture together thoroughly. It should be thick and sticky. Allow mixture to cool for about 10 minutes before filling (adding the German chocolate filling between the two layers of cake) and frosting the cake.
3. Store any remaining cake in the refrigerator for 2–3 days.

Raspberry Coulis for Cakes and Cheesecakes

Coulis can be served over a cheesecake, a simple yellow cake, or a pound cake. You can use any berry to create a coulis. Heavily seeded berries should be strained though a fine sieve or cheesecloth to remove the seeds.

INGREDIENTS | YIELDS 1½ CUPS

1 pint raspberries

½ cup sugar

¼ cup water, orange juice, or fruit liqueur such as peach or cherry

1. Place raspberries in a medium saucepan with the sugar and water, juice, or liqueur. Bring to a boil and cook for 3–5 minutes until mixture has slightly thickened.
2. Remove from heat and cool on a potholder for 30 minutes. Strain the coulis with a wire strainer, whisk together well, and serve warm or cold. Store in a glass jar in the refrigerator for up to 2 weeks.

Classic Pavlova Cake

This delicate and delicious cake is enhanced by sweet bananas and strawberries.

INGREDIENTS | SERVES 6

4 large egg whites

1 teaspoon vinegar

½ cup sugar

1 cup heavy cream

3 tablespoons confectioners' sugar

½ teaspoon vanilla

1 banana, sliced

1 quart strawberries, washed, hulled, and halved, 8 left whole for decoration

Origins of the Pavlova

There is some debate as to who invented this cake. It was designed to honor the famed ballerina Anna Pavlova, whose admirers came from around the world. Some say it was created in Australia; others say the cake originated in the United States.

1. Preheat oven to 200°F.
2. In a medium bowl whip the egg whites, and as they stiffen, add the vinegar and slowly add the sugar. Pour into a 9" glass pie pan that you've treated with nonstick spray.
3. Bake the meringue for 2 hours. Then, turn off the oven and crack the door. Let the meringue rest for another hour. It should become very crisp and lightly browned.
4. In a small bowl, whip the cream and mix in the confectioners' sugar and vanilla.
5. Slice a layer of bananas onto the bottom of the cooled meringue crust. Add a layer of whipped cream. Sprinkle with halved strawberries.
6. Add another layer of whipped cream and decorate with the whole strawberries. Serve immediately or it will get soggy.

Hummingbird Cake with Cream Cheese Icing

This old-fashioned fruit-filled cake is perfect for birthdays.
It's delicious topped with the cream cheese frosting.

INGREDIENTS | SERVES 8–10

Cake

1 cup plus 2 tablespoons brown rice flour

1 cup arrowroot starch or tapioca starch

1 cup sugar

2 teaspoons baking powder

1 teaspoon baking soda

1 teaspoon xanthan gum

1 teaspoon ground cinnamon

½ teaspoon sea salt

1 (8-ounce) can crushed pineapple in juice, undrained

1 cup mashed bananas (2–3 very ripe bananas)

½ cup water

½ cup light-tasting olive oil

3 large eggs

1 teaspoon vanilla extract

Cream Cheese Frosting

1½ cups butter, softened

8 ounces cream cheese, softened

3 cups confectioners' sugar

1 teaspoon vanilla extract

1. Preheat oven to 350°F. Line two 9" round baking pans with parchment paper and then grease with oil or non-stick cooking spray. Dust pans lightly with brown rice flour.

2. In a medium-sized bowl, whisk together brown rice flour, arrowroot starch or tapioca starch, sugar, baking powder, baking soda, xanthan gum, ground cinnamon, and salt.

3. In a smaller bowl whisk together crushed pineapple in juice, mashed bananas, water, oil, eggs, and vanilla until fully combined.

4. Slowly add the wet ingredients into the dry ingredients and stir until fully incorporated. Pour into baking pans.

5. Bake cakes for 30–35 minutes until a toothpick inserted in the middle comes out clean, they are golden-brown, and the top springs back when touched lightly.

6. Cool cakes for 5 minutes in their pans and then transfer to a wire rack to cool completely for 1–2 hours before icing with the cream cheese frosting.

7. In a large bowl, using a hand mixer, cream together the butter and cream cheese. Stir in confectioners' sugar and vanilla extract. Mix until the frosting is thick enough to spread and very creamy. Use to fill the middle layer of the cake and to frost outside of cake.

Fresh Strawberry Cake

This is a perfect cake for baby showers or tea parties! Fresh strawberries are added to a white cake base to create a light, fruit-filled, and elegant cake.

INGREDIENTS | SERVES 8–10

1 cup plus 2 tablespoons brown rice flour

1 cup plus 2 tablespoons arrowroot starch

1 teaspoon xanthan gum

3 tablespoons baking powder

½ teaspoon sea salt

1½ cups sugar

¾ cup fresh strawberries, stems removed, and diced

4 large egg whites

1 cup almond milk or other nondairy milk

½ cup light-tasting olive oil or melted coconut oil

1 teaspoon almond extract

16 ounces whipped topping or 3 cups fresh whipped heavy cream mixed with ⅓ cup sugar

1. Preheat oven to 350°F. Line 2 (8") round cake pans with a circle of parchment paper on the bottom of each pan. Spritz each pan with nonstick cooking spray or brush with light-tasting olive oil and set aside.
2. In a medium bowl whisk together the brown rice flour, arrowroot starch, xanthan gum, baking powder, and sea salt.
3. In a large bowl mix together sugar and fresh strawberries until they are fully coated in the sugar (this will help keep the strawberries from sinking to the bottom of the cake). Add the egg whites, almond milk, olive oil, and almond extract. Whisk wet ingredients together thoroughly. Slowly stir in dry mixture a little at a time, until it's thoroughly mixed into the wet ingredients.
4. Pour cake batter evenly between the greased cake pans. Bake for 25–35 minutes until the cake is golden brown on top and a toothpick inserted in the middle comes out clean.
5. Allow cakes to cool completely on a wire rack before frosting. Use whipped topping to fill the center of the layers and to frost the outside. Top cake with additional fresh strawberries if desired.

Lemon Cream Cake

This recipe transforms the white cake recipe in this chapter into a rich, delicious, and creamy lemon dessert.

INGREDIENTS | SERVES 8–10

12 ounces cream cheese, softened

3½ cups confectioners' sugar, divided

1½ tablespoons plus ½ teaspoon fresh lemon juice, divided

2 teaspoons freshly grated lemon zest

1½ cups heavy whipping cream

½ cup crumbled gluten-free graham crackers

3 tablespoons cold butter

½ teaspoon vanilla extract

1 recipe White Cake (see recipe in this chapter) made as two 8" or 9" round layers

1. Make the filling: Mix together cream cheese, 3 cups confectioners' sugar, 1½ tablespoons lemon juice, and lemon zest in a medium bowl.
2. In another bowl whip cream until stiff peaks form. Fold the whipped cream gently into the cream cheese filling. Place in fridge until assembling cake.
3. In a small bowl mix together crumbled graham crackers and remaining confectioners' sugar. Cut in butter, remaining lemon juice, and vanilla extract until you have a crumbly mixture.
4. To assemble cake, divide filling into three parts. Place about a tablespoon of the filling in the center of a cardboard cake round or large plate. Place one layer, centered on the cake round or plate. Spread ⅓ of the filling on the top of the cake layer. Gently place the second layer on top of the filling; add another ⅓ of the filling and spread evenly over top of the cake. Use the remaining ⅓ of the filling to frost the sides of the cake.
5. Sprinkle the crumbly topping evenly over the top of the cake. Refrigerate for at least 3 hours before slicing into 10–12 pieces and serving. Refrigerate any remaining cake for up to 3 days.

Cherry Dump Cake

This versatile cake can be made with any fruit pie filling. Most store-bought canned pie fillings are thickened with cornstarch and therefore gluten-free, but read the ingredients to make sure.

INGREDIENTS | SERVES 12–16

½ cup plus 1 tablespoon brown rice flour

½ cup arrowroot starch or tapioca starch

½ cup sugar

1 teaspoon baking powder

½ teaspoon baking soda

½ teaspoon xanthan gum

¼ teaspoon sea salt

2 (21-ounce) cans cherry pie filling

8 ounces chopped walnuts or pecans

½ cup butter, melted

1. Preheat oven to 350°F. Heavily grease a 9" × 13" cake pan with oil or nonstick cooking spray.
2. In a large bowl whisk together the brown rice flour, arrowroot starch, sugar, baking powder, baking soda, xanthan gum, and salt. Set aside.
3. Pour filling into cake pan. Sprinkle flour mixture evenly over the filling. Top with chopped nuts and drizzle the melted butter over all.
4. Bake for 35–40 minutes until the top of the cake is golden-brown and the filling is bubbling. Allow to cool for 30 minutes before serving.

Jennifer's Twinkie Cake

My coworker Jennifer always makes this cake for her husband's birthday. It's a tasty, light yellow cake with a delicious, creamy whipped filling and topping.

INGREDIENTS | SERVES 12

1 (3.9-ounce) package of instant vanilla pudding and pie filling

1 cup cold milk

1 (12-ounce) container whipped topping

1 recipe Basic Yellow Cake (see recipe in this chapter), baked as two 8" or 9" layers and cooled

1. In a large bowl whisk together the instant pudding and milk. Chill thick pudding mixture for 20 minutes. After chilling, fold in the whipped topping.
2. Frost and fill cake with the whipped pudding mixture. Refrigerate for at least 2–3 hours and then slice and serve. Store any remaining cake in the refrigerator for up to 3 days.

Suzy-Q Cake

Use 1 (3.9-ounce) package of instant chocolate pudding and pie filling instead of vanilla for a Suzy-Q Cake. For another flavor option, add sliced fruit such as strawberries on top of the filling in the middle of the cake, and as a garnish on top of each slice of cake.

Classic Coconut Cake

This super "coconutty" cake is great for family potlucks and barbecues.
If you make it in a large sheet pan, you can store the cake right in the baking dish for easy traveling.

INGREDIENTS | SERVES 12

1½ cups brown rice flour

¾ cup arrowroot starch or tapioca starch

1 teaspoon xanthan gum

1½ cups sugar

2 teaspoons baking powder

1 teaspoon baking soda

½ teaspoon salt

½ cup unsalted butter, softened

¾ cup light coconut milk

2 teaspoons vanilla extract

½ teaspoon coconut extract

4 large egg whites

1–2 cups flaked sweetened coconut, for sprinkling on top of the cake

Coconut Frosting

In a large bowl cream together 1 cup Spectrum Palm Shortening or butter, 1 teaspoon coconut or vanilla extract, 4 cups confectioners' sugar, and ¼ cup of light coconut milk. Stir together well with a whisk or a fork until you have a smooth, creamy frosting.

1. Preheat oven to 350°F. Spray a 13" × 9" pan with non-stick cooking spray and set aside.
2. In a large bowl, combine rice flour, arrowroot starch or tapioca starch, xanthan gum, sugar, baking powder, baking soda, and salt and mix well with a wire whisk.
3. In a stand mixer fitted with a paddle attachment, beat the butter until fluffy. Add the flour mixture, along with the milk, vanilla, and coconut extract. Beat until blended, and then beat on medium speed for 2 minutes.
4. Add the unbeaten egg whites, all at once, and beat 2 minutes longer. Pour batter into prepared pan. Bake 35–40 minutes, or until cake is beginning to pull away from edges and is light golden-brown. Cool completely on wire rack.
5. Once cake is completely cooled, fill and frost the cake with the coconut frosting. Generously sprinkle sweetened coconut flakes on top. If you have time, chill cake for 2–3 hours before serving for the best flavor. Store any remaining cake in the refrigerator for up to 3 days.

Gluten-Free Pound Cake

There are dozens of variations for this cake, such as adding 2 tablespoons of cocoa,
or 1 teaspoon of cinnamon, or even a swirl of strawberry preserves.
But try it just as it is at least once to savor the vintage flavors of butter and vanilla.

INGREDIENTS | SERVES 12

1½ cups brown rice flour

1½ cups arrowroot starch or tapioca starch

1 teaspoon xanthan gum

2 teaspoons baking powder

2 cups sugar

1 cup butter, melted

1 tablespoon vanilla extract

4 large eggs

1 cup milk

1. Preheat oven to 350°F. Grease a 12-cup Bundt pan or a 10-inch angel food tube pan; sprinkle it with a little brown rice flour and set aside.
2. In a medium bowl whisk together brown rice flour, arrowroot starch or tapioca starch, xanthan gum, and baking powder. In a large bowl cream together sugar and melted butter, until light and fluffy. Stir in vanilla extract. Add the eggs one at a time, stirring thoroughly each time. Add the flour mixture and the milk alternately to the creamed sugar-egg mixture. Stir together well until you have a stiff but smooth cake batter.
3. Pour the batter into pan. Using a spatula, spread the batter evenly around the pan. Bake for 50–60 minutes until the top of the cake is golden-brown and a knife inserted in the center comes out clean.
4. Cool the cake 10 minutes in the pan, then turn out and cool for an additional hour on a wire rack before slicing.
5. Serve cake plain, or with whipped cream and strawberries, or with a drizzle of chocolate syrup. Store any leftover cake in the refrigerator for up to 3 days. After three days freeze individual slices for up to 3 months.

Strawberry Poke Cake

This fun and easy cake is made with either the basic yellow cake or the white cake in a sheet pan. It's a great cake for children's birthday parties.

INGREDIENTS | SERVES 12

1 Basic Yellow Cake or White Cake recipe (see recipes in this chapter), prepared in a well-greased 9" × 13" cake pan and cooled

1 (3-ounce) box of strawberry gelatin dessert

½ cup boiling water

½ cup cold water

1 (8-ounce) container whipped topping

½ pint fresh strawberries, hulled and sliced (optional)

Try Lemon, Lime, or Grape Poke Cake

You can use different flavors of gelatin to make a different type of poke cake for every occasion. Use half lime and half grape gelatin to make a fun birthday party cake with green and purple colors! Decorate with colored sprinkles.

1. Pierce the cake all over with chopsticks for smaller holes or with the handle of a wooden spoon for larger holes.
2. In a small bowl stir together the strawberry gelatin powder, boiling water, and cold water. When the gelatin is dissolved thoroughly into the water mixture, pour over the entire cake.
3. Cover the sheet pan with plastic wrap and refrigerate at least 2 hours or until fully chilled. When ready to serve, frost cake with whipped topping. Add strawberries, if desired. Cut into squares and serve.
4. Store any leftover cake covered in plastic wrap in the refrigerator for up to 3 days.

Red Velvet Cupcakes

The traditional recipe is made with buttermilk, but this version uses regular milk or nondairy milk mixed with apple cider vinegar. This helps the batter rise and assists the cocoa and food coloring in giving these cupcakes their distinctive red hue.

INGREDIENTS | SERVES 12

1 cup brown rice flour

¾ cup arrowroot starch or tapioca starch

1 teaspoon xanthan gum

½ teaspoon sea salt

¾ teaspoon baking soda

2 tablespoons cocoa powder

1 cup sugar

6 tablespoons butter or Spectrum Palm Shortening

2 large eggs, room temperature

1 tablespoon vanilla extract

1 teaspoon apple cider vinegar

1½ tablespoons red food coloring

1 cup milk or nondairy substitution

1. Preheat oven to 350°F. Line a muffin pan with paper liners and then spritz them with oil or nonstick cooking spray.
2. In small bowl whisk together brown rice flour, arrowroot or tapioca starch, xanthan gum, salt, baking soda, and cocoa powder.
3. In a large bowl cream together the sugar and butter thoroughly until light and fluffy. Add the eggs, vanilla, vinegar, and food coloring and mix together well.
4. Add the dry ingredients alternately in thirds with the milk, beginning and ending with the flour mixture.
5. Pour batter evenly into paper liners and bake for 22–25 minutes until a toothpick inserted in the center of the cupcakes comes out clean and the top of the cake is reddish-brown.
6. Allow cupcakes to cool in the pans for 5 minutes then transfer to a wire rack to cool completely before frosting with the cream cheese frosting for the Hummingbird Cake (see recipe in this chapter).

Dreamy Key Lime Cupcakes

Lime isn't a common flavor in most cupcakes. These tangy sweet cupcakes are a fun and nontraditional flavor to try for a birthday party or special dinner. If you can find packaged premade royal icing flowers, they make a very cute topping on these cupcakes.

INGREDIENTS | YIELDS 24 CUPCAKES

1 cup plus 2 tablespoons brown rice flour

1 cup plus 2 tablespoons arrowroot starch or tapioca starch

1 teaspoon xanthan gum

3 teaspoons baking powder

½ teaspoon sea salt

1½ cups sugar

2 tablespoons fresh lime zest

1¼ cups almond milk or other nondairy milk

4 large egg whites

½ cup light-tasting olive oil or melted coconut oil

3 tablespoons fresh lime juice

Creamy Lime Frosting

In a large bowl or stand mixer, combine 1 cup Spectrum Palm Shortening with 4 cups of confectioners' sugar. Add 4 teaspoons of fresh lime juice and 1 tablespoon fresh lemon zest. Stir and combine until you have a thick frosting. Add 3 or 4 tablespoons of ice-water to smooth out the frosting to a spreadable consistency. Add frosting to an icing bag and frost each cupcake as desired.

1. Preheat oven to 350°F. Line a muffin pan with paper liners and then spritz them with oil or nonstick cooking spray.
2. In small bowl whisk together brown rice flour, arrowroot starch or tapioca starch, xanthan gum, baking powder, and sea salt.
3. In a large bowl cream together the sugar with the lime zest and then add the almond milk, egg whites, olive oil, and fresh lime juice.
4. Add the dry ingredients a little at a time into the wet ingredients until you have a thoroughly mixed cake batter.
5. Pour batter evenly into 24 paper liners and bake for 18–20 minutes until a toothpick inserted in the center of the cupcakes comes out clean and the top of the cupcakes are just starting to brown.
6. Allow cupcakes to cool in the pans for 5 minutes then transfer to a wire rack to cool completely before frosting with the Creamy Lime Frosting in the sidebar.

Black Bottom Cupcakes

This recipe makes no-fuss cupcakes that don't need any frosting at all!
They are great for potlucks because they travel well.

INGREDIENTS | SERVES 24

Cream Cheese Filling

1 (8-ounce) package cream cheese, softened

1 large egg

⅓ cup sugar

⅛ teaspoon sea salt

1 cup mini semisweet chocolate chips

Cake

¾ cup brown rice flour

¾ cup arrowroot starch or tapioca starch

½ teaspoon xanthan gum

1 cup sugar

¼ cup unsweetened cocoa powder

1 teaspoon baking soda

½ teaspoon sea salt

1 cup water

⅓ cup light-tasting olive oil

1 tablespoon apple cider vinegar

1 teaspoon vanilla extract

1. Preheat oven to 350°F. Line muffin tins with 24 paper liners and spritz with olive oil or nonstick cooking spray.
2. In a medium bowl stir together the cream cheese, egg, sugar, and salt. Beat until mixture is rich and creamy. Stir in the chocolate chips and set aside.
3. In a large bowl whisk together the brown rice flour, arrowroot starch or tapioca starch, xanthan gum, 1 cup sugar, cocoa powder, baking soda, and salt. Make a well in the center of the dry ingredients and add the water, oil, vinegar, and vanilla extract. Stir the wet ingredients into the dry ingredients.
4. Fill muffin tins ⅔ full of batter. On top of the batter add a small spoonful of the cream cheese mixture.
5. Bake for 25–30 minutes until a toothpick inserted in the middle of a cupcake comes out clean and the edges are beginning to pull away from the paper liners. Cool for 5 minutes in the pan and then turn out cupcakes to cool completely on wire racks before serving. Store any remaining cupcakes in the refrigerator for up to 3 days.

Apple Spice Cupcakes

This vintage spiced-apple cake recipe is perfect served in cupcake portions. You could also make it in a 12-cup Bundt pan or a 10-inch angel food cake pan, baked at 350°F for 60–80 minutes.

INGREDIENTS | SERVES 24

1½ cups sorghum flour

1½ cups arrowroot starch or tapioca starch

1 teaspoon xanthan gum

½ teaspoon ground nutmeg

2 teaspoons ground cinnamon

½ teaspoon ground cloves

½ teaspoon ground ginger

1 teaspoon baking soda

½ teaspoon baking powder

½ teaspoon sea salt

1½ cups light-tasting olive oil or canola oil

1½ cups sugar

½ cup brown sugar

3 large eggs

1 tablespoon vanilla extract

5 medium apples, peeled, cored, and roughly chopped

1 cup chopped walnuts or pecans

1. Preheat oven to 350°F. Line muffin tins with 24 paper liners and spritz with olive oil or nonstick cooking spray.
2. In a large bowl whisk together the flour, arrowroot starch or tapioca starch, xanthan gum, nutmeg, cinnamon, cloves, ginger, baking soda, baking powder, and salt.
3. In a medium bowl stir together the oil, sugar, brown sugar, eggs, and vanilla extract. Stir the wet ingredients into the dry ingredients. Fold in chopped apples and nuts.
4. Fill muffin tins ⅔ full of batter. Bake for 25–30 minutes until a toothpick inserted in the middle of a cupcake comes out clean and the cupcakes are a light golden-brown.
5. Cool for 5 minutes in the pan and then turn out cupcakes to cool completely on wire racks before serving. Store any remaining cupcakes in the refrigerator for up to 3 days.

Baking with Apples

When baking, choose apples with firm flesh such as Granny Smith, Jonathan, McIntosh, Cortland, Pink Lady, Pippin, or Winesap. They will hold up to baking without turning to mush. You can leave the skins on, which adds extra fiber.

Chai Latte Cupcakes with Nutmeg Cardamom Icing

These heavily spiced cupcakes are wonderful during the fall, served with a hot cup of coffee or tea. They are vegan, as well as being gluten-free.

INGREDIENTS | SERVES 24

Cupcakes

1 cup sorghum flour

⅓ cup arrowroot starch or tapioca starch

½ teaspoon xanthan gum

¼ teaspoon baking soda

1 teaspoon baking powder

½ teaspoon sea salt

2 teaspoons ground cinnamon

1 teaspoon ground cardamom

½ teaspoon ground ginger

¼ teaspoon ground cloves

⅛ teaspoon ground white pepper

1 cup almond milk, warmed to 110°F

4 black tea bags

¼ cup light-tasting olive oil or canola oil

½ cup unsweetened applesauce or plain pumpkin purée

¾ cup sugar

1 teaspoon vanilla extract

Frosting

1 cup Spectrum Palm Shortening

4 cups confectioners' sugar

1 teaspoon ground cinnamon

1 teaspoon ground nutmeg

1 teaspoon ground cardamom

1 teaspoon ground ginger

3–5 tablespoons ice water

1. Preheat oven to 350°F. Line muffin tins with 24 paper liners and spritz with olive oil or nonstick cooking spray.

2. In a large bowl whisk together the sorghum flour, arrowroot starch or tapioca starch, xanthan gum, baking soda, baking powder, salt, cinnamon, cardamom, ginger, cloves, and pepper. Set dry ingredients aside.

3. In a small bowl or glass measuring cup, heat almond milk in the microwave to 110°F. Add the tea bags and allow to steep for 10 minutes. Remove tea bags.

4. In a medium bowl mix together the tea-steeped milk, oil, applesauce, sugar, and vanilla. Stir the wet ingredients into the dry ingredients until you have a thick cake batter.

5. Fill the muffin tins ⅔ full of batter.

6. Bake for 25–30 minutes until a toothpick inserted in the middle of a cupcake comes out clean and the tops are golden-brown. Cool for 5 minutes in the pan and then turn out cupcakes onto wire racks to cool completely.

7. Make the frosting: In a medium bowl, cut shortening into confectioners' sugar with a pastry blender. Stir in spices. (If you prefer a less-spicy frosting, use only ½ teaspoon of each.) Mixture will be crumbly. Thin the frosting with ice water, 1 tablespoon at a time, until you get the consistency you desire to frost the cupcakes.

8. Store any remaining cupcakes in the refrigerator for up to 3 days.

Sugar Plum Cupcakes

These cupcakes have a secret ingredient: puréed plum baby food. The plums give these cupcakes their unique flavor and help keep them super moist for 3–4 days after they are baked.

INGREDIENTS | SERVES 24

Cupcakes

1 cup brown rice flour
1 cup arrowroot starch or tapioca starch
1 teaspoon xanthan gum
2 teaspoons baking powder
1 teaspoon ground cinnamon
2 cups sugar
2 (6-ounce) jars puréed plum baby food
¾ cup light-tasting olive oil or canola oil
3 large eggs
1 cup chopped pecans (optional)

Plum Glaze

1 cup confectioners' sugar
1 (4-ounce) jar puréed plum baby food
2 tablespoons milk or nondairy milk substitute

1. Preheat oven to 350°F. Line muffin tins with 24 paper liners and spritz with olive oil or nonstick cooking spray.
2. In a large bowl whisk together the brown rice flour, arrowroot starch or tapioca starch, xanthan gum, baking powder, and cinnamon.
3. In a medium bowl whisk together the sugar, plum baby food, oil, and eggs. Stir the wet ingredients into the dry ingredients. Fold in the chopped pecans, if desired.
4. Fill muffin tins ⅔ full of cake batter.
5. Bake for 25–30 minutes until a toothpick inserted in the middle of a cupcake comes out clean and the tops are golden-brown. Cool for 5 minutes in the pan and then turn out cupcakes onto wire racks to cool completely.
6. Make the glaze: In a medium bowl whisk together confectioners' sugar, baby food, and milk. Whisk until you have a thin, sweet glaze. Drizzle generously over completely cooled cupcakes. Store any remaining cupcakes in the refrigerator for up to 3 days.

Light and Lovely Angel Food Cake

You could make endless variations of this cloudlike angel food cake. Add a few tablespoons of cocoa powder to the dry ingredients. Add the zest of 1 large lemon. Or, fold in ⅓ cup mini chocolate chips right before pouring batter into the pan.

INGREDIENTS | SERVES 12

½ cup sorghum flour

½ cup arrowroot starch or tapioca starch

12 large egg whites, room temperature

1½ teaspoons cream of tartar

¼ teaspoon sea salt

1 cup sugar

1 tablespoon vanilla extract

1. Preheat oven to 350°F. Grease a 12-cup Bundt pan or a 10-inch angel food tube pan; sprinkle with a little sorghum flour and set aside.
2. In a small bowl whisk together sorghum flour and arrowroot or tapioca starch.
3. In the bowl of a stand mixer, using the whisk attachment (or use a hand mixer), whip egg whites until foamy. Add in the cream of tartar and sea salt and continue to mix until soft peaks form. Beat in the sugar a little at a time until stiff peaks form and the egg whites look slightly glossy.
4. Stop the mixer and remove the whisk attachment. Using a hand whisk slowly fold in the vanilla. Continuing using the hand whisk, slowly folding in flour mixture about ¼ cup at a time. Slowly pour the cake batter into the tube pan. Bake for 50–55 minutes until the cake is golden-brown and a toothpick inserted in the middle comes out clean; the sides of the cake will also pull away from the pan.
5. Allow to cool for 10–20 minutes. Run a knife around the edge of the cake and turn out onto a cake plate. Serve plain or with sliced strawberries and whipped cream.

CHAPTER 9

Pies

Basic Gluten-Free Pie and Tart Pastry

It takes a little practice to learn how to roll out dough, but because this crust doesn't contain gluten, you can never overwork the dough.

INGREDIENTS | YIELDS 1 (8" OR 9") PIE CRUST OR TART PASTRY

¾ cup sorghum flour
¾ cup arrowroot starch
½ teaspoon sea salt
¼ teaspoon xanthan gum
½ cup Spectrum Palm Shortening
1 large egg
2 tablespoons ice-cold water, as needed

Measurements for a Double-Crusted Pie

Most of the pie recipes in this book only use a bottom crust, but occasionally it's fun to have a top crust or a lattice crust. For double-crusted pies use 1½ cups sorghum flour, 1½ cups arrowroot starch, 1 teaspoon sea salt, ½ teaspoon xanthan gum, 1 cup Spectrum Palm Shortening, 2 large eggs, 4 tablespoons ice-cold water.

1. In a large bowl whisk together sorghum flour, arrowroot starch, salt, and xanthan gum. Using a pastry blender or a knife and fork, cut in shortening throughout the flour until it resembles small peas. Make a well in the center of the flour and add the egg and 1 tablespoon of water. Mix with a fork until the dough gathers up into a ball. Shape dough into a round disk, cover with plastic wrap, and refrigerate at least 1 hour. Dough can be frozen at this point for up to 1 month.

2. Roll out dough onto a flat surface liberally dusted with sorghum flour.

3. Gently unroll the crust into the pan. It's okay if the dough cracks and doesn't transfer perfectly. This dough is very forgiving and you can patch it with your fingers. Cut off any extra dough around the pan and flute the edges of the crust. Or, mark the edges with a fork for a rustic look. Another option is to reroll the scraps of dough and cut out shapes with cookie cutters. Place these decorative shapes on top of the filling right before baking. Now the unbaked crust is ready for making a pie. The crust can also be frozen at this point in an air-tight, zip-top plastic bag or container for up to 1 month.

4. Make a prebaked crust: Heat oven to 350°F and prick small holes in the bottom of the crust with a fork. Bake for 10–15 minutes until crust is golden-brown. Crust can be frozen for up to 1 month.

Easy Pat-in-the-Pan Pie Crust

If you don't have the time or energy to make your own crust, but still want a pie, try this delicious and easy recipe. It makes a bottom crust for an 8" or 9" pie. You cannot make a top crust with this recipe.

INGREDIENTS | YIELDS 1 (8" OR 9") PIE CRUST

¾ cup sorghum flour

¾ cup arrowroot starch

1½ teaspoons sugar

¼ teaspoon xanthan gum

½ teaspoon salt

⅓ cup vegetable oil

1 large egg white

2 tablespoons ice-cold almond milk or ice-cold water

Soak-Proof Crust

With fruit pies especially, the bottom crust can get a bit soggy after a day or two. To prevent that from happening, spread a thin layer of cream cheese over the crust after prebaking it. Then add fillings as directed. This will protect the crust and keep it flaky for several days.

1. Pour sorghum flour, arrowroot starch, sugar, xanthan gum, and salt into an 8" or 9" pie pan. Whisk together thoroughly. Make a well in the center of ingredients and add vegetable oil, egg white, and almond milk. Stir wet ingredients into the dry ingredients to create a crumbly dough.
2. Place a sheet of plastic wrap over the dough to keep your fingers clean; press the dough evenly over the bottom and up the sides of the pie pan. Flute edges of the crust or use a fork to decorate the edges. You can now use this crust for any pie recipe calling for an unbaked pie crust. The crust can also be frozen in an airtight zip-top plastic bag for up to 1 month.
3. Make a prebaked crust: Use a fork to prick very small holes in the bottom of the crust. Heat oven to 350°F. Bake pie crust for 10–15 minutes until it is golden-brown and flaky. Allow crust to cool before adding a custard or pudding filling.

Gluten-Free "Graham" Cracker Crust

You can use either store-bought gluten-free "graham" crackers for this recipe or the Cinnamon "Graham" Crackers in Chapter 7.

INGREDIENTS | YIELDS 1 (8" OR 9") PIE OR TART CRUST

20–30 gluten-free graham-style crackers

2 tablespoons Spectrum Palm Shortening

2 tablespoons sugar

1. Place about 20–25 crackers into a zip-top plastic bag. Remove all the air from the bag and use a rolling pin to crush the crackers into fine crumbles. You can also do this in a food processor if you have one. Measure out 1¾ cups crumbs. (Repeat the process if you need additional cookie crumbs or save any leftover crumbs in the freezer for future pies.)
2. Pour cookie crumbs into a large bowl and mix with the shortening and the sugar until you have a crumbly mixture. Press the mixture into an 8" or 9" pie pan or a 9" tart pan. You can use the unbaked crust for any pie recipe calling for a graham cracker crust.
3. Make a prebaked crust: Heat oven to 350°F. Bake crust for 5–8 minutes until golden-brown. Remove from oven and allow to cool completely before adding a pudding or fruit filling. This crust does not freeze well.

Chocolate Wafer Pie Crust

You can make this pie crust with the Mint Chocolate Wafer Cookies in Chapter 7,
with or without the peppermint extract. Or, use store-bought gluten-free chocolate cookies.

INGREDIENTS | YIELDS 1 (8" OR 9") PIE CRUST

20–30 gluten-free chocolate wafer cookies

2 tablespoons Spectrum Palm Shortening

2 tablespoons sugar

Use Shortbread or Vanilla Cookies Instead

You can also use homemade shortbread or plain vanilla gluten-free cookies if you prefer. Crush the cookies in a zip-top plastic bag or in a food processor and make the crust as directed.

1. Place about 20–25 cookies into a zip-top plastic bag. Remove all the air from the bag and use a rolling pin to crush the cookies into fine crumbles. You can also do this in a food processor if you have one. Measure out 1¾ cups crumbs. (Repeat the process if you need additional cookie crumbs or save any leftover crumbs in the freezer for future pies.)
2. Pour cookie crumbs into a large bowl and mix with the shortening and the sugar until you have a crumbly mixture. Press the mixture into an 8" or 9" pie pan or a 9" tart pan. You can use the unbaked crust for any pie recipe calling for a graham cracker crust.
3. Make a prebaked crust: Heat oven to 350°F. Bake crust for 5–8 minutes until golden-brown. Remove from oven and allow to cool completely before adding a pudding or fruit filling. This crust does not freeze well.

Amish Apple Crumble Pie

This simple apple pie has a crumbly, cinnamony streusel topping.

INGREDIENTS | SERVES 8–10

Pie

7 medium apples, peeled, cored, and thinly sliced

Juice and zest of 1 fresh lemon (about 2–3 tablespoons juice)

¾ cup brown sugar

¾ cup brown rice flour

1 teaspoon ground cinnamon

½ teaspoon ground nutmeg

1 prepared, unbaked Basic Gluten-Free Pie and Tart Pastry (see recipe in this chapter)

Crumble Topping

⅓ cup sugar

2 tablespoons brown sugar

¼ cup brown rice flour

¼ cup gluten-free rolled oats

¼ teaspoon sea salt

1 teaspoon ground cinnamon

1 teaspoon ground nutmeg

3 tablespoons Spectrum Palm Shortening or butter

1. Preheat oven to 350°F.
2. In a large bowl mix together apples with lemon juice. Add the remainder of the pie ingredients. Toss to combine and pour apple filling into a prepared 8" or 9" pie shell.
3. Make the crumble topping: In a medium bowl mix together sugar, brown sugar, brown rice flour, oats, salt, cinnamon, and nutmeg. Add shortening and stir together until a crumbly mix forms. Sprinkle crumble topping evenly over the entire pie.
4. Bake pie on a cookie sheet (to catch drips) for 40–50 minutes until the apples are cooked through and the top is golden-brown. If the crust appears to be getting too brown, place a ring of foil around the edges to prevent burning.
5. Allow pie to cool completely before slicing. Store any leftovers in the refrigerator in an airtight container for up to 5 days.

Double-Crusted Apple Pecan Pie

An American classic; it doesn't get better than baseball and apple pie.
Feel free to change or add additional spices such as cardamom, allspice, or ginger.

INGREDIENTS | SERVES 8–10

7 medium apples, peeled, cored, and thinly sliced

Juice and zest of 1 fresh lemon (about 2–3 tablespoons juice)

¾ cup brown sugar

¾ cup brown rice flour

1 teaspoon ground cinnamon

½ teaspoon ground nutmeg

¾ cup pecans, coarsely chopped

2 prepared, unbaked Basic Gluten-Free Pie and Tart Pastries (see recipe in this chapter)

1 large egg white

2 tablespoons cold water

2 tablespoons sanding sugar or coarse evaporated cane sugar crystals (optional)

Whipped cream or ice cream (optional)

How to Flute the Edge of a Pie Crust

To create a "wave" pattern on the edge of a pie crust, pinch a piece of dough between your thumb and forefinger to create two smooth dips with an edge of dough between each dip. Continue shaping the edge of the crust this way around the entire pie. For a picture tutorial, visit *http://ow.ly/laiJo.*

1. Preheat oven to 375°F.
2. In a large bowl mix together apples with lemon juice. Add brown sugar, brown rice flour, cinnamon, nutmeg, and chopped pecans. Toss to combine and pour apple filling into one of the prepared 8" or 9" pie crusts.
3. Roll out the second pie crust on a well-floured surface to make an 11" or 12" circle. Carefully place the crust over the pie. Run a sharp knife along the rim and trim off any crust that is hanging over the edges. Flute the edges of the crust or use a fork and gently press down along the edges to seal the crust. If you wish, roll out scraps of dough and cut out shapes with a cookie cutter to place decoratively on the crust.
4. Decoratively prick the top crust in several places to allow air to escape from the pie filling while baking. Cover the pie with foil and place on a cookie sheet. Bake for 20 minutes.
5. Whisk the egg white with water. Carefully remove pie from the oven, remove foil, and brush the top crust lightly with the egg mixture. If desired, sprinkle sugar lightly over the pie. Place pie back in the oven and bake for an additional 25–30 minutes until the pie is uniformly golden-brown. Remove from oven and place pie on a cooling rack. Allow to cool completely before slicing. Serve with whipped cream or ice cream, if desired.

Lattice-Topped Cherry Pie

Making the lattice top for this pie can take a bit of patience and time, but if you're willing to work with the dough you will have a show-stopping, gluten-free dessert.

INGREDIENTS | SERVES 8–10

⅔ cup sugar

¼ cup cornstarch

¼ teaspoon salt

4 cups fresh or frozen tart red cherries, pitted

1½ cups water

2 tablespoons lemon juice

2 prepared, unbaked Basic Gluten-Free Pie and Tart Pastries (see recipe in this chapter)

Sorghum flour, for rolling out the top crust

Sanding sugar or coarse evaporated cane juice crystals (optional)

In a Pinch

If you can't find fresh or frozen cherries, you can use Dole canned dark cherries, which come in a 14½-ounce can. Use 3 cans of drained dark cherries. They are packed in syrup, but are not maraschino-flavored cherries, so they will work well in this pie.

1. Preheat oven to 350°F.
2. In a medium saucepan combine sugar, cornstarch, salt, cherries, water, and lemon juice. Cook over medium heat, stirring constantly for 5–7 minutes until mixture thickens. Pour cherry mixture into a pie crust that has been pressed into a 9" deep-dish pan.
3. Roll out the remaining pie crust onto a flat sorghum-floured surface into a large rectangle at least 10" long. Gently cut 12–14 long (1" wide) strips of dough. Very carefully place the strips over the pie in a crisscross pattern. The easiest way to do this is to place 6–7 strips in one direction and then place the remaining 6–7 strips in the opposite direction in a # (hatch) pattern. If the strips break while putting them on the pie, gently patch them back together. No one will notice on the finished pie.
4. When you've placed all the strips on the pie, use a knife and cut off excess crust around the edge of the pie. Flute edges of crust and sprinkle sanding sugar or coarse evaporated cane juice over the crust, if desired. Cover the edges of the pie with foil to prevent burning. Place pie on a cookie sheet and bake for 40–50 minutes until filling is hot and bubbly and the crust is golden-brown.
5. Move cake to a wire rack to cool for 30–40 minutes. Do not cut pie until completely cooled. Store any remaining pie in a tightly sealed container in the refrigerator for up to 5 days. This pie does not freeze well.

Lemon Chiffon Pie

A chiffon is a sweet lemon custard lightened with beaten egg whites and served with whipped cream.

INGREDIENTS | SERVES 8–10

1 (.25-ounce) package unflavored gelatin

¼ cup cold water

4 large egg yolks

1 cup sugar, divided

½ cup fresh lemon juice

½ teaspoon salt

1 teaspoon lemon zest

4 large egg whites

1 (9-inch) prepared, prebaked Gluten-Free "Graham" Cracker Crust (see recipe in this chapter)

Whipped cream (optional)

1. In a small bowl whisk together gelatin and water. Allow to set for 5 minutes.
2. In another small bowl beat the egg yolks, ½ cup sugar, lemon juice, and salt. Cook in a double boiler over medium heat, stirring constantly for 5–6 minutes, until the mixture thickens to a custard consistency. Add lemon zest and gelatin and whisk the mixture thoroughly. Cool the custard.
3. While the custard cools and thickens, in a clean bowl beat the egg whites until stiff peaks form. While beating, slowly add the remaining ½ cup of sugar. Gently fold the beaten egg whites into the lemon curd mixture. Pour the filling into the baked pie crust and chill in the refrigerator overnight.
4. Do not slice until completely chilled. Serve with whipped cream, if desired.

Georgia Peach Pie

There's nothing quite like fresh, juicy peaches in the heat of deep summer.
This old-fashioned peach pie creates a smooth filling as it bakes.

INGREDIENTS | SERVES 8–10

8 large (ripe, but firm) sweet Georgia peaches, peeled, pitted, and thinly sliced

¾ cup sugar

1½ teaspoons lemon juice

¼ cup plus 1 tablespoon sorghum flour

1 teaspoon vanilla extract

2 prepared, unbaked Basic Gluten-Free Pie and Tart Pastries (see recipe in this chapter)

4 tablespoons butter, thinly sliced

Additional sorghum flour, for rolling pie crust

1 large egg white

2 tablespoons cold water

2 tablespoons sanding sugar or coarse evaporated cane sugar crystals (optional)

Whipped cream or ice cream (optional)

In a Pinch

If you don't have fresh peaches available you can substitute 4 cups of frozen peaches or canned peaches that have been drained from the syrup in the can.

1. Preheat oven to 350°F.
2. In a large bowl mix together peaches, sugar, lemon juice, sorghum flour, and vanilla extract. Stir to combine and pour peach filling into one 9" gluten-free pie shell. Place slices of butter evenly over the top of filling.
3. Roll out the second pie crust on a well-floured surface into an 11" or 12" circle. Carefully place the crust over the pie. Run a sharp knife along the rim and trim off any crust hanging over the edges. Flute the edges of the crust or use a fork and gently press down along the edges to seal the crust. At this point you can roll out scraps of dough and cut shapes with a cookie cutter to place decoratively on the crust.
4. Decoratively prick the top crust in several places to allow air to escape from the pie filling while baking. Cover the pie with foil and place on a cookie sheet. Bake for 30 minutes.
5. In a small bowl, whisk the egg white with water. Carefully remove pie from the oven, remove foil, and brush the top crust lightly with the egg mixture. If desired, sprinkle sugar lightly over the pie.
6. Place pie back in the oven and bake for an additional 25 minutes until the pie is uniformly golden-brown. Remove from oven and place pie on a cooling rack. Allow to cool completely before slicing. Serve with whipped cream or ice cream, if desired.

Creamy Key Lime Pie

If you can find key limes or key lime juice in your local grocery store, it's worth spending the extra money. The tart flavor of key limes is quite different from that of regular limes and gives this pie its signature flavor.

INGREDIENTS | SERVES 8–10

1 (.25-ounce) package unflavored gelatin or 2 teaspoons unflavored gelatin

¼ cup cold water

4 large egg yolks

1 cup sugar, divided

½ cup fresh key lime juice

½ teaspoon salt

1 teaspoon key lime zest

4 large egg whites

1 (9-inch) prepared, prebaked Gluten-Free "Graham" Cracker Crust (see recipe in this chapter)

Whipped cream (optional)

1. In a small bowl whisk together gelatin and water. Allow to set for 5 minutes.
2. In another small bowl beat the egg yolks, ½ cup sugar, lime juice, and salt. Cook in a double boiler over medium heat, stirring constantly for 5–6 minutes, until the mixture thickens to custard consistency. Add key lime zest and gelatin and whisk the mixture thoroughly. Cool the custard.
3. While the custard cools and thickens, in a clean bowl beat the egg whites until stiff peaks form. While beating, slowly add the remaining ½ cup of sugar. Gently fold the beaten egg whites into the lime curd mixture. Pour the filling into pie crust and chill in the refrigerator overnight.
4. Do not slice until completely chilled. Serve with whipped cream, if desired.

Blueberry Pie

Make this perfect summer pie when fresh blueberries are abundant and cheap.
If you don't have fresh blueberries, frozen will work as well.

INGREDIENTS | SERVES 8–10

¼ cup sugar

1½ tablespoons cornstarch

1 teaspoon cinnamon

2 teaspoons lemon juice

¼ cup water

6 cups (about 3 pints) fresh blueberries

1 prepared, unbaked Basic Gluten-Free Pie and Tart Pastry (see recipe in this chapter)

3 tablespoons butter, thinly sliced

1. Preheat oven to 350°F.
2. In a medium saucepan combine sugar, cornstarch, cinnamon, lemon juice, and water. Cook over medium heat, stirring constantly for 5–7 minutes until mixture thickens. Add blueberries and cook for 2 additional minutes, stirring constantly. Pour blueberry mixture into a gluten-free pie crust that has been pressed into a 9" pie pan.
3. Evenly place slices of butter over pie filling. Place the pie on a cookie sheet and bake for 25–30 minutes until the filling is hot and bubbly. Remove from the oven and place on a wire rack. Cool pie for 30–40 minutes and then chill for 3–4 hours or overnight before serving. Store leftovers in an airtight container in the refrigerator for up to 5 days.

Strawberry Rhubarb Pie

Strawberries and rhubarb are a delicious tangy-sweet summer combination.
If you can't find fresh rhubarb, you can use frozen.

INGREDIENTS | SERVES 8–10

2½ cups chopped rhubarb, fresh or frozen

2½ cups fresh strawberries, washed, stems removed, and sliced

1½ cups sugar

3 tablespoons cornstarch

1 teaspoon lemon zest

½ teaspoon lemon juice

½ teaspoon ground cinnamon

1 teaspoon vanilla extract

¼ cup water

1 prepared, unbaked Basic Gluten-Free Pie and Tart Pastry (see recipe in this chapter)

3 tablespoons butter, thinly sliced

1. Preheat oven to 350°F.
2. In a medium saucepan combine rhubarb, strawberries, sugar, cornstarch, lemon zest, lemon juice, cinnamon, vanilla, and water. Cook over medium heat, stirring constantly for 5–7 minutes until mixture thickens. Pour mixture into a gluten-free pie crust that has been pressed into a 9" pie pan.
3. Evenly place slices of butter over pie filling. Place the pie on a cookie sheet and bake for 25–30 minutes until the filling is hot and bubbly.
4. Remove from the oven and place on a wire rack. Cool pie for 30–40 minutes and then chill for 3–4 hours or overnight before serving. Store leftovers in an airtight container in the refrigerator for up to 5 days.

Butterscotch Pie

*My great-grandmother shared this recipe from the 1930s with me.
Homemade butterscotch pie is a chilled brown sugar pudding served in flaky crust.*

INGREDIENTS | SERVES 8–10

3 tablespoons butter or Spectrum Palm Shortening

1 cup brown sugar

¼ cup brown rice flour

¼ cup arrowroot starch

3½ cups milk or coconut milk

2 large eggs

1 tablespoon vanilla extract

1 prepared, baked Gluten-Free "Graham" Cracker Crust or 1 prepared, Basic Gluten-Free Pie and Tart Pastry (see recipes in this chapter)

Don't Cry over Scalded Milk

This recipe originally called for scalded milk, or milk that is gently heated to remove harmful bacteria—a home method of pasteurization. In the process many proteins are denatured and enzymes destroyed. Because the milk you buy today is already pasteurized, you don't need to scald milk before using it in a pudding recipe.

1. Melt butter in a medium saucepan, over medium heat. Add brown sugar and stir until sugar is dissolved. In a small bowl whisk together brown rice flour, arrowroot starch, milk, and eggs into a smooth paste.
2. Slowly pour flour-egg mixture into melted sugar-butter mixture in the saucepan, whisking constantly. Continue to cook over medium heat for 5–6 minutes, whisking constantly, until pudding thickens. When pudding is thick enough to cover the back of a spoon, remove from heat. Whisk in vanilla extract.
3. Pour pudding into pie crust and chill for at least 8 hours. Slice and serve. Store leftovers in an airtight container in the refrigerator for up to 5 days.

Creamy Peanut Butter Pie

This recipe creates a dairy-free, vegan peanut butter pie thickened with chia seed gel. Chia seeds have a gelatinous quality when mixed with warm water. This helps the filling set and thicken when it's chilled, as if it were made with gelatin.

INGREDIENTS | SERVES 8–10

2 teaspoons chia seeds

⅓ cup boiling water

1 (13½-ounce) can full-fat coconut milk

1 cup creamy natural peanut butter

¾ cup sugar

2 teaspoons vanilla extract

1 prepared Chocolate Wafer Pie Crust (see recipe in this chapter)

Make "Other" Butter Pie

This pie can just as easily be made with almond butter, cashew butter, walnut butter, or a combination of nut butters. It's also delicious made with Sunbutter, a seed butter made from sunflower seeds. Simply replace the peanut butter called for with the "other" butter of your choice.

1. In a small bowl mix together the chia seeds and boiling water and set aside for 5 minutes to "gel."
2. Once the chia has created a gel in the water, add to a high-powered blender. Turn to high and purée for 10–20 seconds. Turn off blender, then add the coconut milk and blend on high again for 30–40 seconds. Turn off blender and then add the peanut butter, sugar, and vanilla extract. Blend again on high for 3–4 minutes until the mixture is super creamy and thick.
3. Make the filling without using a high-powered blender: Add the chia seeds mixed with water to a regular blender and blend on high until the mixture has been thoroughly puréed, about 1–2 minutes. Pour puréed chia seeds and water into a large bowl and whisk in the coconut milk, peanut butter, sugar, and vanilla. Whisk together until creamy and very thick.
4. Pour filling into the crust. If desired, sprinkle mini chocolate chips over the filling. Chill pie for 8 hours before serving. Store any remaining pie in an airtight container in the refrigerator for up to 5 days. This pie does not freeze well.

Chocolate Pecan Pie

This super-rich, chocolaty pie will impress any chocolate lover you know.

INGREDIENTS | SERVES 8–10

1 cup light brown sugar

¼ cup sugar

1 tablespoon sorghum flour

½ cup butter, melted

2 large eggs

1 tablespoon almond milk

1½ teaspoons vanilla extract

1⅓ cups chopped pecans

¾ cup semisweet chocolate chips

1 prepared, prebaked Basic Gluten-Free Pie and Tart Pastry (see recipe in this chapter)

1. Preheat oven to 350°F.
2. In a large bowl mix together the brown sugar, sugar, and sorghum flour. Stir in the melted butter, eggs, almond milk, and vanilla. Then stir in the pecans.
3. Pour chocolate chips evenly over the bottom of the pie crust. Pour filling into crust right on top of the chocolate chips. Place a pie shield on the crust or use strips of foil to make a ring around the edge of the crust, so it doesn't burn while baking.
4. Place pie on a cookie sheet (just in case it bubbles over while baking) and bake for 35–40 minutes until set. Allow pie to cool completely on the counter before slicing. This pie can be frozen for up to 1 month.

How about a Pine Nut Pie?

Pecans are popular for pies because of their mild flavor and taste. However, if you enjoy other types of nuts, such as cashews, walnuts, brazil nuts, or pine nuts (which are actually seeds), they can also make a delicious holiday pie. Chop the nuts into small pieces (unnecessary for pine nuts) and use 1⅓ cups and bake as directed. See if your friends can tell the difference in your pie's unique taste.

Shoofly Pie

Shoofly pie is a favorite dessert in Amish country. It's basically a molasses brownie baked in a flaky pie shell. Or, you can pour the pie filling into an 8" × 8" pan and bake 25–30 minutes, slice into squares, and serve.

INGREDIENTS | SERVES 8–10

¾ cup sorghum flour

½ cup arrowroot starch

½ teaspoon xanthan gum

½ cup brown sugar

1 tablespoon Spectrum Palm Shortening

1 cup molasses

1 teaspoon baking soda

¾ cup boiling water

1 large egg, slightly beaten

1 prepared, unbaked Basic Gluten-Free Pie and Tart Pastry (see recipe in this chapter)

1. Preheat oven to 350°F. In a medium bowl, whisk together sorghum flour, arrowroot starch, xanthan gum, and brown sugar. Cut in shortening with a pastry blender and stir together. Reserve ½ cup of the crumbly flour mixture to sprinkle on top of the pie.
2. In a large bowl stir together molasses, baking soda, and boiling water. The mixture will bubble and foam as the baking soda activates. Allow the molasses mixture to cool and then whisk in the flour mixture and the egg. Pour batter into the unbaked pie shell. Sprinkle reserved crumbs evenly over the top of the pie.
3. Place pie on a cookie sheet and bake for 45 minutes until golden-brown. Allow pie to cool for 30–40 minutes before serving. Store leftovers in an airtight container on the counter for up to 5 days. This pie freezes well.

Coconut Custard Cream Pie

This creamy pie is super easy to make. You can purchase plain, unsweetened, shredded coconut online or at many high-end grocery stores.

INGREDIENTS | YIELDS 1 (8"–9") PIE

⅓ cup Spectrum Palm Shortening

1½ cups sugar

2 tablespoons sorghum flour

2 large eggs

1 cup coconut milk

1¼ cups unsweetened shredded or flaked coconut, divided

2 teaspoons vanilla extract

1 prepared, unbaked Basic Gluten-Free Pie and Tart Pastry (see recipe in this chapter)

1. Preheat oven to 350°F.
2. In a large bowl cream together shortening and sugar. Add sorghum flour and stir to combine. Whisk in eggs, coconut milk, shredded coconut, and vanilla extract. Pour mixture into pie shell. Sprinkle additional shredded coconut on top.
3. Place pie on a cookie sheet and bake for 40–50 minutes until pie is golden-brown.
4. Place pie on a wire rack and cool for 30–40 minutes. Chill 8 hours before serving. Store any remaining pie in an airtight container in the refrigerator for up to 5 days.

French Silk Pie

This traditional French pie requires quite a few steps. You can take a shortcut and use boxed chocolate pudding, but you won't enjoy it as much as this rich, velvety dessert.

INGREDIENTS | SERVES 8–10

⅔ cup sugar

2 large eggs

2 ounces dark chocolate, melted

1 teaspoon vanilla extract

⅓ cup butter, softened

⅔ cup heavy whipping cream

2 teaspoons confectioners' sugar

1 prepared, prebaked Basic Gluten-Free Pie and Tart Pastry (see recipe in this chapter)

1. In a double boiler, whisk together the sugar and eggs and cook over medium heat slowly for 3–5 minutes, until slightly thickened. Add chocolate and cook an additional 1–2 minutes until chocolate is completely melted into the mixture. Remove from heat and stir in vanilla. Set aside and allow to cool to room temperature.

2. In a small bowl, cream the butter until light and fluffy. Add cooled chocolate mixture and continue to beat until light and fluffy, about 5–6 minutes.

3. In a large bowl beat whipping cream until the mixture begins to thicken. Add confectioners' sugar and continue beating until stiff peaks form. Fold whipped cream into the chocolate mixture and pour into pie crust. Chill for at least 8 hours before slicing and serving. Store any leftovers in an airtight container in the refrigerator for up to 5 days.

CHAPTER 10

Potluck and Bake Sale Favorites

Chewy Granola Bars

These granola bars are perfect to grab and go. This large recipe is a great option for bake sales.

INGREDIENTS | SERVES 26

2 cups gluten-free quick-cook oats

¾ cup rice bran (such as Ener-G brand)

¼ cup ground flaxseed

¼ cup slivered almonds

¼ cup uncooked quinoa

¼ cup shelled sunflower seeds

¼ cup sesame seeds

¼ cup flaked coconut

⅔ cup brown sugar

½ cup honey

4 tablespoons butter or Spectrum Palm Shortening

½ teaspoon ground cinnamon

½ teaspoon salt

2 teaspoons vanilla extract

1 cup chopped dried fruit (cherries, cranberries, blueberries, apricots, etc.)

Change Things Up

Substitute dry ingredients, fruit, and nuts to suit your taste. Be sure to use equal amounts so that the ratio of dry ingredients to syrup remains the same. If you add too many dry ingredients, the bars will not stick together; if you have too few, the bars will be overly sticky.

1. Preheat oven to 400°F. Line a large, rimmed baking sheet with foil.
2. In a large bowl mix together: quick cooking oats, rice bran, ground flaxseed, slivered almonds, uncooked quinoa, shelled sunflower seeds, sesame seeds, and flaked coconut. Stir to combine and then pour onto the baking sheet. Place in the oven and toast for 10–12 minutes, stirring every few minutes to prevent burning. As soon as the ingredients are toasted, remove the pan from the oven.
3. Place a small saucepan over medium-high heat and add the brown sugar, honey, butter, cinnamon, and salt. Bring the mixture to a strong boil for 2 minutes, stirring constantly. Turn off the heat and stir in vanilla.
4. Place the toasted ingredients in a large bowl, and stir in the dried fruit. Pour the hot liquids into the bowl and stir aggressively until all the ingredients are moist and well combined.
5. Using a wooden spoon, scrape the mixture onto the baking sheet, pressing down to evenly spread out the mixture. Using a wet rubber spatula helps to keep the granola from sticking, allowing you to press the mixture down enough. Set the baking sheet aside and let the mixture cool for 2–3 hours until hardened.
6. Once the mixture is hard, remove it from the pan and turn it out onto a cutting board. Remove the parchment paper. Cut the granola into bars by pressing straight down with a long knife (don't saw or they will crumble). Cut approximately 26 bars, 1" × 5½".
7. Wrap the bars individually in plastic wrap and store in an airtight container at room temperature for up to a week.

Gluten-Free Crispy Rice Treats

This is a fun and easy "no-bake" recipe for crispy rice bars. Make sure you buy a gluten-free variety of rice cereal when you make these tasty treats.

INGREDIENTS | SERVES 12

3 tablespoons butter or Spectrum Palm Shortening

1 (10-ounce) package marshmallows (most are already gluten-free, but check package to make sure)

6 cups gluten-free crispy rice cereal

1. Grease a 9" × 13" baking dish with nonstick cooking spray or melted butter and set aside.
2. In a large saucepan melt the butter and marshmallows over medium-low heat, stirring constantly so the mixture doesn't burn. When completely melted remove from heat.
3. Stir in rice cereal and stir until all the cereal is completely coated in the mixture. Pour the sticky mixture into baking dish and pat down with wax paper or plastic wrap.
4. Cool for at least 1 hour and then cut into 2" squares to serve. These are best eaten the same day, but can be kept on the counter in an airtight container for up to 3 days.

Nutty Caramel Corn

A fun snack for fall, this favorite is commonly seen around Halloween. Try it along with some caramel apples at a party.

INGREDIENTS | SERVES 6

1 (3½-ounce) bag plain microwave popcorn, popped

1 cup dry-roasted, salted peanuts

1 cup brown sugar

½ cup butter

½ cup corn syrup or honey

¼ teaspoon salt

1. Preheat the oven to 200°F. Spray a 9" × 13" baking pan with cooking spray. In a large bowl, combine the popped popcorn and nuts.
2. In a medium saucepan, combine the brown sugar, butter, corn syrup, and salt. Heat over medium-high heat until mixture is melted and smooth, stirring constantly, about 4–5 minutes.
3. Remove from heat and pour caramel mixture over the popcorn and nuts, mixing well. Spread mixture on the prepared baking pan. Bake 1 hour, stirring every 15 minutes. Remove from oven and allow mixture to cool on the baking sheet for 30 minutes. Store in an airtight container on the counter for up to 3 days.

No-Bake Honey Balls

Let the kids get their hands dirty. These sweet and chewy no-bake cookies are a good choice for beginning cooks.

INGREDIENTS | SERVES 15

½ cup honey

½ cup golden raisins

½ cup dry milk powder or blanched almond flour

2 cups gluten-free crushed crisp rice cereal, divided

¼ cup confectioners' sugar

1 cup finely chopped dates

1. In a food processor, combine honey and raisins; process until smooth. Scrape into a small bowl and add milk powder, 1 cup crushed cereal, confectioners' sugar, and dates; mix well. You may need to add more confectioners' sugar or honey for desired consistency.
2. Form mixture into ¾" balls and roll in remaining crushed cereal. Store in airtight container at room temperature.

Gluten-Free Chex Snack Bars

In the past few years several major cereal companies have jumped onboard and created safe, affordable gluten-free cereals. For example, many Chex cereals are now gluten-free.

INGREDIENTS | SERVES 24

4 cups Chocolate Chex gluten-free cereal

½ cup salted peanuts

½ cup light corn syrup or honey

¼ cup sugar

½ cup all-natural creamy peanut butter

¼ cup candy-coated chocolate candies (like M&Ms)

1. Line a 9" × 9" square pan with parchment paper and spritz with nonstick cooking spray or butter. Set aside. In a large bowl mix together cereal and peanuts.
2. In a medium saucepan heat corn syrup or honey and sugar over medium heat, stirring constantly, just until it starts to boil. Remove from heat and stir in peanut butter.
3. Pour mixture over the cereal and peanuts. Stir to coat thoroughly. Stir in the chocolate candies, and then pour the entire mixture into pan. Press the mixture down flat with wax paper or plastic wrap. Cover lightly and cool for at least 1 hour.
4. When completely cooled, cut into 24 small squares. Store any remaining bars in an airtight container on the counter for 3–4 days.

Take-Along Trail Mix

Trail mix is so versatile you can create your own versions. Try adding some yogurt-covered raisins, dry gluten-free cereal, candy-coated chocolate, or even popcorn.

INGREDIENTS | SERVES 4

½ cup small gluten-free pretzel sticks or twists

½ cup raisins

½ cup peanuts or almonds

¼ cup sunflower seeds

¼ cup gluten-free chocolate chips

In a large bowl, combine all ingredients. Store in an airtight container or resealable plastic bag.

Mini Cherry Cheesecakes

These individual cheesecakes are decadent and delicious. Feel free to use a dairy-free cream cheese substitute such as Tofutti (if you can tolerate soy), instead of regular cream cheese.

INGREDIENTS | SERVES 12

1 cup crumbs made from Spritz Cookies (see Chapter 11) or 1 cup blanched almond flour

3 tablespoons butter or Spectrum Palm Shortening

1 (8-ounce) package cream cheese, softened

⅓ cup sugar

2 teaspoons lemon juice

1½ teaspoons vanilla extract

1 egg

1 (20-ounce) can cherry pie filling

Make It Blueberry or Apple

Most brands of canned pie filling are gluten-free, but always double-check ingredients to make sure. If you don't like cherries or just don't have any in your pantry, use canned apple pie filling or blueberry pie filling instead. Both will work perfectly in this recipe.

1. Preheat oven to 375°F. Line a muffin pan with heavy-duty paper liners. Spritz the liners with nonstick cooking spray or butter.
2. In a small bowl mix together the cookie crumbs or almond flour and butter. Divide the mixture evenly among the 12 paper-lined muffin cups and press down the mixture with your fingers to create a crust.
3. In a small bowl whisk together the cream cheese, sugar, lemon juice, and vanilla extract. Whisk in the egg so you have a thick cheesecake batter. Divide the batter evenly over the crusts in muffin cups.
4. Bake for 12–15 minutes or until cheesecake centers are almost set. Set on a wire rack and cool for at least 1 hour before transferring to the fridge to cool completely.
5. When the cheesecakes are cooled, spoon about 3–4 cherries from the pie filling over each. Chill for 1 hour or so and then serve.
6. Store any remaining cakes in the refrigerator for up to 3 days.

No-Bake Peanut Butter Oatmeal Bars

Here's an easy, no-bake snack bar that's super simple to put together for your kids.
These bars travel well and are full of healthy plant proteins and fiber.

INGREDIENTS | SERVES 12

2 cups, gluten-free rolled oats
½ cup ground flaxseed
½ cup raisins
½ cup flaked coconut
¼ teaspoon sea salt
¾ cup all-natural peanut butter
½ cup honey
¼ cup chocolate chips

1. Line a 9" × 13" baking dish with parchment paper. Spritz with nonstick cooking spray and set aside.
2. In a large bowl mix together oats, flaxseeds, raisins, flaked coconut, and sea salt. Set aside.
3. In a medium saucepan heat peanut butter and honey just until they are warmed through and stir together well. Pour mixture over the dry ingredients and mix together well.
4. Pour the mixture into baking dish and place a piece of wax paper or plastic wrap over the mixture; press down into the pan to set. Sprinkle chocolate chips on top of mixture. Refrigerate for 3–4 hours until set and then slice into bars.
5. Store remaining bars in the refrigerator for up to 2 weeks.

Mini Flourless Cupcakes

Flourless cupcakes are always fun to make, but they are incredibly rich.
These mini cupcakes are the perfect portion size.

INGREDIENTS | YIELDS 2½ DOZEN MINI CUPCAKES

¾ cup semisweet chocolate chips
½ cup butter
½ cup sugar
½ cup unsweetened cocoa powder
3 large eggs

Easy Chocolate Ganache

This recipe is for a small amount of chocolate ganache, when you just need a little to decorate cupcakes like this. In a small bowl mix together ¼ cup semisweet chocolate chips, ¼ cup heavy cream, and 1 teaspoon butter. Heat in the microwave for 30 seconds at a time until chips are just melted through. Whisk the mixture together and you have an easy chocolate ganache to drizzle over cheesecake, flourless cake, or fruit.

1. Preheat oven to 375°F. Line a mini-muffin pan with heavy-duty foil liners and spritz with nonstick cooking spray.
2. Heat chocolate and butter in a saucepan or microwave until just melted. In a medium bowl whisk together sugar and cocoa powder. Add in the eggs and whisk until combined. Pour in the melted chocolate and butter and whisk just until mixed.
3. Scoop batter about 1–1½ tablespoons at a time into each mini-muffin cup.
4. Bake about 7–8 minutes until cupcakes are just set. The centers may still be a tiny bit jiggly. Allow to cool completely on a wire rack before serving. If desired, drizzle chocolate ganache over cupcakes.

Gluten-Free Snack Mix

You can make this savory snack mix either in your slow cooker or your oven. Serve at a holiday party or share with friends in small gift jars.

INGREDIENTS | SERVES 20

2 tablespoons melted butter

1 teaspoon garlic powder

1 teaspoon onion powder

1 teaspoon paprika

1 teaspoon dried thyme

1 teaspoon dill weed

1 teaspoon chili powder

1 teaspoon gluten-free Worcestershire sauce

2¼ cups gluten-free corn Chex cereal

2¼ cups gluten-free rice Chex cereal

1 cup gluten-free Glutino pretzels

1 cup roasted peanuts or almonds

Snack Mix Variations

Mexican: Substitute 1 teaspoon each cayenne pepper, ground chipotle, hot New Mexico chili powder, and oregano for the thyme, dill weed, and Worcestershire sauce. Asian: Substitute 1 teaspoon each sesame seeds, gluten-free soy sauce, ground ginger, and white pepper for the paprika, thyme, dill weed, and Worcestershire sauce.

1. Make in a slow cooker: Pour the butter, spices, and Worcestershire sauce into the bottom of a 6-quart slow cooker. Stir. Add the cereal, pretzels, and nuts. Cook uncovered on low for 2–3 hours, stirring every 30 minutes. Pour onto a baking sheet and allow to cool. Store in an airtight container for up to 1 week.
2. Make in the oven: Preheat oven to 250°F and line a large cookie sheet with parchment paper. Mix all ingredients in a large bowl. Stir to coat the cereal and nuts evenly with the butter and spices. Pour mixture onto the cookie sheet and spread evenly. Bake for about 1 hour stirring every 15 minutes or so until the mixture is golden and toasty.

Pumpkin Whoopie Pies

This pumpkin version of a whoopie pie is soft and cakelike. Fill it with your favorite icing or marshmallow filling. It's great for bake sales because it makes at least 2 dozen whoopie pies.

INGREDIENTS | YIELDS 24 WHOOPIE PIES

Cookies

2 cups plus 2 tablespoons brown rice flour

2 cups plus 2 tablespoons arrowroot starch

1½ teaspoons xanthan gum

½ teaspoon ground cinnamon

1½ teaspoons baking powder

½ teaspoon baking soda

1 teaspoon sea salt

½ cup Spectrum Palm Shortening

¾ cup brown sugar

2 large eggs

¾ cup pure pumpkin purée

½ cup plus 2 tablespoons almond milk

1 teaspoon vanilla extract

Marshmallow Filling

1 cup marshmallow creme (such as Marshmallow Fluff)

1 cup butter or shortening

1 cup confectioners' sugar

1 teaspoon vanilla extract

1. Preheat oven to 350°F. Line 2 large, rimmed baking sheets with parchment paper and set aside.
2. In a medium-sized bowl whisk together the brown rice flour, arrowroot starch, xanthan gum, cinnamon, baking powder, baking soda, and salt.
3. In a large bowl cream the shortening and brown sugar together, until well incorporated. Add in the eggs, pumpkin, milk, and vanilla extract. Stir the wet ingredients into the dry ingredients. You will have a very thick cake-like batter.
4. Scoop 1 tablespoon of batter per cookie and separate each by 2". Bake for 12–14 minutes until cookies start to brown.
5. Make the filling: In a large bowl mix marshmallow creme and butter or shortening for 3–4 minutes until light and fluffy (this is easier to do in a stand mixer if you have one). Slowly stir in confectioners' sugar and vanilla extract. Spoon or use an icing tip to place about 2 tablespoons of icing between two cookies and then sandwich them together.

Moist Chocolate Chip Banana Muffins

These muffins are soft, moist, and studded with chocolate chips. They are perfect for a quick breakfast or snack, and are a great choice for kids' lunches as well.

INGREDIENTS | SERVES 15

1 cup sorghum flour

½ cup gluten-free oat flour

¼ cup tapioca starch

1 teaspoon xanthan gum

½ cup packed brown sugar

2 teaspoons baking powder

1 teaspoon baking soda

½ teaspoon salt

2 large eggs

⅓ cup oil

½ cup sour cream or plain yogurt

1 teaspoon vanilla extract

1 cup ripe bananas, mashed (approximately 2 medium bananas)

¾ cup gluten-free semisweet chocolate chips

1. Grease a muffin tin or line with paper liners. Preheat the oven to 350°F.
2. In a large mixing bowl combine the sorghum flour, oat flour, tapioca starch, xanthan gum, brown sugar, baking powder, baking soda, and salt. Set aside.
3. In a medium mixing bowl, whisk together the eggs, oil, sour cream, vanilla extract, and mashed bananas. Pour the wet ingredients into the dry ingredients, and stir just to combine. Fold in the chocolate chips.
4. Spoon the batter into muffin tin. Bake for 20–22 minutes, or until a toothpick inserted into the middle comes out clean.
5. Remove muffins from the oven and allow to sit for 5 minutes before removing from the muffin tin to a wire cooling rack. Cool completely before storing in an airtight container for up to 5 days.

Change Things Up

To change things up a bit, you can add either ½ teaspoon of ground cinnamon or ground espresso powder to the batter. Adding ½ cup of chopped pecans or walnuts is another great option.

Corn Bread Muffins

These muffins stay fresh for several days after they are made, so they're a perfect travel snack for after-school games and potlucks. You can cut the sugar down to ⅓ cup and still have great results.

INGREDIENTS | SERVES 12

½ cup butter or margarine

⅔ cup sugar

2 large eggs

1 cup buttermilk

½ teaspoon baking soda

1 cup cornmeal

⅔ cup brown rice flour

⅓ cup arrowroot starch or tapioca starch

½ teaspoon xanthan gum

½ teaspoon salt

1. Preheat oven to 350°F. Lightly grease a muffin pan and set aside.
2. In a large microwave-safe bowl, melt butter. Stir in the sugar. Add eggs and stir to combine. Stir in buttermilk.
3. In a medium-sized mixing bowl, whisk the remaining ingredients. Add to wet ingredients and stir until few lumps remain.
4. Scoop batter into prepared muffin tin.
5. Bake for 20 minutes, or until a toothpick inserted into the center comes out clean.
6. Allow to cool in the muffin pan for 5 minutes before removing to cooling rack. Serve warm.

Oatmeal Cinnamon Raisin Buns

Toasted and topped with butter, cinnamon, and sugar, these buns are sure to be a hit at the breakfast table. Or, fancy things up a bit and use any leftover buns to make the Classic French Toast in Chapter 2.

INGREDIENTS | SERVES 12

½ cup gluten-free quick-cooking oats

1 cup raisins

Hot water, enough to cover oats and raisins

¾ cup warm water

2 tablespoons sugar

1 tablespoon instant yeast

2 teaspoons apple cider vinegar

2 tablespoons vegetable oil

2 large eggs

2 large egg whites

1 cup brown rice flour

1 cup arrowroot starch or tapioca starch

¼ cup dry milk powder or blanched almond flour

2 teaspoons ground cinnamon

2½ teaspoons xanthan gum

1 teaspoon salt

Why Apple Cider Vinegar?

Apple cider vinegar is used in a lot of gluten-free bread recipes. It helps give a greater rise and more tender crumb to the bread by acting as a dough enhancer, increasing the amount of ascorbic acid in the dough.

1. Place oats and raisins in a bowl and cover with hot water. Set aside and let soak for 10 minutes. Drain water using a sieve or strainer.
2. In a small bowl, combine warm water, sugar, and yeast. Stir and let sit until foamy on top. Then add the cider vinegar, vegetable oil, eggs, and egg whites.
3. Combine the rest of the dry ingredients in the bowl of a stand mixer until well mixed.
4. Add the soaked oats and raisins to the dry ingredients. Turn the mixer (with the paddle attachment) on low speed, and slowly add the wet ingredients. Once combined, scrape down the sides of the bowl with a rubber spatula. Turn the mixer on medium and beat for 3 minutes.
5. Spoon the dough equally into a 12-cup muffin pan that has been lined with cupcake liners and greased. Let rise, uncovered, in a warm, draft-free place for 25 minutes or until the individual buns have doubled in size.
6. Place the muffin pan in preheated 350°F oven, and bake for 18–22 minutes, or until the buns are nicely browned and a toothpick inserted in the middle of a bun comes out clean.
7. Remove buns from oven, and leave in pan for 5 minutes. Remove from pan and cool on wire cooling rack. When the buns are completely cool, store in an airtight bag. They can be left on the counter for 3 days, or frozen (wrap in additional plastic wrap if freezing) for up to 1 month.

Oatmeal Chocolate Chip Cookies

These big, soft oatmeal cookies are loaded with chocolate chips. To change things up a bit, use chopped nuts or different flavored baking chips, such as cinnamon or butterscotch.

INGREDIENTS | SERVES 48

1 cup butter or margarine, softened

2 cups brown sugar, packed

2 large eggs

1 teaspoon vanilla

1½ cups brown rice flour

¾ cup arrowroot starch or tapioca starch

½ teaspoon xanthan gum

1 teaspoon baking powder

½ teaspoon baking soda

2 cups gluten-free quick-cook oats

2 cups gluten-free chocolate chips

Freezing Cookies

These cookies freeze remarkably well. Placed in an airtight container they keep in the freezer for 3–4 weeks. You can also freeze the dough before baking. Scoop dough onto a baking sheet lined with wax paper and place in freezer. Once cookies are completely frozen, you can place them in a resealable freezer bag. Frozen dough should be used within 4–6 weeks. To bake frozen cookies, place cookies on parchment-lined baking sheets, and let the dough come to room temperature before baking as per instructions.

1. Preheat oven to 350°F.
2. Cream together the butter and the brown sugar.
3. Add eggs, one at a time. Mix until blended. Stir in vanilla.
4. In a large bowl, combine brown rice flour, arrowroot starch or tapioca starch, xanthan gum, baking powder, and baking soda. Stir to blend. Stir dry ingredients into butter-sugar mixture.
5. Add the oats and chocolate chips, and stir to combine all ingredients.
6. Using a cookie scoop (or 2 tablespoons), drop cookies onto parchment-lined cookie sheets. Bake cookies for 11–12 minutes, or until they are slightly brown around the outside, but still slightly moist in the middle.
7. Allow to cool on cookie sheets for 5 minutes before transferring to a wire rack.
8. Cool completely before storing in an airtight container on the counter for up to 5 days.

Fruity Pear Citrus Muffins

Pears add moisture and flavor to this simple quick bread. You can omit the glaze if you'd like.

INGREDIENTS | SERVES 12

1½ cups brown rice flour

½ cup arrowroot starch or tapioca starch

1 teaspoon xanthan gum

½ cup sugar

2 teaspoons baking powder

1 teaspoon baking soda

¼ teaspoon salt

1 teaspoon vanilla extract

½ cup puréed pears

1 teaspoon grated orange zest

½ cup orange juice

¼ cup oil

3 tablespoons lemon juice

1 cup confectioners' sugar

Storing Quick Breads

Most quick breads—breads made with baking powder or soda instead of yeast—improve in texture and flavor if allowed to stand overnight at room temperature. Cool the bread completely, then either wrap in plastic wrap or place the bread in a resealable bag. Quick breads can also be frozen.

1. Preheat oven to 375°F. Line a 12-cup muffin pan with paper liners and then spritz with nonstick cooking spray.
2. In a large bowl combine brown rice flour, arrowroot starch, xanthan gum, sugar, baking powder, baking soda, and salt; mix well.
3. In a small bowl combine vanilla, pears, orange zest, orange juice, and oil; mix well. Add to dry ingredients and stir just until combined. Pour into prepared paper liners, filling them ⅔ full.
4. Bake for 18–25 minutes, or until muffins are golden-brown and firm. While muffins are baking, combine lemon juice and confectioners' sugar in a small bowl. Drizzle half of mixture over muffins when they come out of the oven.
5. Let muffins cool 10 minutes in pan; remove to wire rack. Drizzle with remaining half of lemon mixture; cool completely.

Chocolate Meringue and Nut Cookies

Nuts add a wonderful crunch to these crisp and delicious cookies.
Use either the hazelnuts or blanched almonds.

INGREDIENTS | YIELDS ABOUT 40 COOKIES

½ cup sugar, divided
¼ cup unsweetened cocoa powder
⅛ teaspoon salt
3 egg whites (from extra-large eggs)
⅛ teaspoon cream of tartar
½ cup hazelnuts, lightly toasted, skinned, and coarsely chopped

1. Preheat oven to 275°F. Line 2 cookie sheets with parchment paper.
2. Sift ¼ cup of sugar and cocoa together in a bowl. Add salt.
3. In a medium bowl, beat egg whites with cream of tartar. When peaks begin to form, add the remaining ¼ cup sugar, a teaspoon at a time. Slowly beat in the cocoa mixture. The meringue should be stiff and shiny.
4. Add chopped nuts. Drop by teaspoonfuls on the parchment paper. Bake for 45–50 minutes. Cool on baking sheets. You can place these in an airtight cookie tin on the counter for up to 3 days or serve them the same day.

Orange Crispy Cookies

This adaptation of a classic Italian cookie is easy to make ahead of time.
You can change the recipe by adding currants, raisins, or chopped pecans.

INGREDIENTS | YIELDS 30 COOKIES

3 large eggs
1 cup sugar
1½ cups gluten-free cornmeal
¾ cup brown rice flour
¾ cup arrowroot starch or tapioca starch
½ teaspoon salt
¾ teaspoon xanthan gum
¾ cup unsalted butter, melted
1 tablespoon concentrated orange juice
Zest of ½ orange, minced very finely

1. In the bowl of your food processor, blend the eggs and sugar. Slowly add the rest of the ingredients, stopping occasionally to scrape the bowl. Don't over process. When the dough comes together, remove from the food processor.
2. Divide the dough in half and place on a sheet of plastic wrap. Roll the 2 balls of dough into logs. Refrigerate for at least 3–4 hours.
3. Preheat oven to 350°F. Prepare a cookie sheet with non-stick spray or parchment paper.
4. Remove the plastic wrap from the dough and slice each log into 15 round cookies. Place cookies 1" apart on baking sheets. Bake for 10 minutes, or until golden-brown.

Key Lime Bars

These sweet and tart bars are a unique treat to offer at a bake sale or potluck.
If the lime filling isn't quite green enough, add a drop or two of green food coloring.

INGREDIENTS | SERVES 15

Crust

1 cup unsalted butter, at room temperature

½ cup sugar

1¼ cups plus 2 tablespoons brown rice flour

½ cup plus 2 tablespoons arrowroot starch or tapioca starch

½ teaspoon xanthan gum

Pinch salt

Filling

7 large eggs, at room temperature

2½ cups sugar

2 tablespoons grated key lime zest (approximately 4–6 key limes)

1 cup freshly squeezed key lime juice (approximately 6 key limes)

⅔ cup brown rice flour

⅓ cup arrowroot starch or tapioca starch

Confectioners' sugar for dusting

Best Made Ahead

Key Lime Bars are best if you can make them one day before you serve them. Refrigerating will make them easier to cut. Do not sprinkle with confectioners' sugar until you are ready to serve, as it tends to dissolve from the moisture of the lime layer.

1. Preheat oven to 350°F. Line a 9" × 13" baking pan with parchment paper, so the paper rises up the sides. This will make removing the squares much easier, as you can lift them out once they are cooled.

2. Make the crust: In the bowl of a stand mixer, cream the butter and sugar until light and fluffy. In medium-sized bowl, combine brown rice flour, arrowroot starch, xanthan gum, and salt. Slowly add to the butter-sugar mixture while the mixer is on low. Mix just until combined. Dump the dough into the baking pan, and using hands dusted with brown rice flour, press the dough evenly over the bottom of the pan, building up ½" edge on all sides.

3. Bake for 20 minutes, or until very lightly browned. Remove from oven and cool on wire rack. Do not turn the oven off yet.

4. While the crust is baking, whisk the filling ingredients together in a medium bowl. Gently pour over the crust and bake for 30–35 minutes, until the filling is set. Let cool completely and refrigerate for at least 3 hours.

5. To remove from pan, cut along 9" edges, and use the parchment paper to lift the bars out to a cutting board. Using a sifter or wire sieve, dust bars with confectioners' sugar. Cut into squares and serve.

Salted Caramel Brownies

These brownies have a surprise layer of caramel in the middle and coarse sea salt sprinkled on top.

INGREDIENTS | SERVES 16

½ cup butter or Spectrum Palm Shortening

1 cup sugar

1 tablespoon vanilla extract

2 large eggs

¾ cup unsweetened cocoa powder

¼ teaspoon sea salt

½ cup sorghum flour

¼ teaspoon xanthan gum

¾ cup caramel squares (unwrapped) or caramel bits

½ teaspoon coarse sea salt

1. Preheat oven to 325°F. Line an 8" × 8" baking pan with parchment paper and then grease with nonstick cooking spray or light-tasting olive oil.
2. In a microwave-safe bowl, heat butter or shortening for about 30 seconds, just until melted. Stir in sugar. Allow mixture to cool 5 minutes and then stir in vanilla and eggs.
3. In a small bowl whisk together cocoa powder, sea salt, sorghum flour, and xanthan gum. Slowly stir dry ingredients into wet ingredients. Pour half of the batter into pan. Sprinkle the caramel squares or bits evenly over the bottom layer of batter, and then pour the remaining batter on top of the caramel. It doesn't have to be perfectly even.
4. Place in oven and bake for 20–25 minutes until the edges are crispy and deep brown and starting to just pull away from the pan. Sprinkle hot brownies with coarse sea salt and place the entire pan on a wire rack to cool for at least 1 hour.
5. Slice into 16 small brownies to serve. Store any remaining brownies in an airtight container on the counter for up to 3 days.

Chocolate Chip Blondies

This recipe is great for potlucks and bake sales because it makes a huge batch of blondies.

INGREDIENTS | YIELDS 32 BARS

1 cup butter, softened or 1 cup Spectrum Palm Shortening

1 cup sugar

1⅔ cups brown sugar

4 large eggs

2 tablespoons vanilla extract

1¼ cups brown rice flour

1¼ cups arrowroot starch

1 teaspoon xanthan gum

2 teaspoons baking powder

½ teaspoon sea salt

1 cup chocolate chips

Oatmeal Butterscotch Blondies

Instead of chocolate chips you could add 1 cup gluten-free rolled oats and 1 cup butterscotch chips to create a completely different flavor for these bars. Read ingredient labels carefully to make sure butterscotch chips are gluten-free.

1. Preheat oven to 350°F. Line a 9" × 13" baking dish with parchment paper and set aside.
2. In a large bowl cream butter and sugars until light and fluffy. Stir in eggs and vanilla until well incorporated.
3. In a medium bowl whisk together brown rice flour, arrowroot starch, xanthan gum, baking powder, and sea salt. Slowly stir the flour mixture into the creamed sugar mixture, until fully incorporated. Fold in chocolate chips.
4. Pour batter into baking dish. Bake for 40–45 minutes until golden-brown. Allow to cool completely before cutting. Store brownies in an airtight container in the refrigerator for up to 5 days. Blondie batter and bars will freeze well for up to 1 month.

Neapolitan Cupcakes with Strawberry-Swirl Buttercream

Which is your favorite? Chocolate? Vanilla? Strawberry? Now you don't have to pick just one—you can enjoy all three flavors in these delectable cupcakes.

INGREDIENTS | SERVES 12

Cupcakes
⅓ cup brown rice flour
⅓ cup arrowroot starch or tapioca starch
⅓ cup sorghum flour
½ teaspoon xanthan gum
¾ cup sugar
1½ teaspoons baking powder
½ teaspoon baking soda
¼ teaspoon salt
¾ cup buttermilk
¼ cup oil
2 large eggs
2 tablespoons cocoa powder
1 teaspoon vanilla extract
1 teaspoon strawberry extract
5 drops red food coloring

Frosting
3 cups confectioners' sugar, sifted
¾ cup unsalted butter, softened
3 tablespoons heavy cream
Pinch salt
1 teaspoon vanilla extract
½ teaspoon strawberry extract

1. Preheat oven to 350°F. Line 12 muffin cups with paper liners. Set aside.
2. In a large bowl, whisk together the brown rice flour, arrowroot starch, sorghum flour, xanthan gum, sugar, baking powder, baking soda, and salt.
3. In a smaller bowl, whisk together the buttermilk, oil, and eggs. Pour into the dry ingredients and stir just until mixed. Divide the batter between three medium bowls.
4. To the batter in the first bowl, stir in the cocoa powder. To the batter in the second bowl, stir in vanilla extract. To the batter in the third bowl, stir in strawberry extract and food coloring.
5. Scoop batter into prepared muffin cups, layering each flavor of batter. You will need about 1½ tablespoons of each flavor to fill the baking pans evenly.
6. Bake for 18–20 minutes, or until a toothpick inserted into the middle of the cupcake comes out clean. Remove from oven and allow to cool for 5 minutes before removing to wire cooling rack. Cool completely before frosting.
7. To make the buttercream, beat together the confectioners' sugar, butter, cream, and salt until smooth and fluffy (3–5 minutes with a stand mixer).
8. Divide buttercream between two bowls. In one bowl, incorporate vanilla extract. In the second bowl, incorporate strawberry extract.
9. Place the buttercream in a piping bag fitted with a large star tip. Place vanilla buttercream on one side of the piping bag and strawberry on the other—the two will mix in a beautiful swirl pattern when you pipe it onto the cupcakes.
10. Store frosted cupcakes in an airtight container on the counter for up to 3 days.

Oat Almond Bars

Make sure your oats, nuts, and dried fruit are all gluten-free. These sweet treats are also egg-free and can easily be made dairy-free using the tip in the sidebar.

INGREDIENTS | SERVES 12

1 (14-ounce) can sweetened condensed milk

2⅓ cups gluten-free old-fashioned oats

1 cup raw almonds

¾ cup unsweetened dried cherries, cranberries, or blueberries

¾ cup shredded unsweetened coconut

¼ teaspoon sea salt

¼ teaspoon ground ginger

1 teaspoon vanilla extract

Homemade Dairy-Free Sweetened Condensed Milk

If you can't use the canned version of sweetened condensed milk make your own by adding 3 cups of almond milk or soy milk to a saucepan. Mix in ¾ cup sugar or coconut palm sugar, 1 tablespoon vanilla extract, and ¼ teaspoon sea salt. Cook, stirring constantly, until the volume has been reduced to about 1½ cups of sweetened milk. Then use as directed in this recipe.

1. Preheat oven to 250°F. Oil an 11" × 7" baking pan. Set aside.
2. In a medium saucepan, heat the condensed milk. Do not boil. Stir in the remaining ingredients.
3. Pour the mixture into baking pan. Flatten with the back of a spoon or spatula, being sure the mixture reaches all four corners of the pan.
4. Bake for 60–70 minutes or until the mixture looks dry but is not browned. The mixture should only be slightly sticky at this point. Remove from the oven and place on a wire rack. Allow the mixture to cool completely in the pan. Slice into bars.

Big Batch Fudgy Brownies

*Here's a recipe you won't need to double or triple for a large group—
it makes 35 (2-inch) fudgy gluten-free brownies, enough for a crowd!*

INGREDIENTS | SERVES 35

6 ounces unsweetened chocolate

1 cup butter or Spectrum Palm Shortening

6 large eggs

2½ cups sugar

1 tablespoon vanilla extract

1 cup brown rice flour

¾ cup arrowroot starch or tapioca starch

½ teaspoon xanthan gum

½ teaspoon sea salt

Plain Jane or Dress 'Em Up?

You can leave these brownies plain, or add chopped nuts or chocolate chips on half the brownies (for people who aren't allergic to nuts). Or, have a toppings bar with chocolate syrup, walnuts, chocolate chips, and other choices that people can add to their brownies if they like.

1. Preheat oven to 325°F. Line a 10" × 15" jelly roll pan with parchment paper and then grease with nonstick cooking spray or butter.
2. In a large microwave-safe bowl heat chocolate and butter 30 seconds at a time until they are just melted. Whisk together and set aside to cool for 5 minutes. Once mixture has cooled slightly add in the eggs, sugar, and vanilla and whisk until the mixture is slightly frothy.
3. In a small bowl whisk together the brown rice flour, arrowroot starch, xanthan gum, and salt. Slowly stir the flour mixture into the wet ingredients, until just combined; do not over mix.
4. Pour the batter into jelly roll pan and with a spatula spread it out evenly over the whole pan. Bake for 25–30 minutes just until the centers of the brownies are set. Place pan on a wire rack and allow to cool completely before cutting into 2" squares.
5. Store any leftover brownies in an airtight container on the counter for up to 3 days.

CHAPTER 11

Gluten-Free Holiday Classics

Natural Dried-Fruit Fruitcake

*This recipe has less sugar than a traditional fruitcake because
it is sweetened naturally with real dried fruit.*

INGREDIENTS | YIELDS 3 (8½" × 4½") LOAVES

½ cup each: raisins, golden raisins, dried cherries, dried apples, dried apricots, and dried pineapple (chop larger fruits with a knife or scissors into a small pieces)

⅔ cup each: macadamia nuts, pecans or walnuts, and pistachios, all unsalted and coarsely chopped

½ cup rum

½ cup Triple Sec liqueur

12 tablespoons butter

⅔ cup packed brown sugar

2 large eggs

2 tablespoons freshly grated orange zest

¼ cup maple syrup

⅔ brown rice flour

⅔ arrowroot starch

½ teaspoon xanthan gum

¼ teaspoon baking soda

¼ teaspoon cream of tartar

¼ teaspoon salt

1 teaspoon cinnamon

½ teaspoon freshly grated nutmeg

¼ teaspoon cloves

¼ teaspoon allspice

Stays Fresh for Weeks

The alcohol in this cake helps it stay fresh for a month or so. The cake is best the first few days after it's made (as most baked goods are), but by dousing with rum or brandy once a week this cake can technically stay fresh for several weeks, which is why it was popular in the days before refrigeration. A cook could make this cake weeks before Christmas and have one big task out of the way.

1. The day before baking the cake, in a large bowl mix together all fruits, nuts, rum, and liqueur; allow to sit for 24 hours.

2. When you're ready to make the cake, preheat oven to 325°F. Grease or line 3 (8½" × 4½") loaf pans with parchment paper.

3. In a large bowl cream together the butter and brown sugar. Add the eggs, orange zest, and maple syrup and stir until combined. In a small bowl whisk together the brown rice flour, arrowroot starch, xanthan gum, baking soda, cream of tartar, salt, and spices. Add dry ingredients into the creamed sugar mixture. Stir to combine thoroughly. Fold soaked fruits and nuts into cake batter. Spoon the batter into loaf pans.

4. Bake for about 1 hour and 20 minutes until the top of the cake is golden-brown and a toothpick inserted into the center comes out clean. Allow cake to cool in the pans for 20 minutes before transferring to a wire rack to cool completely. The cake can be eaten immediately and it contains very little alcohol due to the heat of baking.

5. If you want to age the fruitcake, soak a cheesecloth in brandy or rum and wrap over the cake tightly. Place the cake in an airtight container, such as a metal tin, and every few days pour a few tablespoons of brandy or rum over the cake.

6. If you're eating the cake immediately after baking, store leftovers in an airtight container on the counter for 2–3 days. This cake freezes well for up to 2 months.

Boston Cream Pie

*This recipe includes steps for making your own vanilla cream to fill the cake.
To take a shortcut, make a small box of your favorite store-bought vanilla pudding
and chill for at least 8 hours before you make the cake.*

INGREDIENTS | SERVES 8–12

Vanilla Cream Filling

⅔ cup milk
⅓ cup sugar
¾ cup heavy cream
4 tablespoons cornstarch
1 large egg yolk
2 teaspoons vanilla

Cake

1 recipe Basic Yellow Cake batter (see Chapter 8)

Ganache

½ cup semisweet chocolate chips
½ cup heavy cream

1. Make the vanilla cream the day before baking the cake. In a medium bowl mix the milk with the sugar and heat over medium heat until the sugar has dissolved. In a small bowl whisk together the cream, cornstarch, and egg yolk. Whisk into the cream mixture very, very slowly and turn the heat down to low. Cook, whisking constantly, for 3–5 minutes until the mixtures thickens to a pudding-like texture.

2. Remove the cream from the heat, stir in the vanilla, and pour into a plastic or glass bowl. Place a sheet of plastic wrap over the cream so it does not develop a protein film on top as it cools. Refrigerate overnight.

3. Pour the cake batter into an 8" cake pan lined with parchment paper. Bake in a preheated 350°F oven for 20–25 minutes until springy and a toothpick inserted in the middle comes out clean. Cool in the pan for 5–10 minutes, then place on a wire rack to cool completely.

4. While the cake is cooling, prepare the chocolate ganache. Place chocolate chips in a large bowl. Using a saucepan or the microwave, bring the cream to a boil. Pour the cream over the chocolate and stir until chocolate is thoroughly melted with no lumps.

5. To assemble cake, use a serrated knife to cut the cooled cake in half horizontally. Remove the top portion of the cake and spoon the chilled vanilla cream over cake. Gently add the top of the cake and then pour warm ganache over the top of the cake. Chill the cake for a few hours before serving. Store cake in the refrigerator for up to 5 days. The fully assembled cake will not freeze well.

Red-and-Green Poke Cake

This is a fun cake to make for children's birthday parties. The simple yellow cake has different flavors of gelatin poured over it for flavor and a pop of bright color.

INGREDIENTS | SERVES 10–12

1 cup plus 2 tablespoons brown rice flour

1 cup arrowroot starch

1 cup sugar

2 teaspoon baking powder

1 teaspoon baking soda

1 teaspoon xanthan gum

½ teaspoon sea salt

½ cup light-tasting olive oil or canola oil

1½ cups almond milk

4 large eggs

1 tablespoon vanilla extract

½ (3-ounce) package strawberry or cherry gelatin

1 cup boiling water, divided

½ cup cold water, halved

½ (3-ounce) package lime gelatin

1 (8-ounce) tub whipped topping

1. Preheat oven to 350°F. Line a 9" × 13" baking dish with parchment paper and grease the edges that are not covered by the paper.
2. In a large mixing bowl whisk together brown rice flour, arrowroot starch, sugar, baking powder, baking soda, xanthan gum, and salt. In a smaller bowl mix together oil, milk, eggs, and vanilla. Whisk wet ingredients together thoroughly and then add to dry ingredients and whisk together until you have a thick batter.
3. Pour cake mix into baking dish. Bake for 25–30 minutes until cake is golden-brown, springy, and a toothpick inserted in the middle comes out clean. Allow the cake to cool completely in the pan.
4. Once the cake has cooled, poke holes all around the top using a fork for tiny holes or the handle of a wooden spoon for larger holes.
5. Next, prepare gelatin mixtures. In a small bowl mix together the strawberry or cherry gelatin with ½ cup boiling water and ¼ cup cold water. Pour mixture sporadically over the cake. In another small bowl mix together the lime gelatin with ½ cup boiling water and ¼ cup cold water and pour sporadically over the cake. Cover the cake pan with foil or plastic wrap and place in the refrigerator to chill for at least 4 hours.
6. When ready to serve, frost cake with whipped topping and cut into squares. Store any leftover cake in the refrigerator for up to 4 days. This cake does not freeze well.

Classic Pumpkin Roll

There is something decadent about this sweet, spicy pumpkin cake rolled around a smooth cream cheese icing. A rolled cake takes more time and effort than a regular cake, so be patient.

INGREDIENTS | SERVES 16

½ cup arrowroot starch

¼ cup sorghum flour

½ teaspoon xanthan gum

½ teaspoon baking powder

½ teaspoon baking soda

1 teaspoon cinnamon

½ teaspoon ginger

¼ teaspoon cloves

¼ teaspoon sea salt

1 cup sugar

3 large eggs

3 tablespoons water

⅔ cup pure pumpkin purée

¼ cup confectioners' sugar

8 ounces cream cheese

1 cup confectioners' sugar

6 tablespoons Spectrum Palm Shortening

1 teaspoon vanilla

Tea Towel versus Kitchen Towel

You generally need to roll the cake while it's still hot. This task is easiest with the help of a tea towel and confectioners' sugar. A tea towel is a flat, often thin, towel used in the kitchen. It's not the most absorbent towel (like fluffy towels with tiny loops of cotton to soak up liquids), but it's incredible useful for tasks like this. Tea towels also dry quickly when hung and don't need to be machine dried.

1. Preheat oven to 375°F. Line a 15" × 10" jelly roll pan with parchment paper. Grease the parchment paper with butter or nonstick cooking spray. This cake is apt to stick, so make sure to grease the paper adequately.

2. In a large bowl whisk together arrowroot starch, sorghum flour, xanthan gum, baking powder, baking soda, cinnamon, ginger, cloves, salt, and sugar.

3. In a smaller bowl mix eggs, water, and pumpkin. Pour the egg mixture into the dry ingredients and mix together thoroughly into a batter.

4. Pour the batter into jelly roll pan. Roll the batter around so it covers the whole pan. Tap the pan on the counter to remove any air bubbles from the batter. Bake batter for 15 minutes until the cake is firm and springy.

5. This step can be a bit tricky but it's very important. Sprinkle ¼ cup confectioners' sugar liberally onto a tea towel. Place a fold of tea towel onto the edge of the cake and gently remove parchment paper from the back of the cake while rolling the cake up into the tea towel. The cake will probably crack just a little on the edges—that's perfectly okay. Move towel-wrapped pumpkin roll to a wire rack and allow to cook completely.

6. While the cake is cooling make the cream cheese filling. In a medium bowl beat together cream cheese and shortening until light and fluffy. Beat in 1 cup confectioners' sugar a little at a time until fully incorporated. Stir in vanilla. Refrigerate filling until the roll is completely cool.

7. Once the cake is completely cool, gently unroll it and remove the tea towel. The roll should want to roll up on its own. Spread the cream cheese filling over the entire cake leaving about ½" around the edge so the cake will seal. Roll the cake up lengthwise. Cover roll with plastic wrap and chill for several hours or several days until serving. The cake can be stored in the fridge for up to 1 week. It does not freeze well.

Cranberry Squares

The tart dried cranberries in this recipe are cooked in brown sugar syrup laced with a hint of cinnamon. Leftovers, should there be any, can be covered in an airtight container and stored on the counter.

INGREDIENTS | SERVES 15

Crust
½ cup butter, softened
⅔ cup packed brown sugar
1¼ cups brown rice flour
¾ cup arrowroot starch
1 teaspoon xanthan gum
½ teaspoon salt

Filling
1½ cups packed brown sugar
2 tablespoons brown rice flour
½ teaspoon baking powder
¼ teaspoon salt
1 teaspoon ground cinnamon
¼ cup butter, softened
4 large eggs, beaten
2 teaspoons vanilla
3 cups dried sweetened cranberries

1. Preheat oven to 350°F.
2. Make the crust: Cream butter and brown sugar together in a medium bowl. Add brown rice flour, arrowroot starch, xanthan gum, and salt. Stir until well combined and crumbly. Reserve 1 cup of the crumbs to sprinkle over the tops of squares. Press remaining crumbs into the bottom of a 9" × 13" baking pan. Bake the crust for 12–15 minutes, or until it is a pale gold around the edges.
3. Make the filling: In a medium bowl, combine brown sugar, brown rice flour, baking powder, salt, and cinnamon. Add butter, eggs, and vanilla and stir until well blended. Stir in the dried cranberries.
4. Pour filling over the crust, top with reserved crumbles, and bake for 20–25 minutes, or until golden and bubbly around the edges but still slightly jiggly in the center. Cool completely in the pan on a wire rack. Slice into squares.

Pumpkin Cheesecake

This combination of cheesecake and pumpkin pie is the perfect dessert to enjoy during fall celebrations.

¾ cup crushed Cinnamon Chex or gluten-free graham cracker crumbs

½ cup ground pecans

2 tablespoons sugar

2 tablespoons brown sugar

¼ cup butter, melted

¾ cup sugar

¾ cup pumpkin purée (not pie filling)

3 large egg yolks

1½ teaspoons ground cinnamon

½ teaspoon ground nutmeg

½ teaspoon ground ginger

¼ teaspoon salt

3 (8-ounce) packages cream cheese

⅜ cup sugar

1 large egg

1 large egg yolk

2 tablespoons whipping cream

1 tablespoon cornstarch

1 teaspoon vanilla extract

½ cup whole pecans

1 (15-ounce) jar dulce de leche

Keeping Things Clean

To keep your oven clean when baking anything in a springform pan, place the pan on a foil-lined baking sheet. If the pan does not seal properly and some of the batter leaks out, it will not get on the bottom of your oven.

1. Preheat oven to 350°F.
2. Combine the Cinnamon Chex crumbs, ground pecans, 2 tablespoons sugar, 2 tablespoons brown sugar, and the melted butter and mix well. Firmly press into one 9" springform pan.
3. Combine ¾ cup sugar, pumpkin purée, 3 egg yolks, spices, and salt in a medium bowl. Mix well and set aside.
4. Beat the cream cheese with an electric mixer until light and fluffy; gradually add ⅜ cup sugar and mix well. Add the whole egg, remaining egg yolk, and the whipping cream, beating well. Add cornstarch and vanilla extract, and beat batter until smooth. Add pumpkin purée mixture and mix well. Pour batter into prepared pan.
5. Bake for 50–55 minutes. Do not over bake. The center may be soft but it will firm up when chilled. Turn oven off and open oven door, but leave the cake in the oven for the next hour. This will help prevent the top from cracking.
6. Cover and refrigerate until ready to serve. Remove the springform pan and decorate cake top with whole pecans and dulce de leche a few hours before serving. Refrigerate until ready to serve.

Creamy Cranberry Orange Pie

This creamy cranberry pudding has just a hint of orange zest for a different and delicious holiday pie.

INGREDIENTS | SERVES 8

4 cups fresh or frozen cranberries
½ cup orange juice
2 tablespoons lemon juice
1¼ cups sugar
¼ teaspoon salt
1 tablespoon orange zest
6 large egg yolks
½ cup butter, melted
1 prebaked 8" or 9" Basic Gluten-Free Pie and Tart Pastry (see Chapter 9)

1. Cook cranberries, orange juice, lemon juice, sugar, and salt in a medium saucepan until cranberries have "popped" and the mixture has thickened slightly. Allow mixture to cool for 10 minutes and purée in a blender.
2. Add cranberry mixture and orange zest back into the saucepan and cook on very low heat. Whisk egg yolks in a small bowl and slowly stir into warm cranberry mixture. Carefully stream butter into the pudding and continue stirring for 3–5 minutes until mixture has thickened.
3. Pour pudding into pie crust. Chill at least 6 hours before serving. Store in refrigerator for up to 5 days.

Gingersnap Pumpkin Pie

To give this traditional pie a different flavor add 1 tablespoon orange zest to the pumpkin filling.
This recipe is dairy-free, but if you prefer the traditional dairy-based pie,
use a 12-ounce can of evaporated milk instead of coconut milk.

INGREDIENTS | SERVES 8

Crust

1¾ cups gluten-free gingerbread cookie crumbs

2 tablespoons Spectrum Palm Shortening

2 tablespoons sugar

Filling

¾ cup sugar

½ teaspoon salt

2 teaspoons ground cinnamon

½ teaspoon ground ginger

¼ teaspoon cloves

2 large eggs

1 (15-ounce) can pure pumpkin purée

1 (13½-ounce) can full-fat coconut milk

1. Preheat oven to 325°F. In a glass or metal pie pan combine crust ingredients. Press to the sides and bottom of the pan to create a crust. Bake for 5 minutes, to set the crust. Cool crust completely.
2. In a large bowl combine sugar, salt, cinnamon, ginger, and cloves. Whisk together well. Add eggs, pumpkin purée, and coconut milk. Whisk all ingredients together until you have a smooth batter. Pour batter into the crust.
3. Bake for 1 hour until pie has set. Allow pie to cool for 1–2 hours on a wire rack, then transfer pie to refrigerator to cool completely before serving. This pie can be frozen for up to 1 month.

Crustless Pumpkin Pie

This pie has the same fantastic flavor as traditional pumpkin pie,
but it is much easier to make because it does not have a crust.

INGREDIENTS | SERVES 8

1 (15-ounce) can pumpkin purée (not pie filling)

½ cup packed brown sugar

½ cup sugar

⅛ teaspoon ground cloves

½ tablespoon ground cinnamon

1 teaspoon ground ginger

½ teaspoon salt

2 teaspoons baking powder

½ cup sorghum flour

2 tablespoons tapioca starch

2 teaspoons vanilla

2 tablespoons olive oil

2 large eggs, beaten

1 cup evaporated milk or full-fat coconut milk

Whipped cream (optional)

1. Preheat oven to 350°F.
2. Grease a 9½" pie plate with oil.
3. Combine all ingredients and mix until well combined.
4. Pour into prepared pie plate, and bake for 60–70 minutes. The pie is done when a knife inserted into the middle comes out clean.
5. Cool completely before serving. Serve with a dollop of whipped cream.

The Skinny on Crustless Pies

Go ahead and have that scoop of whipped cream with your pie without feeling guilty. By removing the crust from this pie, you save nearly 1,000 calories per pie, or 125 calories per slice.

Brown Sugar Pecan Pie

Brown sugar, butter, a little gluten-free flour, and nondairy milk give this pie a gooey center. Feel free to use regular milk, if you are not intolerant of dairy.

INGREDIENTS | SERVES 8–10

1 cup light brown sugar

¼ cup sugar

1 tablespoon sorghum flour

½ cup butter, melted

2 large eggs

1 tablespoon almond milk

1½ teaspoons vanilla extract

1⅓ cups chopped pecans

1 prebaked 8" or 9" Basic Gluten-Free Pie and Tart Pastry (see Chapter 9)

1. Preheat oven to 350°F.
2. In a large bowl mix together the brown sugar, sugar, and sorghum flour. Stir in the melted butter, eggs, almond milk, and vanilla. Stir in the pecans.
3. Pour filling into pie crust. Place a pie shield on the crust or use strips of foil to make a ring around the edge of the crust, so it doesn't burn while baking.
4. Place pie on a cookie sheet (just in case it bubbles over while baking) and bake for 35–40 minutes until set. Allow pie to cool completely on the counter before slicing. This pie can be frozen for up to 1 month.

Old-Fashioned Oatmeal Pie

Pecans can be expensive and some years they are more available than others. If you don't have or can't afford to buy freshly shelled pecans, try making an oatmeal pie instead. This is a very popular pie in the Amish community. All you do is replace the chopped pecans with 1½ cups gluten-free rolled oats and bake as directed.

Cranberry Cobbler

Even people who don't like cranberries will change their minds when they taste this dessert. Stock up on cranberries during the fall-winter holidays and freeze them for later use.

INGREDIENTS | SERVES 6–8

2 cups whole, raw cranberries

1 cup sugar, divided

½ cup pecans, finely chopped

½ cup crushed pineapple with juice

2 tablespoons grated orange zest (1 medium orange)

3 tablespoons melted butter or coconut oil

Fresh juice from half of a medium-sized orange (about 2 tablespoons)

1 large egg, beaten

¼ cup brown rice flour

1. Preheat oven to 350°F. Grease an 8" pie pan or a 2-quart baking dish.
2. Pour cranberries, ½ cup sugar, pecans, pineapple, and orange zest into pie pan. Mix together well.
3. In a small bowl whisk together remaining sugar, butter, orange juice, egg, and brown rice flour, until you have a thin batter. Pour the batter over the cranberry mixture in the pie pan.
4. Bake for 45 minutes until cranberries are hot and bubbly. Allow pan to cool on the counter for at least an hour before serving. Serve hot or cold, as a side dish or a dessert. Store covered in the refrigerator for up to 5 days. This dish does not freeze well.

Sweet Potato Pie

Although similar in taste to pumpkin pie, the filling for this pie is slightly more dense and heartier than pumpkin. Experiment with the spices to find a blend you enjoy.

INGREDIENTS | SERVES 8–12

2 cups fresh sweet potatoes, peeled, cooked, and mashed

2 large eggs

1 (13½-ounce) can full-fat coconut milk

1 teaspoon vanilla extract

¾ cup sugar

1½ teaspoons ground cinnamon

½ teaspoon ground ginger

¼ teaspoon ground cloves

½ teaspoon freshly grated nutmeg

¼ teaspoon ground cardamom

½ teaspoon sea salt

1 prebaked 9" Basic Gluten-Free Pie and Tart Pastry (see Chapter 9)

1. Preheat oven to 425°F.
2. In a large bowl whisk together sweet potatoes, eggs, coconut milk, and vanilla.
3. In a smaller bowl mix together the sugar, cinnamon, ginger, cloves, nutmeg, cardamom, and salt. Whisk the sugar mixture into the sweet potato mixture, until fully incorporated.
4. Pour sweet potato filling into pie crust. Place pie crust on a cookie sheet and bake for 15 minutes at 425°F. Then reduce temperature to 350°F and bake for an additional 40–50 minutes until the pie is set and a knife inserted in the middle comes out clean. If you notice the crust is starting to brown too much, add a ring of foil strips to prevent burning. Cool completely before slicing. Store covered pie in the refrigerator for up to 5 days. This pie freezes well for up to 1 month.

Soft Gingersnap Cookies

The tantalizing aroma of these spicy cookies is enough to draw people into the kitchen to see what's baking. Refrigerate dough for 1 hour before baking your cookies.

INGREDIENTS | SERVES 48

¾ cup butter, softened

1 cup sugar, plus more for rolling cookies

1 large egg

¼ cup molasses

1 cup brown rice flour

¾ cup sorghum flour

¾ cup arrowroot starch or tapioca starch

1 teaspoon xanthan gum

1 teaspoon baking soda

2 teaspoons ground ginger

¾ teaspoon ground cinnamon

½ teaspoon ground cloves

¼ teaspoon salt

1. Preheat oven to 350°F. Line baking sheets with parchment paper. Set aside.
2. In a stand mixer, beat the butter and sugar until light and fluffy. Add in the egg and molasses. Mix until blended.
3. In a mixing bowl, whisk together the brown rice flour, sorghum flour, arrowroot or tapioca starch, xanthan gum, baking soda, ginger, cinnamon, cloves, and salt.
4. Gradually add the dry ingredients to the butter mixture, mixing until well blended. Cover and refrigerate dough for 1 hour.
5. Roll the dough into ¾" balls and then roll in the additional sugar to coat. Place on baking sheet 2" apart.
6. Bake for 10–12 minutes or until puffy and lightly browned. Remove to wire racks to cool. Store in an airtight container once completely cool.

Pfeffernüsse Cookies

These peppery cookies are a wonderful holiday tradition, especially in Germany. Don't shy away from the long list of ingredients—most are spices that give these cookies their distinctive flavor.

INGREDIENTS | YIELDS 4–5 DOZEN COOKIES

½ cup molasses
¼ cup honey
½ cup Spectrum Palm Shortening
2 teaspoons anise extract
2 large eggs
2 cups brown rice flour
2 cups arrowroot starch
1½ teaspoons xanthan gum
¾ cup sugar
½ cup brown sugar
1½ teaspoons ground cardamom (optional)
1 teaspoon ground nutmeg
1 teaspoon ground cloves
1 teaspoon ground ginger
2 teaspoons ground cinnamon
1 teaspoon ground black pepper
1½ teaspoons baking soda
½ teaspoon salt
1 cup confectioners' sugar

1. In a medium saucepan stir together molasses, honey, shortening, and anise extract. Cook over medium heat, stirring until ingredients are fully melted and creamy. Remove from heat and allow to cool for 5–10 minutes. Once cool, stir in eggs and set aside.
2. In a large bowl whisk together brown rice flour, arrowroot starch, xanthan gum, sugar, brown sugar, cardamom, nutmeg, cloves, ginger, cinnamon, black pepper, baking soda, and salt. Add molasses-egg mixture and stir until thoroughly combined into a thick batter. Cover and refrigerate batter for at least 2 hours.
3. When ready to make cookies, heat oven to 325°F. Line 2–3 large baking sheets with parchment paper. Roll dough into 1" balls. Place balls of dough on baking sheets at least 1" apart. Bake for 10–15 minutes until cookies have spread a little and are starting to look a bit dry on the edges.
4. Allow cookies to cool for 5 minutes on the cookie sheet and then move to a wire rack to completely cool. Dust cooled cookies with confectioners' sugar. Store in an airtight container on the counter for up to 3 weeks. These cookies freeze well for up to 2 months and are also sturdy enough for shipping.

An Old-Fashioned Christmas Cookie

Pfeffernüsse cookies are German/Dutch cookies that date back to the 1700s. The spicy cookies or biscuits sometimes contained bits of pepper (pfeffer) along with other warm holiday spices. Some old recipes produce a hard cookie with a long shelf life because it doesn't have a lot of moisture. This recipe makes a moist cookie that still holds up well for 2–3 weeks.

Pumpkin Snickerdoodles

These cookies are light as air, but big on flavor. Kids will love to find them nestled in their lunchboxes.

INGREDIENTS | SERVES 40

½ cup butter, softened

¾ cup sugar

⅓ cup pumpkin purée (not pie filling)

1 large egg

1 teaspoon vanilla extract

1¼ cups plus 2 tablespoons brown rice flour

½ cup plus 2 tablespoons arrowroot starch

1 teaspoon xanthan gum

1 teaspoon baking powder

¼ teaspoon salt

¼ teaspoon ground cinnamon

½ cup sugar

1 teaspoon pumpkin pie spice

Pumpkin Pie Spice

You can make your own pumpkin pie spice by combining 2 tablespoons ground cinnamon, 2 teaspoons each ground nutmeg and ground ginger, ½ teaspoon ground allspice, and ¼ teaspoon ground cloves. Store in an airtight container in a cool, dark place.

1. In a stand mixer fitted with a paddle attachment, beat the butter and ¾ cup sugar until light and fluffy. Add the pumpkin purée, egg, and vanilla extract, and beat until well mixed, then scrape down the bowl and mix again.
2. In a separate mixing bowl, whisk together the brown rice flour, arrowroot starch, xanthan gum, baking powder, salt, and ground cinnamon.
3. With the mixer running on low, slowly add the dry ingredients to the wet ingredients. Mix until well combined. Chill dough for 1 hour.
4. Preheat oven to 350°F and line baking sheets with parchment paper.
5. In a small bowl, stir together the ½ cup sugar and the pumpkin pie spice.
6. Form dough into 1" balls and roll dough in the sugar-spice mixture. Place cookies on prepared baking sheets, with about 2" between cookies, leaving room for them to spread. Lightly press down on the tops of the cookies with the bottom of a drinking glass.
7. Bake for 10–14 minutes, or until the cookies are just starting to lightly brown.
8. Allow to cool on the pan for 5 minutes before transferring to a cooling rack. Store in an airtight container, once they are fully cooled.

Linzer Cookies

These beautiful holiday cookies have your favorite jam sandwiched between two cookie layers. They look much harder to make than they really are!

INGREDIENTS | YIELDS 12–14 COOKIES

1¼ cups brown rice flour

¾ cup arrowroot starch

3 tablespoons blanched almond flour

1 teaspoon sea salt

1 teaspoon xanthan gum

1 teaspoon freshly grated lemon zest

6 tablespoons Spectrum Palm Shortening

1¼ cups sugar

2 large eggs

1 teaspoon vanilla extract

Confectioners' sugar

1 (10-ounce) jar strawberry jam

An Easier Way to Roll Out Cookies

Rolling out gluten-free dough can be a challenge. The best way to do this is to lay out two sheets of parchment paper (about the size of a large baking sheet) or sturdy sheets of good plastic wrap and secure them to a hard, dry surface (your counters or kitchen table). Generously sprinkle gluten-free flour on the paper and then place dough on top. Sprinkle more gluten-free flour on top of dough and then place a large sheet of plastic wrap on top of dough. Roll out dough with a rolling pin. The sheet of plastic wrap between dough and rolling pin will keep dough from sticking to the pin, preventing a big mess.

1. Preheat oven to 350°F. Line 2 large baking sheets with parchment paper.
2. In a medium bowl whisk together brown rice flour, arrowroot starch, blanched almond flour, sea salt, xanthan gum, and lemon zest.
3. In a large bowl cream together the shortening and sugar until light and fluffy. Add the eggs and vanilla; stir until creamy. Add dry ingredients ½ cup at a time and stir together into a stiff dough. Roll out cookies between ¼" and ½" thickness and cut out using nesting heart or circle cookie cutters. Make sure to cut out two cookies for each Linzer "sandwich." You'll have one regular cut-out cookie and another cookie in the same shape, but with a hole in the center made from the smaller nesting cookie cutter. When the cookies are assembled you'll see the jam between the layers.
4. Place cookies 1" apart on lined cookie sheets and bake for 12–15 minutes until cookies are just beginning to brown on the edges. Allow cookies to cool on the baking sheets for 5–10 minutes then move to a wire rack to cool completely.
5. To assemble cookies, dust tops of the cookies with the holes in the middle with confectioners' sugar. Spread 1–2 teaspoons jam over the bottom cookie layer and then add the top cookie. These cookies are best the day they are made. Keep 1–2 days on the kitchen counter in a tightly sealed container. These cookies will freeze well for up to 1 month.

White Chocolate Cranberry Cookies

These easy drop cookies have festive colors for the holiday season. Both crunchy and chewy at the same time, they're sure to be a hit.

INGREDIENTS | SERVES 24

¼ cup Spectrum Palm Shortening
¼ cup sugar
¾ cup brown sugar
1 large egg
1 tablespoon vanilla extract
½ cup arrowroot starch
¾ cup sorghum flour
½ teaspoon sea salt
¼ teaspoon xanthan gum
1 teaspoon baking powder
½ teaspoon baking soda
1 cup white chocolate baking pieces
1 cup dried cranberries

1. Preheat oven to 350°F. Line 2 baking sheets with parchment paper and set aside.
2. In a large bowl cream together shortening, sugar, and brown sugar. When thoroughly combined, stir in the egg and vanilla.
3. In a smaller bowl whisk together arrowroot starch, sorghum flour, sea salt, xanthan gum, baking powder, and baking soda. Slowly stir dry ingredients into the creamed sugar mixture. Stir white chocolate pieces and dried cranberries into the thick batter.
4. Drop batter 1 teaspoon at a time about 2" apart onto baking sheets. Bake for 7–9 minutes, just until the cookies' edges are golden-brown and tops are slightly brown.
5. Remove from oven and allow to cool on baking sheets for 15–20 minutes before removing to cooling rack.
6. Store cookies in an airtight container on the counter for up to 2 days. These cookies are best the day they are made. They can also be frozen (either as raw dough or as baked cookies) for up to 2 months.

Spritz Cookies

These will remind you of the buttery, crisp cookies that come in a metal tin at Christmas. To get specific shapes you have to use a cookie press, but if you don't have one simply chill the dough in a log, then slice and bake.

INGREDIENTS | YIELDS 3–4 DOZEN COOKIES

1¼ cups brown rice flour

1 cup arrowroot starch

1 teaspoon xanthan gum

½ teaspoon baking powder

¼ teaspoon salt

1 cup Spectrum Palm Shortening

¾ cup sugar

1 large egg

1 teaspoon lemon, vanilla, or butter extract

2–4 tablespoons of ice-cold water, as needed

Colored sanding sugar (optional)

1. Preheat oven to 350°F. Line 2 baking sheets with parchment paper.
2. In a medium bowl whisk together brown rice flour, arrowroot starch, xanthan gum, baking powder, and salt. Set aside. In a large bowl cream shortening and sugar. Mix in the egg and 1 teaspoon of your favorite flavor extract. Slowly add the dry ingredients until you have a soft cookie dough. You may need to add 2–4 tablespoons of ice-cold water to the dough to make it pliable and workable.
3. Using a cookie press, choose your shapes and press out dough according to press's directions. It is easier to press the cookies onto a plate (instead of straight onto the cookie sheet) and then transfer them to a cookie sheet for baking. Place cookies 1" apart on baking sheets. Sprinkle with colored sanding sugar, if desired.
4. Bake for 7–9 minutes until the edges of cookies are light golden-brown. Do not over bake. Cool for 10 minutes and then store in an airtight container on the counter for up to 2 weeks. These cookies freeze well for up to 2 months. They're also sturdy enough for shipping.

Roll-Out Holiday Sugar Cookies

Butter and cream cheese are combined in this recipe to create a delicious, easy-to-roll-out sugar cookie. If you're dairy intolerant, use the recipe for Spritz Cookies and roll out as directed here.

INGREDIENTS | YIELDS 2–3 DOZEN COOKIES

4 ounces cream cheese

½ cup butter

½ cup confectioners' sugar

1 teaspoon almond extract or vanilla extract

1¼ cups arrowroot starch or cornstarch

½ cup brown rice flour

Quick Vanilla Glaze

In a small bowl combine ½ cup confectioners' sugar with 1 tablespoon pure vanilla extract, and 1–2 tablespoons milk or water. Mix well with a fork and drizzle over cooled cookies. Leave cookies undisturbed for several minutes to allow the glaze to harden and set.

1. Preheat oven to 350°F. Line 2 baking sheets with parchment paper.
2. In a large bowl cream together cream cheese, butter, and confectioners' sugar for several minutes until light and fluffy. Add flavoring extract. In a smaller bowl whisk together arrowroot starch and brown rice flour. Stir flour mixture slowly into butter-sugar mixture.
3. Refrigerate dough for at least 1 hour. When ready to bake, heat oven to 350°F. Line 2 baking sheets with parchment paper. Roll out refrigerated dough on a flat surface to ⅓" thickness. Cut out cookies with your favorite cookie cutters and carefully transfer to baking sheets.
4. Bake for 12–14 minutes until the edges of the cookies are lightly browned. Allow to cool on baking sheets for 5–10 minutes and then move to wire rack to cool completely. Store in an airtight container on the counter for up to 2 weeks. Cookies (and dough) will also freeze well for up to 2 months.

Chocolate Crackle Cookies

A soft super-chocolaty treat that children especially love, these cookies are coated in confectioners' sugar before baking and "crackle" as they cook. If the confectioners' sugar melts after the cookies are finished baking, coat them again and serve.

INGREDIENTS | YIELDS 2–3 DOZEN COOKIES

½ cup Spectrum Palm Shortening

1⅓ cups light brown sugar

2 large eggs

1 teaspoon vanilla extract

⅓ cup almond milk

1 cup semisweet chocolate chips, melted and cooled

¾ cup brown rice flour

½ cup arrowroot starch

½ cup cocoa powder

¼ teaspoon xanthan gum

2 teaspoons baking powder

Confectioners' sugar, for coating

1. In a large bowl cream together shortening and brown sugar for several minutes until light and fluffy. Add eggs, vanilla extract, and almond milk. Stir to combine. Whisk in chocolate.
2. In a smaller bowl whisk together brown rice flour, arrowroot starch, cocoa powder, xanthan gum, and baking powder. Slowly stir dry ingredients into chocolate-and-sugar mixture. Refrigerate dough for at least 2 hours.
3. When ready to bake heat oven to 325°F. Line 2 baking sheets with parchment paper. Roll cookie dough into 1" balls and roll each ball in confectioners' sugar to thoroughly coat. Place cookie balls onto baking sheets at least 1" apart. Bake for 10–12 minutes until cookies spread a little and "crackle" apart so you can see the dark cookies in between the confectioners' sugar cracks. Move to wire rack and cool completely. Store cookies in an airtight container on the counter for up to 5 days. These cookies freeze well, but you may need to recoat them in confectioners' sugar after defrosting.

Pecan Pumpkin Crunch Bars

These portable little bars are a great alternative to pumpkin pie, especially if you are traveling and need a less-fragile dessert. Try them topped with whipped cream or ice cream.

INGREDIENTS | YIELDS 16–20 BARS

Crust

½ cup blanched almond flour

¼ cup brown rice flour

¼ cup arrowroot starch

½ cup gluten-free rolled oats

1 tablespoon brown sugar

¼ cup Spectrum Palm Shortening

Filling

½ cup sugar

1 (15-ounce) can pumpkin purée (or 2 cups cooked pumpkin)

¾ cup coconut milk

2 large eggs

1 teaspoon cinnamon

¼ teaspoon nutmeg

½ teaspoon ground cloves

¼ teaspoon ground ginger

Topping

½ cup pecans, chopped

¼ cup sugar

1. Preheat oven to 350°F. Grease a 9" × 13" baking dish.
2. In a small bowl, combine crust ingredients. Pour into the baking dish and press to create the crust.
3. In a medium bowl whisk the filling ingredients together. Pour batter over crust. In another small bowl combine chopped pecans and ¼ cup sugar, and sprinkle evenly over the pumpkin filling.
4. Bake for 40–50 minutes until a knife inserted into the middle of the filling comes out clean. Let cool completely before slicing into bars. Store leftovers in an airtight container in the refrigerator for up to 5 days. Bars will also freeze for up to 1 month.

Candy Cane Brownies

These cute, minty, and decadent holiday brownies are made in cupcake liners for individual servings. You can use a box of gluten-free brownie mix instead of the Basic Cocoa Brownies if you like.

INGREDIENTS | YIELDS 12 BROWNIES

1 recipe Basic Cocoa Brownies batter (see Chapter 7)

12 mini chocolate-covered peppermint candies (like York Peppermint Patties)

¾ cup chocolate chips

3 (2-inch) candy canes, crushed

1. Preheat oven to 350°F. Line a muffin tin with 12 paper liners. Grease paper liners with nonstick cooking spray.
2. Spoon brownie batter into paper liners. Unwrap peppermint candies and push one candy into the center of each brownie. Bake brownies for 13–15 minutes until a toothpick inserted in the center comes out clean. Allow brownies to cool for 20–30 minutes.
3. In a microwaveable bowl melt chocolate chips for about 1 minute until smooth. Drizzle melted chocolate decoratively over each brownie. Top brownies with crushed candy canes and serve. Brownies can be stored up to 5 days in an airtight container on the counter. They freeze well for up to 1 month.

Pumpkin Swirl Brownies

You can never have too many pumpkin-infused holiday recipes. Chocolate and pumpkin create a delicious creamy combination in these classic fudgy brownies.

Sweet Potato or Butternut Squash Swirl

If you don't have any fresh or canned pumpkin purée, you can use ½ cup cooked and mashed butternut squash or sweet potatoes for these brownies. Nobody will know the difference and both are healthy, nutrient-rich foods.

1. Preheat oven to 350°F. Line an 8" × 8" baking dish with parchment paper or grease with nonstick cooking spray.
2. Pour brownie batter into baking dish. In small bowl whisk together the egg white, pumpkin purée, sugar, pumpkin pie spice, and vanilla extract. Pour pumpkin mixture in a swirl pattern over the brownies. Gently run a kitchen knife through brownies and swirl once or twice. Don't overdo this, as you still want to be able to see the pumpkin mixture through brownies.
3. Bake for 30–35 minutes until a toothpick inserted in the middle of the brownies comes out clean. Let brownies cool in the pan for 30–40 minutes before slicing. Store brownies in an airtight container in the refrigerator for up to 5 days. These brownies freeze well for up to 1 month.

CHAPTER 12

Low-Glycemic Gluten-Free Goodies

Grain-Free "Buttermilk" Biscuits

These flaky "buttery" biscuits can be made with or without butter.
Use coconut oil instead of butter for a casein-free biscuit.

INGREDIENTS | SERVES 8

2½ cups blanched almond flour

½ teaspoon sea salt

½ teaspoon baking soda

3 tablespoons softened butter or coconut oil

1 tablespoon honey

2 tablespoons almond milk

1 teaspoon apple cider vinegar

2 large eggs

1. Preheat oven to 350°F and line a baking sheet with parchment paper.
2. In a medium bowl whisk together almond flour, sea salt, and baking soda. Cut in the butter or coconut oil with a pastry blender or a knife and fork until it resembles small peas throughout the dry ingredients.
3. Make a well in the center of the dry ingredients and stir in honey, almond milk, vinegar, and eggs until you have a thick dough.
4. Scoop dough into 8 equal-size balls. Place balls about 2" apart and shape them into traditional-looking biscuits with your hands.
5. Bake for 15–20 minutes until biscuits are golden-brown. Allow to cool for several minutes and serve warm.

Blueberry Almond Scones

These slightly sweet scones have a light texture with a soft crumb. Try different types of fruit, such as strawberries—or even chocolate chips—in place of the blueberries.

INGREDIENTS | SERVES 8

3 cups blanched almond flour

¾ cup arrowroot starch or tapioca starch

½ teaspoon baking soda

¼ teaspoon sea salt

¼ cup coconut palm sugar or regular sugar

⅓ cup butter or Spectrum Palm Shortening

1 large egg, slightly whisked

⅔ cup almond milk

1 teaspoon vanilla extract

½ teaspoon lemon juice or apple cider vinegar

1 cup fresh or frozen blueberries (do not defrost if frozen)

Traditional Scones versus Almond Flour Scones

Traditional scones are created by shaping the dough into a round loaf and slicing it before baking. These scones, however, are made in a cake pan and then sliced into triangles after they are cooked because almond flour dough is not quite thick enough to support itself baking without a pan. You could use a scone baking pan, but it's just as easy to bake the dough in a cake pan and then slice it.

1. Preheat oven to 350°F. Line a 9" cake pan with parchment paper and spritz with nonstick cooking spray. Set aside.
2. In a large bowl whisk together almond flour, arrowroot starch, baking soda, salt, and coconut or regular sugar. Using a fork and knife or a pastry cutter, cut butter or shortening evenly into the flour mixture until it resembles small peas. Set aside. In a small bowl mix together egg, almond milk, vanilla extract, and lemon juice.
3. Mix wet ingredients with dry ingredients until thoroughly incorporated. Add blueberries and mix. Batter will be thick. Pour batter into cake pan and smooth the top with a spatula.
4. Bake for 25–30 minutes until edges of the scone are golden-brown and a toothpick inserted in the middle comes out mostly clean with few crumbs.
5. When scone is done, remove from oven and set aside to cool for several minutes. Cut round scone into 8 triangular scones.

Grain-Free, Egg-Free Pancakes

A common challenge with grain-free or low-glycemic gluten-free baking is figuring out how to make recipes without eggs. These pancakes use chia seeds as the binding ingredient instead of eggs.

INGREDIENTS | SERVES 4

2 tablespoons chia seeds

6 tablespoons warm water

1½ cups blanched almond flour

1 tablespoon arrowroot starch or tapioca starch

½ teaspoon sea salt

½ teaspoon baking soda

½ teaspoon ground cinnamon

¼ cup unsweetened applesauce or plain pumpkin purée

½ cup almond milk

1½ teaspoons vanilla extract

Coconut oil, butter, or nonstick cooking spray

1. In a small bowl whisk together chia seeds and warm water. Set aside to gel.
2. In a larger bowl whisk together almond flour, arrowroot starch, sea salt, baking soda, and cinnamon. Make a well in the center of the dry ingredients and pour in the gelled chia seed mixture, applesauce, almond milk, and vanilla. Whisk all ingredients together into a thick batter.
3. Heat a little coconut oil, butter, or nonstick cooking spray on an electric griddle or heavy skillet over medium-high heat until sizzling. Drop 1½ tablespoons of batter per pancake and cook for 3–4 minutes on one side until the bottom has browned. Then flip and cook for an additional 1–2 minutes until the underside has browned. Serve hot with butter and pure maple syrup or honey.

Fluffy Coconut Flour Pancakes

Coconut flour is extremely dry and acts almost like a sponge in baking.
You need a lot of liquid to make these pancakes moist and delicious.

INGREDIENTS | SERVES 2–3

½ cup coconut flour

1 teaspoon baking soda

½ teaspoon sea salt

4 large eggs, room temperature

1 cup almond milk or coconut milk

1 tablespoon vanilla extract

1 tablespoon honey

Coconut oil, butter, or nonstick cooking spray for frying

Keeping Pancakes Fluffy

Making grain-free pancakes can be a challenge if you aren't familiar with how to use the flours and how they work in recipes. The best way to keep these pancakes soft and fluffy is to make them relatively small, no more than 2–3" in diameter. If they are larger than that, they take too long to cook through and will become dry, instead of light and fluffy.

1. In a large bowl whisk together coconut flour, baking soda, and sea salt. Make a well in the center of the dry ingredients and pour in the eggs, almond milk, vanilla, and honey. Whisk all ingredients together into a thick batter.

2. Heat a little coconut oil, butter, or nonstick cooking spray on an electric griddle or heavy skillet over medium-high heat until sizzling. Drop 1½ tablespoons of batter per pancake and cook for 3–4 minutes on one side until the bottom has browned. Then flip and cook for an additional 1–2 minutes until the underside has browned.

3. Serve hot with butter or coconut oil and pure maple syrup, honey, or fresh strawberry jam.

Lemon Poppy Seed Muffins

These muffins are flavored with lemon gelatin dessert. However, if you're not a fan of gelatin, you can replace it with 1 tablespoon fresh lemon zest and 2 teaspoons lemon extract.

INGREDIENTS | SERVES 12

2 cups blanched almond flour

½ cup arrowroot starch or tapioca starch

½ teaspoon sea salt

½ teaspoon baking soda

¾ cup coconut palm sugar (or sugar)

½ teaspoon freshly grated nutmeg

2 tablespoons poppy seeds

3 tablespoons lemon gelatin (about half of a 3-ounce package)

1 teaspoon lemon extract

3 large eggs

½ cup almond milk

Coconut Palm Sugar

Most recipes in this book that call for sugar can be made with coconut palm sugar instead. Palm sugar has a lower glycemic index than white table sugar, which means it doesn't digest in the body as quickly as cane sugar and therefore doesn't create a large spike of insulin in the body while it's being digested.

1. Preheat oven to 350°F. Line a 12-cup muffin pan with paper liners.
2. In a large mixing bowl whisk together flour, arrowroot starch, salt, baking soda, coconut palm sugar, grated nutmeg, poppy seeds, and gelatin.
3. In a smaller bowl whisk together the lemon extract, eggs, and almond milk. Pour wet ingredients into dry ingredients and whisk until thoroughly combined. Pour batter into muffin pan.
4. Bake for 18–20 minutes until golden-brown or until a toothpick inserted in the middle of a cupcake comes out clean.
5. Allow to cool in pan for 10 minutes then transfer to a wire rack until completely cool.
6. If desired, make a lemon glaze by whisking together 3 tablespoons fresh lemon juice, 1 tablespoon fresh lemon zest, scrapings from 1 vanilla bean pod, 4 tablespoons honey, and 2 tablespoons melted coconut oil. Drizzle over cooled muffins.

Cinnamon Bun Muffins

Do you miss the big, sweet swirl of a cinnamon bun? These muffins carry all the amazing flavor, but with less sugar, fat, and refined flours than a traditional cinnamon bun.

INGREDIENTS | SERVES 12

Muffins
1 cup blanched almond flour
2 tablespoons coconut flour
¼ teaspoon baking soda
¼ teaspoon sea salt
½ cup coconut palm sugar
¼ teaspoon ground cinnamon
½ cup unsweetened applesauce
3 large eggs
1 tablespoon vanilla extract

Cinnamon Swirl
¼ cup coconut palm sugar
1 tablespoon ground cinnamon
2 tablespoons melted butter or coconut oil

1. Preheat oven to 350°F. Line a muffin pan with 12 paper liners and grease with butter, coconut oil, or nonstick cooking spray.
2. In a large bowl whisk together the almond flour, coconut flour, baking soda, salt, ½ cup coconut palm sugar, and ¼ teaspoon cinnamon. In a smaller bowl whisk together the applesauce, eggs, and vanilla. Mix the wet ingredients into the dry ingredients until you have a thick, but smooth batter. Fill each paper liner ⅔ full with batter.
3. In another small bowl whisk together cinnamon swirl ingredients. Spoon 1½ teaspoons of mixture over each muffin. Use a toothpick or a knife to gently swirl the cinnamon and sugar over the top of the batter.
4. Bake for 25–30 minutes until the tops of the muffins are golden-brown and a toothpick inserted in the middle comes out mostly clean with just a small amount of crumbs.
5. Cool for 10–15 minutes before serving.

Almond Flour Loaf Bread

Many people miss sandwich bread when they cannot eat grains or gluten.
This high-protein sandwich bread is supplemented with ground flaxseeds.

INGREDIENTS | YIELDS 1 (7½" × 3½")
LOAF

1½ cups blanched almond flour

¾ cup arrowroot starch or tapioca starch

¼ cup ground flaxseeds

½ teaspoon sea salt

½ teaspoon baking soda

4 large eggs

1 teaspoon honey

1 teaspoon apple cider vinegar

Pan Size Matters

When baking gluten-free recipes of any kind, use the correct pan size listed if you can. It's especially important in bread and cake recipes. For this almond flour loaf, the bread will rise much higher in a 7½" × 3½" loaf pan than it would in a larger loaf pan. The pan used for testing this recipe is available at this website: *http://ow.ly/kUrZ3.*

1. Preheat oven to 350°F. Grease loaf pan generously with olive oil or nonstick cooking spray and set aside.
2. In a medium-sized mixing bowl whisk together almond flour, arrowroot starch, flaxseeds, salt, and baking soda.
3. In a smaller bowl whisk together eggs, honey, and vinegar.
4. Pour wet ingredients into dry ingredients and stir until you have a wet batter. Pour batter into loaf pan. Bake for 30–35 minutes until a toothpick inserted into the middle of the loaf comes out clean.
5. Allow bread to cool in pan for 5 minutes, then move to a wire rack to cool completely. Wait until bread has cooled completely before slicing with a sharp, serrated bread knife.

Almond Flour Irish Soda Bread

This loaf is fun to make and attractive, and has just a hint of sweetness.
Feel free to vary seasonings and add-ins for a different flavor.

INGREDIENTS | YIELDS 1 (8" OR 9")
ROUND LOAF

2 cups blanched almond flour

¾ cup arrowroot starch or tapioca starch

1½ teaspoons baking soda

¼ teaspoon sea salt

¼ teaspoon caraway seeds

½ cup raisins

2 large eggs

2 tablespoons honey

1 tablespoon apple cider vinegar

1 tablespoon water

1 large egg white mixed with 1 tablespoon warm water

Coarse gray sea salt (optional)

Alternatives

Instead of using raisins and caraway seeds, try these alternatives: For a Greek-inspired loaf use ½ cup chopped and seeded kalamata olives with 1–2 teaspoons crushed rosemary; for an Italian-inspired loaf use ¾ cup finely chopped sun-dried tomatoes and 3 teaspoons julienned fresh basil.

1. Preheat oven to 350°F. Line an 8" cake pan with parchment paper and then grease with olive oil or nonstick cooking spray.
2. In a large bowl whisk together almond flour, arrowroot starch, baking soda, sea salt, caraway seeds, and raisins. In a smaller bowl whisk together eggs, honey, vinegar, and water. Mix the wet ingredients into the dry ingredients and stir together until you have a thick dough.
3. Wet your hands with olive oil or water and pour the dough into pan. Shape the dough gently with your wet hands into a pretty round loaf. Using a very sharp, serrated knife, gently slice a cross into the top of the loaf.
4. Lightly brush the top of the loaf with the egg white and warm water mixture. Bake for 25 minutes until a toothpick inserted in the center of the loaf comes out clean. Sprinkle with coarse gray sea salt, if desired.
5. Allow the bread to cool for 10 minutes in the pan and then transfer to a wire rack to finish cooling completely. Slice bread and serve with butter.

Rosemary Basil Crackers or Crispy Pizza Crust

This versatile recipe can make crispy, crunchy crackers or a cracker-like pizza crust. Either is delicious and incredibly easy to make.

INGREDIENTS | YIELDS 1 (12") PIZZA CRUST OR 30–40 SMALL CRACKERS

1¾ cups blanched almond flour

½ teaspoon sea salt

1 teaspoon dried, crushed rosemary

1 teaspoon dried basil

2 tablespoons olive oil

1 large egg or equivalent egg replacer

Additional blanched almond flour, for rolling out dough

1. Preheat oven to 350°F.
2. In a medium mixing bowl whisk together blanched almond flour, sea salt, dried rosemary, and dried basil. Whisk together. Make a well in the center of dry ingredients and add olive oil and egg.
3. Mix egg and olive oil into the dry ingredients thoroughly until you have a stiff dough.
4. Place a 12" × 16" sheet of parchment paper on a large baking sheet. Lightly sprinkle blanched almond flour over the parchment paper and place the dough in the middle, on top of flour. Place a sheet of plastic wrap gently over the dough as a barrier between the dough and the rolling pin. Roll to ¼" thickness or roughly into a 10" × 14" rectangle. Score crackers by gently rolling a pizza cutter over the dough in a crisscross pattern to create about 30–40 (1") squares. For a pizza crust, roll into an 11" × 11" circle.
5. For crackers: Bake for 12–15 minutes until crackers are lightly golden-brown around the edges. Remove from oven and allow to cool for 20 minutes before breaking into individual crackers. Cool completely on the parchment paper and store any leftover crackers in an airtight container for up to 1 week on the counter. Baked crackers will freeze well for up to 2 months in an airtight container.
6. For pizza: Pre-bake crust for 10 minutes until it's just crispy. Add toppings and bake an additional 10–12 minutes until toppings have heated through. Allow to cool for 5 minutes and then cut and serve with salad.

Thick and Chewy Almond Flour Pizza Crust

This pizza crust has a secret ingredient! In addition to almond flour, this recipe contains mashed white beans for extra protein and fiber. The beans give the dough a great texture.

INGREDIENTS | YIELDS 2 (12"–14") PIZZA CRUSTS

2 cups blanched almond flour

½ teaspoon sea salt

¼ teaspoon baking soda

1 teaspoon dried oregano

1 teaspoon garlic powder

1 teaspoon basil

¾ cup mashed white beans, such as navy beans or cannellini beans

3 large eggs

3 tablespoons olive oil

Focaccia

To make a thick focaccia bread instead of pizza dough, spread dough on a large baking sheet lined with parchment paper. Wet your hands with water or olive oil and make small indentations across dough with your thumbs and fingers. Add sun-dried tomatoes, olives, fresh garlic, and herbs over the dough and drizzle with olive oil. Bake for 15–20 minutes until golden-brown.

1. Preheat oven to 350°F. Line 2 (12") round pizza pans with parchment paper.
2. In a large bowl mix almond flour, sea salt, baking soda, oregano, garlic powder, and basil together. In a small bowl mix together beans, eggs, and olive oil. Mix the wet and dry ingredients together thoroughly. You will have a very wet dough.
3. Spread the dough in pizza pan with a spatula. It may help to wet the spatula with water or spritz it with nonstick cooking spray to keep the dough from sticking.
4. Prebake the dough for 12–15 minutes until golden-brown. Add toppings and bake an additional 10–15 minutes until toppings are cooked through or melted.
5. Cool pizza for about 5 minutes and serve.

Almond Flour Chicken Pot Pie

This savory pie is topped with almond flour pastry dough. If you prefer, you can make a batch of the Grain-Free "Buttermilk" Biscuits in this chapter and top the pie with that instead.

INGREDIENTS | SERVES 6–8

Filling
2 tablespoons olive oil

⅓ cup blanched almond flour or 3 tablespoons arrowroot starch

½ teaspoon sea salt

1 teaspoon ground pepper

2 cups gluten-free chicken broth (or the broth from cooking the chicken)

2½ cups cooked chicken (or the cooked meat from a small roasted chicken)

1 (15-ounce) can peas and carrots, drained

Pastry
1½ cups blanched almond flour

¼ teaspoon sea salt

2 tablespoons olive oil

1 large egg, beaten

Orange Sesame Vinaigrette

A heavy meal like chicken pot pie needs a light side dish or first course, and a simple green salad is a great choice. To top the salad, make a homemade orange sesame vinaigrette by adding the following to a glass jar: ½ cup orange juice, 3 tablespoons olive oil, 1 tablespoon sesame oil, 1 tablespoon honey, and freshly ground salt and pepper. Cover jar and shake vigorously to combine. Drizzle a few tablespoons of vinaigrette over each salad.

1. Preheat oven to 350°F. Grease a 9" deep dish pie pan with olive oil or nonstick cooking spray.
2. In a large saucepan heat olive oil over medium heat. Add almond flour or arrowroot starch to the butter. Stir and cook for several minutes. Add salt, pepper, and chicken broth. Stir until the broth has thickened into a sauce that will coat the back of a spoon. Stir in the chicken and vegetables. Pour the filling into pie pan.
3. Make the pastry: In a medium bowl stir together almond flour and salt. Mix in the olive oil and the egg until you have a thick dough. Place the dough between two sheets of parchment paper or plastic wrap that have been dusted with arrowroot starch. Roll into a 9" circle (about ¼" thick). Gently place pastry over the chicken filling. It doesn't have to be perfect and you can patch the dough as necessary. If you have extra dough, you can roll it out and cut with cookie cutters into small stars or leaves.
4. Place pan on a cookie sheet to prevent spills while baking. Bake for 30–40 minutes until the crust is golden-brown and the sauce is bubbling up around the sides. Let the pot pie rest for at least 10 minutes before serving.

Crustless Kale and Bacon Quiche

This lovely and super-easy quiche makes a beautiful dish that's fancy enough for company.

INGREDIENTS | SERVES 4

5 large eggs

1 (15-ounce) can coconut milk

½ teaspoon sea salt

½ teaspoon freshly ground pepper

6 ounces bacon or turkey bacon

1–2 tablespoons olive oil

1 sweet onion, diced

3 cups fresh kale, rinsed, dried, and chopped

½ cup sun-dried tomatoes, chopped

Use What You Have on Hand

Don't have bacon? Use ½ pound of bulk sausage or ground beef. Don't have kale? Use a bag of fresh baby spinach instead. Don't have sun-dried tomatoes? Use a chopped red bell pepper instead. Don't need to worry about dairy? Add ½ cup shredded Cheddar or mozzarella to the whisked eggs.

1. Preheat oven to 350°F. Grease a 9" deep dish pie pan with nonstick cooking spray or olive oil.
2. In a large bowl whisk together eggs, coconut milk, salt, and pepper. Set aside.
3. In a large, heavy-bottomed skillet cook bacon on medium-high heat, until it's as crispy as you desire. Remove from pan and drain on a plate lined with paper towels.
4. Remove and discard most of the bacon fat from the pan, reserving about a tablespoon. Add olive oil to the pan and heat 1–2 minutes until sizzling. Add onion and cook for 3–5 minutes over medium-high heat until translucent. Add kale and cook for 3–4 minutes until bright green and slightly wilted.
5. Crumble bacon and sprinkle over the bottom of the pie pan. Add cooked onion, chopped sun-dried tomatoes, and kale to pan and spread around evenly. Pour egg mixture over cooked ingredients. Place the pie pan on a large cookie sheet to catch spills while baking.
6. Bake for 35–45 minutes until the center of the quiche is set and a knife inserted in the middle comes out clean. Allow quiche to cool for 10–15 minutes before serving.

Grain-Free "Corn Bread"

If you need a quick bread to serve with dinner or a hot bowl of soup, this is the perfect recipe.
This bread is best the day it's made, but it's perfect for stuffing by day two.

INGREDIENTS | SERVES 9

1½ cups blanched almond flour

⅓ cup arrowroot starch or tapioca starch

⅓ cup plus 1 tablespoon coconut flour

½ teaspoon baking soda

½ teaspoon sea salt

¾ cup almond milk or coconut milk

¼ cup butter or coconut oil, melted

3 large eggs

3 tablespoons honey or coconut palm sugar

1. Preheat oven to 350°F. Line an 8" × 8" baking dish with parchment paper and grease with olive oil or nonstick cooking spray.
2. In a large bowl whisk together blanched almond flour, arrowroot starch, coconut flour, baking soda, and sea salt.
3. Make a well in the center of the dry ingredients and add milk, melted butter, eggs, and honey. Gently stir wet ingredients into dry ingredients until you have a thick batter. Pour batter into baking dish.
4. Bake for 20–25 minutes until golden-brown and a toothpick inserted in the middle comes out clean. Cool in pan for 5–10 minutes and serve warm with butter or coconut oil and jam.

What Can You Substitute for Coconut Flour?

Coconut flour is a magical and unique ingredient. It is extremely porous, meaning it soaks up liquids like a sponge. This property makes it hard to replace with another ingredient in recipes. To make a plain almond flour bread, mix together 1½ cups blanched almond flour, ½ teaspoon baking soda, ½ teaspoon salt, 4 tablespoons honey, and 4 eggs. Place in a greased 8" × 8" baking dish. Bake 25 minutes at 350°F until golden-brown and a toothpick inserted in the middle comes out clean.

Grain-Free Holiday Stuffing or Dressing

Thanksgiving wouldn't be complete without stuffing on the table. The key to a really good gluten-free stuffing is finding or making a gluten-free bread that is very dry and somewhat dense.

INGREDIENTS | SERVES 6–8

6–8 cups toasted, cubed Grain-Free "Corn Bread" (see recipe in this chapter) or Almond Flour Loaf Bread (see recipe in this chapter)

¼–½ cup butter, olive oil, or coconut oil

1 cup finely diced onion

1 cup sliced and finely diced celery

1–2 teaspoons salt

1–2 teaspoons pepper

1–2 tablespoons poultry seasoning

1 pound gluten-free mild sausage (optional)

2½ cups gluten-free chicken broth

Gluten-Free Bread—Is It Worth the Expense?

Store-bought gluten-free bread is expensive and grain-free bread can be nearly impossible to get. It's less expensive to buy gluten-free, grain-free baking ingredients but either way you're spending more money than you would for wheat bread. If you plan on keeping gluten-free bread in your diet (and sometimes that sandwich is just worth it!), save leftover bread in a zip-top plastic bag in your freezer for recipes like this.

1. Preheat oven to 350°F. Line a large 9" × 13" baking dish with parchment paper or foil. Grease pan with nonstick cooking spray or olive oil.
2. Place "corn bread" in a large bowl and set aside.
3. Melt butter in a large pan on the stovetop. When warm and sizzling, add onions and celery. Sauté for 5–6 minutes until onions are translucent. Add salt, pepper, and poultry seasoning. Pour mixture over bread cubes in bowl.
4. If using sausage, add to pan, break into small pieces, and brown for 6–8 minutes until completely cooked through. Pour sausage into stuffing mixture. Stir together thoroughly. Pour stuffing into baking dish. Slowly add chicken broth to bread cube mixture. If you like a moist dressing, add additional chicken broth until desired consistency.
5. Bake stuffing covered with foil for 30 minutes. Remove foil and bake an additional 15 minutes until stuffing is crispy and golden-brown on top.

Almond Flour Savory Crescent Rolls

*This versatile almond flour pastry makes delicious crescent rolls,
pie crusts, or personal-size sweet hand pies.*

INGREDIENTS | SERVES 16

3 cups blanched almond flour

¼ teaspoon baking soda

½ teaspoon sea salt

4 tablespoons cold butter (cut into cubes), or chilled coconut oil

1 teaspoon honey

2 large eggs

Apple Spice Hand Pies

In a medium bowl mix together 3 peeled, cored, and diced apples; ½ teaspoon cinnamon; ¼ teaspoon nutmeg; ⅓ cup brown sugar. Mix and roll out pastry as directed. Cut pastry into 4–6" circles using a cookie cutter. Place 2 tablespoons apple filling on one side of each circle, leaving ½". Fold other half of dough over filling and crimp edges closed with a fork. Brush a little melted butter or coconut oil on top of each pie and sprinkle with cinnamon and sugar. Bake 15–20 minutes until pies are golden-brown. Allow to cool 10–15 minutes before eating.

1. Preheat oven to 400°F. Line a large cookie sheet with parchment paper and set aside.
2. In a large bowl whisk together almond flour, baking soda, and salt. Cut in butter or coconut oil with a pastry blender, until it resembles small peas throughout mixture. Make a well in the center of the dry ingredients and add the honey and eggs. Stir the wet ingredients into the dry ingredients until you have a stiff dough.
3. Shape dough into two large balls. Refrigerate the balls 10–15 minutes before using. Sprinkle additional blanched almond flour onto parchment paper or plastic wrap to help keep the dough from sticking. Place the dough on floured surface. Top with a sheet of parchment paper or plastic wrap and roll out into a 12" circle. Using a pizza cutter, cut into 8 triangles.
4. Roll up triangles starting from the wide end to the point, so they look like crescent rolls. Place each roll about 2" apart on baking sheet. If desired, brush rolls with melted butter or coconut oil.
5. Bake for 12–15 minutes until golden-brown and slightly puffy.

Savory Coconut Flour Popovers

Popovers are sort of a cross between muffins and pancakes, in a baked form. This savory bread is super easy to make and pretty when taken right from the oven to the table for dinner.

INGREDIENTS | SERVES 6

4 large eggs, room temperature
½ cup almond milk
½ teaspoon sea salt
2 tablespoons coconut flour

1. Preheat oven to 400°F. Place a 12-cup muffin tin in the oven while it's preheating to get it very hot.
2. In a large bowl whisk eggs, milk, salt, and coconut flour, just until bubbly. You don't want to break up the protein in the eggs too much.
3. When the oven has reached the correct temperature, carefully remove the muffin tin with oven mitts. Grease the muffin pan with nonstick cooking spray or brush with olive oil. Fill pan ⅔ full with batter. Place in oven immediately and bake for a full 25 minutes without opening the oven door.
4. Remove pan from oven after 25 minutes and prick the popovers with a sharp knife in the middle to allow the steam to escape. Allow popovers to cool for about 5 minutes and then serve hot with butter or coconut oil and jam.

Banana Walnut Bread

This bread is sweetened only with bananas. Add up to ¼ cup honey or coconut palm sugar if you prefer your bread a bit sweeter.

INGREDIENTS | YIELDS 1 (8½" × 4 ½") LOAF

2¼ cups blanched almond flour

¾ cup arrowroot starch or tapioca starch

¼ teaspoon sea salt

1¼ teaspoons baking soda

2 tablespoons melted butter or coconut oil

½ teaspoon apple cider vinegar

3 large eggs

2 cups mashed bananas (about 4 medium)

½ cup chopped walnuts

1. Preheat oven to 350°F. Heavily grease an 8½" × 4½" loaf pan with nonstick cooking spray or olive oil.
2. In a large bowl whisk together the almond flour, arrowroot starch, sea salt, and baking soda. Make a well in the center of the dry ingredients and add butter, vinegar, eggs, and bananas. Mix the wet ingredients into the dry ingredients until you have a thick batter. Fold chopped walnuts into the batter.
3. Pour batter into the greased loaf pan. Smooth the top of the loaf with a spatula dipped in water.
4. Bake for 40–50 minutes until a toothpick inserted in the center of the loaf comes out clean and the top of the bread is golden-brown. Allow to cool in pan for 10 minutes, then place loaf on a wire rack to cool completely. Slice and serve.

Carrot Cake Bread

This is a very lightly sweetened, low-glycemic version of carrot cake.
This bread would be a perfect breakfast on weekday mornings, sliced, toasted
and spread lightly with cream cheese or your favorite low sugar jam.

INGREDIENTS | YIELDS 2 (7½" × 3½")
LOAVES

2¼ cups blanched almond flour

¾ cup arrowroot starch or tapioca starch

½ teaspoon ground cinnamon

¼ teaspoon sea salt

1¼ teaspoons baking soda

2 tablespoons melted butter or coconut oil

¾ cup coconut palm sugar or brown sugar

3 large eggs

2 cups shredded carrots

½ cup almond milk or other nondairy milk

½ teaspoon apple cider vinegar

½ cup raisins (optional)

1. Preheat oven to 350°F. Heavily grease two 7½" × 3½" loaf pans with nonstick cooking spray or olive oil.
2. In a medium bowl whisk together blanched almond flour, arrowroot starch, ground cinnamon, sea salt, and baking soda. Set aside. In a large bowl mix together butter or coconut oil, coconut palm sugar or brown sugar, eggs, carrots, almond milk, and apple cider vinegar. Stir the whisked dry ingredients into the wet ingredients. Fold in the raisins, if desired.
3. Divide the batter evenly between the two pans. Bake for 35–40 minutes until a toothpick inserted in the middle comes out clean and the tops of the loaves are golden brown.
4. Allow loaves to cool on a wire rack for one hour before slicing and serving. Wrap leftover bread in plastic wrap and store in zip-top bags in the freezer for up to one month.

Chocolate Glazed Doughnuts

Just because you're eating grain-free doesn't mean you should give up doughnuts. This recipe uses honey as the sweetener. You can use coconut palm sugar if you prefer.

INGREDIENTS | SERVES 4–5

1¼ cups blanched almond flour

2 tablespoons cocoa powder

¼ teaspoon sea salt

¼ teaspoon baking soda

½ teaspoon ground cinnamon

2 large eggs

¼ cup melted butter, coconut oil, or light-tasting olive oil

4 tablespoons honey

½ teaspoon vanilla extract

Quick Chocolate Icing

In a microwave-safe bowl mix together ½ cup chocolate chips with a high cocoa content and 1½ tablespoons coconut oil. Melt on high power for 15 seconds at a time until chips are melted and can be whisked together with oil. Dip each doughnut into chocolate glaze and set on parchment paper to cool completely. Add toasted chopped nuts or unsweetened flaked coconut as a garnish on each doughnut.

1. Preheat oven to 350°F. Heavily grease a large doughnut pan with nonstick cooking spray or light-tasting olive oil.

2. In a large bowl whisk together almond flour, cocoa powder, sea salt, baking soda, and cinnamon. Make a well in the center of the dry ingredients and add eggs, butter, honey, and vanilla. Stir the wet ingredients into the dry ingredients until you have a thick dough.

3. Spoon the dough evenly into 4–5 doughnut circles in pan. You can also put the dough into a zip-top plastic bag, cut off a 1" tip at an edge of the bag, and pipe the dough into pan.

4. Bake for 10–12 minutes until doughnuts are dark brown and a toothpick inserted in the middle comes out clean. Do not over bake as these doughnuts can dry out quickly. Glaze with chocolate icing, if desired.

Almond Cranberry Biscotti

This lightly sweetened adult cookie is perfect with a hot cup of coffee or tea.
Change the flavors by adding ½ teaspoon each of ground nutmeg and ground cinnamon,
and 2 teaspoons pure vanilla extract in place of the almond extract and cranberries.

INGREDIENTS | YIELDS 24 COOKIES

3 cups blanched almond flour

½ cup coconut palm sugar

¼ teaspoon sea salt

1 teaspoon baking soda

¾ cup dried cranberries

¾ cup toasted, sliced almonds

¼ cup melted butter, coconut oil, or light-tasting olive oil

2 large eggs

1 teaspoon pure almond extract

3 tablespoons cold water

1. Preheat oven to 350°F. Line two large baking sheets with parchment paper. Set aside.
2. In a large bowl whisk together almond flour, coconut palm sugar, sea salt, baking soda, dried cranberries, and sliced almonds.
3. In a smaller bowl whisk together butter, eggs, almond extract, and cold water. Pour the wet ingredients into the dry ingredients and stir together until you have a thick dough.
4. Shape the dough into 2 (9" × 3") logs and place them on one baking sheet. Bake for 25–30 minutes until the logs are golden-brown around the edges. Allow the logs to cool for 1 hour on the baking sheet.
5. Once the logs are completely cool move them to a cutting board and using a very sharp, serrated knife, slice each log into 12 diagonal cookies. Place the cookies back on the baking sheets and bake for 15–18 minutes until very crisp.
6. Cool the cookies on the baking sheets 30 minutes, and then serve. Cookies can be stored in an airtight container on the counter for up to 1 week. These cookies also freeze well for up to 2 months.

Grain-Free Chocolate Chunk Cookies

This recipe was inspired by a series of chocolate chunk cookie recipes posted by Brittany Angell, author of the blog Real Sustenance.

INGREDIENTS | YIELDS 12–15 COOKIES

2 cups blanched almond flour

½ cup coconut palm sugar

3 tablespoons arrowroot starch or tapioca starch

½ teaspoon baking soda

2 heaping tablespoons ground flaxseeds (optional)

¼ teaspoon sea salt

3 tablespoons Spectrum Palm Shortening or butter

1 tablespoon vanilla extract

1 teaspoon almond extract

3–4 tablespoons almond milk or water, as needed

1 (3½-ounce) 70% dark chocolate bar, chopped into chunks

A Few Tips

Do not try to make these cookies with leftover almond pulp from homemade almond milk. It doesn't work—the pulp is too wet and doesn't set up while baking. Instead of coconut palm sugar you can use regular sugar, brown sugar, or honey in these cookies.

1. Preheat oven to 350°F. Line a large cookie sheet with parchment paper or a Silpat mat.
2. In a large bowl whisk together almond flour, coconut palm sugar, arrowroot starch, baking soda, flaxseeds (if using), and salt. Cut shortening or butter into dry ingredients with a pastry blender or a knife and fork until shortening resembles very small peas evenly throughout the dry ingredients.
3. Make a well in the center of the dry ingredients and add the vanilla extract, almond extract, and 3 tablespoons of almond milk. Using a little elbow grease, stir the wet ingredients into the dry ingredients until you have a very thick batter (it might be a bit crumbly).
4. This may take several minutes to incorporate well. If necessary, use an additional tablespoon of almond milk, but don't add too much milk or the cookies will not turn out right. Fold in the chopped chocolate chunks and evenly mix through the dough. Scoop the dough into golf ball–sized mounds and place on cookie sheet about 2" apart. Flatten lightly and shape with your hands into round cookies.
5. Bake for 12–15 minutes depending on how crispy you want your cookies. The edges should be golden-brown when done. Store leftovers in an airtight container on the counter or in the fridge for 2–3 days. These cookies are best the day they are made.

Honey Sesame Cookies

These lightly sweetened cookies are made with sesame seeds that toast as they bake, creating a nutty crunch. These cookies are also egg-free and can easily be made vegan by using maple syrup instead of honey.

INGREDIENTS | YIELDS 2 DOZEN COOKIES

1¼ cups blanched almond flour

¼ teaspoon sea salt

½ teaspoon baking soda

⅓ cup honey

⅓ cup roasted tahini (sesame seed butter)

1 tablespoon butter or Spectrum Palm Shortening

1 tablespoon vanilla extract

¼ cup toasted sesame seeds

A Sunny Variation

You can also make these cookies with Sunbutter, a sunflower seed butter, which is a great crunchy alternative to sesame seed–based tahini. For the outer coating instead of using sesame seeds, roughly chop ⅓ cup sunflower seeds and roll cookies in them before baking.

1. Preheat oven to 350°F. Line a large cookie sheet with parchment paper or a Silpat mat.
2. In a medium mixing bowl whisk together almond flour, sea salt, and baking soda.
3. In a smaller bowl mix together honey, tahini, butter or shortening, and vanilla extract. Stir the wet ingredients into the dry ingredients. Roll the dough into 1" balls. Roll the balls in sesame seeds and place 1" apart on cookie sheet.
4. Using the palm of your hand, gently flatten the cookies. Bake for 8–10 minutes until they are golden-brown and have the scent of toasted sesame seeds. Cool for 5 minutes on the pan and then transfer to a wire rack to cool completely. Store leftover cookies in an airtight container for up to 5 days.

Low Sugar Cocoa Nib Cookies

Cocoa nibs are a healthy low-sugar, dairy-free replacement for chocolate chips. They are basically hulled, roasted and chopped pure cocoa beans. As the primary ingredient in chocolate, these chopped cocoa beans add delicious flavor and crunch to these low-sugar cookies. Cocoa nibs can be purchased online: http://ow.ly/lbEz6.

INGREDIENTS | YIELDS 2 DOZEN COOKIES

1½ cups blanched almond flour

¼ cup arrowroot starch

½ teaspoon baking soda

¼ teaspoon sea salt

1 egg

⅓ cup honey or maple syrup

2 tablespoons softened coconut oil or butter

1 teaspoon pure vanilla extract

¼ cup raw cocoa nibs

1. Preheat oven to 350°F. Line a cookie sheet with parchment paper or a Silpat mat.
2. In a large bowl whisk together almond flour, arrowroot starch, baking soda, and sea salt. Whisk together thoroughly and then make a well in the center of the dry ingredients.
3. Add the egg, honey, softened coconut oil, and vanilla extract into the center of the dry ingredients. Stir the wet ingredients into the dry ingredients to create a sticky cookie dough. Fold in the raw cocoa nibs.
4. Drop cookie dough by tablespoons and place 2" apart onto the lined cookie sheet. Bake for 8–9 minutes until cookies are golden brown. The cookies will be soft and almost cake-like in texture. Allow cookies to cool on the pan for 10–15 minutes and then store in an airtight container on the counter for up to 5 days.

Cinnamon Peach Crisp

A fruit crisp is such an easy dessert to make, and using almond flour makes it even easier because you don't need several flours to create the texture and flavor you want.

INGREDIENTS | SERVES 6–8

1½ cups blanched almond flour

¼ cup coconut palm sugar or brown sugar

1 teaspoon ground cinnamon

½ teaspoon freshly grated nutmeg

¼ teaspoon sea salt

3 tablespoons butter or coconut oil

7–8 medium peaches, peeled, seeded, and sliced (or a 28-ounce can sliced peaches, drained)

3 tablespoons orange juice or apple juice (not necessary if using canned peaches)

1. Preheat oven to 350°F. Grease a 2- or 3-quart casserole dish or an 8" pie plate with nonstick cooking spray or light-tasting olive oil.
2. In a small bowl mix together flour, sugar, cinnamon, nutmeg, and salt. Cut in butter or coconut oil with a pastry blender or with a knife and fork until the mixture is crumbly.
3. Place the peaches in greased casserole dish. Stir in the juice. Sprinkle flour mixture over peaches.
4. Bake for 30–40 minutes until the top is golden-brown and the peaches are starting to bubble around the edges of the dish.

Grain-Free Apple Spice Cupcakes

These down-to-earth cupcakes are perfect for an on-the-go breakfast or a 3 P.M. pick-me-up.

INGREDIENTS | SERVES 12

3 cups blanched almond flour

¾ cup coconut palm sugar

1 teaspoon baking soda

1 teaspoon ground cinnamon

1 teaspoon freshly grated nutmeg

½ teaspoon ground ginger

¼ teaspoon ground cardamom (optional)

¼ teaspoon ground cloves

3 large eggs

¾ cup unsweetened applesauce

3 tablespoons light-tasting olive oil or melted coconut oil

2 tablespoons honey

½ teaspoon apple cider vinegar

1 tablespoon vanilla extract

1. Preheat oven to 350°F. Line a muffin pan with paper liners and grease with nonstick cooking spray or light-tasting olive oil; set aside.
2. Whisk together almond flour, coconut palm sugar, baking soda, and spices in a large bowl and set aside. In another bowl mix together eggs, applesauce, oil, honey, vinegar, and vanilla. Mix wet ingredients into dry ingredients. Do not over mix.
3. Spoon batter into muffin pans until they are at least ¾ full.
4. Bake for 18–25 minutes until a toothpick inserted in the middle comes out clean. Let cupcakes cool on a wire rack. Frost with homemade grain-free vanilla icing, if desired. Store in airtight container in refrigerator as these cupcakes are quite moist.

Almond Flour Devil's Food Cake

This rich chocolate cake is perfect for birthday parties. The recipe also makes 12 regular-sized cupcakes; bake for 18–25 minutes until a toothpick inserted in the middle comes out clean.

INGREDIENTS | SERVES 8–10

Cake

2 cups blanched almond flour

½ cup dark cocoa powder

1¼ cups coconut palm sugar

1 teaspoon baking soda

¼ teaspoon sea salt

3 large eggs

¾ cup unsweetened applesauce or plain pumpkin purée

½ cup water

¼ cup light-tasting olive oil or melted coconut oil

½ teaspoon apple cider vinegar

1 tablespoon vanilla extract

¼ teaspoon pure almond extract

½ cup mini chocolate chips (optional)

Cream Filling

¼ cup chocolate chips

¾ cup heavy cream or coconut cream

1 teaspoon vanilla

Ganache Glaze

4 tablespoons butter or coconut oil

4 ounces unsweetened chocolate

¼ cup chocolate chips

1 tablespoon honey

1. Preheat oven to 350°F. Line an 8" or 9" cake pan with parchment paper and then grease with nonstick cooking spray or light-tasting olive oil.
2. In a large bowl whisk together almond flour, cocoa powder, sugar, baking soda, and salt.
3. In a smaller bowl whisk together eggs, applesauce, water, oil, vinegar, vanilla, and almond extract. Mix the wet ingredients into the dry ingredients until you have a thick batter. If desired, fold in ½ cup mini chocolate chips.
4. Pour the batter into cake pan. Bake for 25–35 minutes until a toothpick inserted in the middle comes out clean and the cake is a deep chocolate brown. Allow cake to cool in pan for 10 minutes. Turn cake out onto a wire rack and continue to cool for an additional 40 minutes to 1 hour.
5. Make cream filling: Melt chocolate chips in a double boiler or the microwave. In another bowl whip heavy cream or coconut cream until light and airy. Fold in vanilla and the melted chocolate.
6. Make chocolate ganache: Melt butter or coconut oil with unsweetened chocolate, chocolate chips, and honey. Stir together until thoroughly melted.
7. To assemble cake, slice in half and spread chocolate cream filling in the center. Place the other half of cake on top of the cream filling and slowly pour the chocolate ganache over the cake. Place cake in fridge until ready to serve.

Coconut Flour Yellow Cake with Creamy White Frosting

*This light, fluffy cake is made primarily with coconut flour, a good option
for people who need to be grain-free, but cannot tolerate almonds.*

INGREDIENTS | SERVES 8–10

Cake

¾ cup sifted coconut flour

¾ teaspoon baking soda

⅛ teaspoon sea salt

½ cup coconut palm sugar

6 tablespoons melted butter or coconut oil

3 large eggs

1 cup almond milk, coconut milk, or hemp milk

1 tablespoon vanilla extract

½ teaspoon apple cider vinegar

Frosting

1 cup unsalted Sunbutter (sunflower seed butter)

1 cup Spectrum Palm Shortening

⅓ cup maple syrup or coconut palm sugar

1. Preheat oven to 350°F. Line an 8" or 9" cake pan with parchment paper and then grease with nonstick cooking spray or light-tasting olive oil.
2. In a large bowl whisk together coconut flour, baking soda, salt, and coconut palm sugar. In a smaller bowl mix together butter, eggs, almond milk, vanilla extract, and vinegar. Pour wet ingredients into dry ingredients and mix until you have a thick batter.
3. Pour batter into the cake pan. Spread batter evenly in the pan with a rubber spatula that's been dipped in water or spritzed with nonstick cooking spray, to get a rounded cake top.
4. Bake for 25–35 minutes until the cake is golden-brown and a toothpick inserted in the middle comes out clean. Be careful not to over bake as coconut flour can dry out quickly.
5. Mix together all frosting ingredients. Blend on high for 1–2 minutes until thick and creamy. Refrigerate for 10 minutes before using to frost cake.
6. Frost top and sides of cake. You can easily make this a 2-layer cake by slicing it through the middle to create 2 smaller layers.

Peanut Butter Chocolate Chip Cupcakes

When I visited relatives who didn't have any gluten-free baking supplies on hand, I used peanut butter, sugar, and eggs to create these gluten-free cupcakes. Now they are one of my favorites.

INGREDIENTS | SERVES 15–18

⅔ cup coconut palm sugar

1 teaspoon baking soda

1¼ cups creamy natural peanut butter

4 large eggs

¼ cup water

½ teaspoon apple cider vinegar

1 tablespoon vanilla extract

¼ cup mini chocolate chips

1. Preheat oven to 350°F. Line cupcake pans with paper liners and then grease with nonstick cooking spray or light-tasting olive oil.
2. In a medium-sized bowl mix together sugar and baking soda. Add peanut butter and cream together.
3. In another medium bowl whisk together the eggs, water, vinegar, and vanilla. Pour the egg mixture into the peanut butter mixture and mix together with a fork until it's very creamy and light.
4. Spoon batter into paper liners until they are no more than ½–¾ full. These cupcakes definitely need room to rise!
5. Lightly sprinkle a few mini chocolate chips on top of the cupcakes and place in the preheated oven. Bake for 15–18 minutes until golden-brown and a toothpick inserted in the middle of a cupcake comes out clean.
6. Allow the cupcakes to cool for about 20 minutes on a wire rack before serving. Cupcakes may deflate slightly as they cool. They are delicious hot or cold. Store leftovers in an airtight container in the refrigerator for up to 5 days.

Honey Pumpkin Pie

This is a low-maintenance, simple, and comforting pumpkin pie for the holidays.
You'll never miss the gluten, grains, dairy, or sugar.

INGREDIENTS | SERVES 8–10

Crust

1½ cups blanched almond flour or finely crushed pecans

¼ teaspoon sea salt

4 tablespoons Spectrum Palm Shortening

Pumpkin Filling

1 (15-ounce) can pumpkin purée

2 teaspoons ground cinnamon

½ teaspoon ground ginger

¼ teaspoon ground cloves

2 large eggs

½ cup honey

½ cup full-fat coconut milk

1. Preheat oven to 350°F. Grease a 9" deep dish pie pan.
2. In a small bowl mix together the crust ingredients until the mixture is crumbly.
3. Pour the crust mixture into pie pan and place a sheet of plastic wrap on top. Use your fingers to press the mixture across the bottom and up the sides of the pie pan to form an easy crust. Remove plastic wrap and pre-bake crust for 10 minutes. Remove from oven and set aside while you make the filling.
4. In a large bowl whisk together the pumpkin, spices, eggs, honey, and coconut milk until thick and creamy. Pour into crust. Bake for 45 minutes until the center is set and a knife inserted in the middle comes out clean. The pie will be slightly jiggly when it's finished. If the pie begins to brown too much or burn, gently place a sheet of aluminum foil over the pie while it's cooking.
5. Allow pie to cool on a wire rack for at least 1 hour. Refrigerate for at least 4–6 hours or overnight before serving.

CHAPTER 13

Gluten-Free Vegan Bake Shoppe

Vegan Yeast-Free Sandwich Bread

This recipe was inspired by Iris Higgins, who first created a similar recipe for The Essential Gluten-Free Baking Guide. *I modified it to work with the flours suggested in this cookbook.*

INGREDIENTS | YIELDS 1 (9" × 5") LOAF

1¾ cups brown rice flour or sorghum flour (or a mix of both)

1¼ cups arrowroot starch or tapioca starch

¼ cup coconut palm sugar or vegan sugar

1 teaspoon baking powder

½ teaspoon baking soda

½ teaspoon sea salt

6 tablespoons whole psyllium husks

2 tablespoons unsweetened applesauce

2 tablespoons light-tasting olive oil

½ teaspoon apple cider vinegar

2¼ cups warm water

What Can You Substitute for Psyllium Husks?

In many gluten-free recipes you can make easy substitutions, but it's very important that you do not substitute *anything* else for the psyllium husks in this recipe. They give this bread the correct texture and structure. You can buy plain, whole psyllium husks at drug stores, health food stores, or online. Psyllium husks are affordable and are a great source of easily digestible natural fiber—they can also be used for laxative purposes.

1. Preheat oven to 350°F. Heavily grease a 9" × 5" loaf pan with nonstick cooking spray or light-tasting olive oil.
2. In a large bowl whisk together brown rice flour, arrowroot starch, sugar, baking powder, baking soda, and salt.
3. In a smaller bowl whisk together psyllium husks, applesauce, olive oil, vinegar, and water. Mix the wet ingredients into the dry ingredients and stir until you have a thick batter. Pour the batter into loaf pan.
4. Bake 1 hour and 10 minutes until the top of the loaf has risen to about ½" over the top of the pan and is golden-brown. Allow the bread to cool in the pan for 10 minutes, then turn out onto a wire rack to cool completely. Don't slice bread until it has completely cooled.
5. Store bread in an airtight container on the counter for up to 2 days. Any leftover bread should be sliced and stored in the freezer for up to 2 months.

Chewy Gluten-Free Vegan Bagels

The egg replacer in this recipe is ground flaxseeds.
See Chapter 1 for instructions on making egg replacers.

INGREDIENTS | SERVES 12

2 cups brown rice flour or sorghum flour

2 cups arrowroot starch or tapioca starch

2 teaspoons xanthan gum

1 tablespoon SAF-Instant Yeast, Red Star Quick-Rise or Bread Machine Yeast, or Fleischmann's Bread Machine Yeast

1 teaspoon baking soda

3 tablespoons coconut palm sugar or vegan sugar, divided

1½ teaspoons sea salt

5 tablespoons ground flaxseeds mixed with 6 tablespoons hot water and 2 tablespoons light-tasting olive oil

1¼ cups warm water

3 tablespoons toasted sesame seeds

¼ cup almond milk

1. In a large bowl whisk together brown rice flour, arrowroot starch, xanthan gum, yeast, baking soda, 1 tablespoon sugar, and salt. In a smaller bowl whisk together flaxseed mixture and warm water. Mix wet ingredients into dry ingredients for 3–4 minutes with a wooden spoon until you have a very thick dough.

2. Cover the bowl of dough with plastic wrap and set in a warm place. Allow the dough to rise for at least 1 hour until it has doubled in size. Line a large cookie sheet with parchment paper and then grease with nonstick cooking spray or light-tasting olive oil; set aside.

3. Once the dough has doubled, divide it into 12 round balls. Using your hands, flatten each ball into a disk and using your index finger, poke a hole in the middle to form the shape of a bagel. Place each bagel on the cookie sheet. Cover the bagels lightly with a gluten-free-floured tea towel or plastic wrap. Set in a warm place to rise for an additional 30 minutes. Preheat oven to 400°F.

4. When the bagels have nearly doubled in size, place a large pot of water on the stove to boil. You should have at least 12 cups of water in the pot. Add 2 tablespoons sugar to the water as it is boiling. When the water has reached a rolling boil, add 2 bagels at a time and boil for 30 seconds–1 minute on each side. Remove bagels carefully from the boiling water with a slotted spoon and place back on cookie sheet. When all bagels have been boiled and placed back on cookie sheet, brush each bagel lightly with almond milk. Sprinkle on sesame seeds and then bake for 25 minutes until bagels are golden-brown.

5. Allow bagels to cool for 10–15 minutes before serving. Bagels can now be sliced and toasted in a toaster, if desired. Eat with your favorite vegan cream cheese or vegan butter and jam.

Cinnamon Raisin Breakfast Bread

This cinnamon bread is easy to whip up. It's versatile too—you can substitute any type of vegan egg replacer you like for the flaxseed mixture.

INGREDIENTS | SERVES 9

¾ cup brown rice flour or sorghum flour

½ cup arrowroot starch or tapioca starch

½ teaspoon xanthan gum

½ teaspoon baking soda

½ teaspoon baking powder

1½ teaspoons ground cinnamon

¼ teaspoon sea salt

¼ cup light-tasting olive oil or canola oil

¼ cup packed coconut palm sugar or vegan brown sugar

1 tablespoon ground flaxseeds mixed with 3 tablespoons warm water

½ cup almond milk

¼ cup unsweetened applesauce

½ cup raisins

½ cup finely chopped pecans

1. Preheat oven to 350°F. Line an 8" × 8" baking pan with parchment paper and then grease with nonstick cooking spray or light-tasting olive oil.
2. In a large bowl whisk together brown rice flour, arrowroot starch, xanthan gum, baking soda, baking powder, cinnamon, and salt.
3. In a smaller bowl whisk together oil, coconut palm sugar, flaxseed mixture, almond milk, and applesauce. Mix the wet ingredients into the dry ingredients until you have a thick batter. Fold in raisins and pecans.
4. Pour batter into baking dish. Smooth the top with a wet spatula, if desired. Bake for 35–40 minutes until the top of the bread is golden-brown and a toothpick inserted in the middle comes out clean.
5. Allow bread to cool for 5–10 minutes before slicing and serving. Serve squares of bread with vegan butter and/or jam. Store remaining bread in an airtight container on the counter for up to 2 days. Freeze remaining bread for up to 2 months.

Hummingbird Morning Muffins

These hearty muffins are chock-full of fruit and nuts. They are very filling and perfect for busy mornings. They also freeze and reheat beautifully.

INGREDIENTS | SERVES 12

1 cup sorghum flour

½ cup arrowroot starch or tapioca starch

½ teaspoon baking soda

1 teaspoon baking powder

½ teaspoon xanthan gum

¼ teaspoon sea salt

1 cup coconut palm sugar or vegan sugar

1½ cups mashed bananas (about 2–3 small bananas)

½ cup crushed pineapple in juice

1 tablespoon vanilla extract

⅓ cup light-tasting olive oil

½ shredded unsweetened coconut

½ cup chopped walnuts

⅓ cup raisins

1. Preheat oven to 350°F. Line a 12-cup muffin pan with paper liners and then grease with nonstick cooking spray or light-tasting olive oil.
2. In a large bowl whisk together sorghum flour, arrowroot starch, baking soda, baking powder, xanthan gum, and sea salt.
3. In a smaller bowl whisk together coconut palm or vegan sugar, bananas, pineapple, vanilla, and olive oil. Mix wet ingredients into dry ingredients until you have a thick batter. Fold in coconut, walnuts, and raisins.
4. Fill muffin tins ¾ full with batter. Smooth tops with a wet spatula, if desired. Bake for 20–25 minutes until muffin tops are golden-brown and a toothpick inserted in the middle comes out clean.
5. Allow muffins to cool in the pan for 5 minutes. Move to a wire rack to cool completely. Store any remaining muffins in an airtight container on the counter for up to 2 days. Freeze leftover muffins for up to 2 months.

Whole-Grain Oat (or Quinoa) Muffins

Just because you are gluten-free doesn't mean you can't enjoy a hearty bran-type muffin. These muffins are based on whole-grain oats. You can use quinoa or teff flour, if you prefer.

INGREDIENTS | SERVES 10–12

⅔ cup gluten-free oat flour or quinoa flour

⅓ cup plus 2 tablespoons arrowroot starch or tapioca starch

½ teaspoon xanthan gum

¼ teaspoon sea salt

1½ teaspoons baking powder

½ teaspoon baking soda

⅓ cup coconut palm sugar or vegan sugar

¼ cup light-tasting olive oil or canola oil

½ cup almond milk

½ cup chopped raisins or nuts

Are Oats Gluten Free?

Pure oats are naturally gluten-free, however while they are being grown or processed they can get cross-contaminated with wheat. It's important to make sure to buy certified gluten-free oats that have been grown away from wheat fields and have been processed in safe factories that either take great care to clean and sanitize their equipment or do not process wheat products at all. You can make your own gluten-free oat flour by grinding rolled oats in your blender or a clean coffee bean grinder.

1. Preheat oven to 350°F. Line a muffin pan with paper liners and then grease with nonstick cooking spray or light-tasting olive oil.
2. In a large bowl whisk together flour, arrowroot starch, xanthan gum, salt, baking powder, and baking soda.
3. In a smaller bowl whisk together coconut palm or vegan sugar, olive oil, and almond milk. Mix the wet ingredients into the dry ingredients until you have a thick batter. Fold in raisins or nuts.
4. Fill muffin tins ⅔ full with batter. Smooth tops with a wet spatula, if desired. Bake for 20–23 minutes until muffin tops are golden-brown and a toothpick inserted in the middle comes out clean.
5. Allow muffins to cool in the pan for 5 minutes. Move to a wire rack to cool completely. Store remaining muffins in an airtight container on the counter for up to 2 days. Freeze leftover muffins for up to 2 months.

Apple Cinnamon Coffee Cake

Coffee cake is a great dessert to make vegan. Because these cakes are a bit more dense than traditional cakes, they work well without eggs or dairy.

INGREDIENTS | SERVES 9

Cake

¾ cup sorghum flour

¾ cup plus 1 tablespoon arrowroot starch or tapioca starch

2¼ teaspoons baking powder

½ teaspoon xanthan gum

½ teaspoon sea salt

½ teaspoon ground cinnamon

¼ cup light-tasting olive oil or canola oil

¾ cup coconut palm sugar or vegan sugar

1 cup almond milk

2 medium Gala apples, peeled, cored, and diced

Topping

1 teaspoon ground cinnamon

4 tablespoons coconut palm sugar or vegan sugar

2 tablespoons sorghum flour

3 tablespoons Spectrum Palm Shortening or vegan butter

1. Preheat oven to 350°F. Line an 8" × 8" baking pan with parchment paper and then grease with nonstick cooking spray or light-tasting olive oil.
2. In a large bowl whisk together sorghum flour, arrowroot starch, baking powder, xanthan gum, salt, and cinnamon.
3. In a smaller bowl whisk together oil, sugar, and almond milk. Mix wet ingredients into dry ingredients until you have a thick batter. Fold in chopped apples.
4. Pour batter into baking dish. In a small bowl mix together all the topping ingredients and sprinkle evenly over the cake. Bake for 35–40 minutes until top of cake is golden-brown and a toothpick inserted in the middle comes out clean.
5. Allow cake to cool for 5–10 minutes before slicing and serving. Serve squares of cake with fresh fruit and hot tea or coffee. Store remaining cake in an airtight container on the counter for up to 2 days. Freeze remaining cake, cut into servings, for up to 2 months.

Blueberry Coffee Cake

Instead of using apples, substitute 1 cup frozen or fresh blueberries in the batter. If using frozen blueberries, don't defrost them. Your batter will turn an unappealing greenish-blue if you use defrosted blueberries! Make the rest of the coffee cake as directed.

Harvest Pumpkin Bread

This lovely loaf of fresh pumpkin bread with dried cranberries and toasted pecans makes a beautiful gift for the holidays.

INGREDIENTS | YIELDS 2 MEDIUM LOAVES

⅔ cup arrowroot starch

⅔ cup brown rice flour

⅔ sorghum flour

½ teaspoon xanthan gum

¾ cup coconut palm sugar or vegan sugar

1¼ teaspoons baking powder

1 teaspoon baking soda

2 teaspoons ground cinnamon

½ teaspoon ground cloves

½ teaspoon ginger

¼ teaspoon salt

1¼ cups plain pumpkin purée

¾ cup light-tasting olive oil or canola oil

½ teaspoon apple cider vinegar

½ cup dried cranberries

½ cup chopped, toasted pecans

1. Preheat oven to 350°F. Line 2 (7½" × 3½") loaf pans with parchment paper and then grease with nonstick cooking spray or light-tasting olive oil.
2. In a large bowl whisk together arrowroot starch, brown rice flour, sorghum flour, xanthan gum, sugar, baking powder, baking soda, spices, and salt.
3. In a medium bowl whisk together the pumpkin purée, olive oil, and vinegar. Pour wet ingredients into dry ingredients and mix to combine. Fold in the cranberries and chopped pecans.
4. Divide batter into loaf pans. Smooth tops of loaves with a wet spatula, if desired. Bake for 35–40 minutes until top of bread is golden-brown and a toothpick inserted in the middle comes out clean.
5. Allow bread to cool for 5–10 minutes in the pan before turning out onto a wire rack to cool completely for 1–2 hours. Slice the bread and serve with vegan butter and jam. Store remaining bread in an airtight container on the counter for up to 2 days. Freeze remaining bread for up to 2 months.

Everyday Vegan Pancakes

For a long time I thought it was nearly impossible to make pancakes vegan and gluten-free. Then, Iris Higgins, author of The Essential Gluten-Free Baking Guide, *tested about 30 different gluten-free flours to find the right mix. I used her guide to create these pancakes.*

INGREDIENTS | SERVES 4–6

1¼ cups brown rice flour

½ cup tapioca starch or cornstarch

2 teaspoons baking powder

½ teaspoon sea salt

2 tablespoons coconut palm sugar or vegan sugar

1 cup almond milk

¼ cup unsweetened applesauce or pure pumpkin purée

2 tablespoons extra-light-tasting olive oil

Note on Starches

Iris Higgins tested many different pancakes using tapioca starch and potato starch. She got the best and fluffiest results with potato starch. Some of her readers tested the recipe with arrowroot starch and felt it created rather gummy pancakes. For this recipe I recommend using tapioca starch, cornstarch, or potato starch, whichever you prefer.

1. In a medium bowl whisk together the brown rice flour, tapioca starch, baking powder, salt, and sugar. Make a well in the center of the dry ingredients and add the almond milk, applesauce, and olive oil. Whisk together until you have a thickened batter.
2. Grease a large, heavy-bottomed skillet or nonstick pan with olive oil or nonstick spray. Heat pan on medium-high heat until it's hot enough to make a drop of water sizzle. Pour a few tablespoons of batter for each pancake.
3. Cook until bubbles form on the top and pop and the edges are slightly dry. Flip with a spatula and cook the opposite side for 1–2 minutes.
4. Serve piping hot with vegan butter or coconut oil and real maple syrup.

Mini Cinnamon Sugar Doughnuts (or Mini Muffins)

Remember mini doughnuts covered in confectioners' sugar or a cinnamon-sugar mixture?
Now you can make your own. If you don't have a mini doughnut pan, use a mini muffin pan instead.

INGREDIENTS | YIELDS 24 MINI DOUGHNUTS

Doughnuts
¾ cup sorghum flour
½ cup arrowroot starch
½ teaspoon xanthan gum
1¼ teaspoons baking powder
½ teaspoon baking soda
1 teaspoon ground cinnamon
½ teaspoon sea salt
5 tablespoons Spectrum Palm Shortening or vegan butter
⅔ cup coconut palm sugar or vegan sugar
⅔ cup plus 3 tablespoons almond milk

Topping
1 teaspoon ground cinnamon
⅓ cup coconut palm sugar or vegan sugar
2 tablespoons almond milk

1. Preheat oven to 350°F. Grease a mini doughnut pan with nonstick cooking spray or light-tasting olive oil.
2. In a large bowl whisk together sorghum flour, arrowroot starch, xanthan gum, baking powder, baking soda, cinnamon, and salt.
3. In a smaller bowl cream together the shortening and coconut palm or vegan sugar. Add the milk and stir until fully incorporated. Pour the wet ingredients into the dry ingredients and mix to combine.
4. Spoon the batter into a zip-top plastic bag and snip off one corner to pipe the batter into pan, filling each doughnut well halfway. Bake for 7–10 minutes until doughnuts are golden-brown and puffy.
5. While doughnuts are baking, place 1 teaspoon ground cinnamon and ⅓ cup coconut palm sugar in a zip-top plastic bag. Zip closed and shake around to mix them up. As soon as you pull doughnuts from the oven, brush them very lightly with almond milk, and then add them to the cinnamon-sugar bag and shake them up until they are coated. Place on a wire rack to cool completely. Store remaining doughnuts in an airtight container on the counter for up to 2 days. Baked doughnuts can be frozen for up to 2 months.

Crispy Vegan Corn Bread

*Corn bread is a staple food in many southern homes—
the perfect accompaniment to a big hot bowl of soup or chili.*

INGREDIENTS | SERVES 9

⅔ cup gluten-free cornmeal

⅓ cup sorghum flour

⅓ cup plus 2 tablespoons arrowroot starch

2 teaspoons baking powder

½ teaspoon xanthan gum

½ teaspoon sea salt

4 tablespoons Spectrum Palm Shortening or vegan butter

3 tablespoons coconut palm sugar or vegan sugar

1 cup plus 2 tablespoons almond milk

1 teaspoon apple cider vinegar or lemon juice

The Versatility of Corn Bread

You can do so many different things with corn bread. Make this recipe a day ahead to make a homemade batch of gluten-free stuffing for the holidays. Use leftover corn bread as a breakfast "cereal" by crumbling it in a bowl and pouring cold almond milk over it. Heat leftover corn bread to eat with a vegan tofu scramble in the morning. Cube leftover corn bread to make a crunchy peach or Apple Brown Betty (see Chapter 6).

1. Preheat oven to 350°F. Line an 8" × 8" baking pan with parchment paper and then grease with nonstick cooking spray or light-tasting olive oil.
2. In a large bowl whisk together cornmeal, sorghum flour, arrowroot starch, baking powder, xanthan gum, and salt.
3. In a smaller bowl cream together shortening and sugar until fluffy. Stir in milk and vinegar. Mix wet ingredients into dry ingredients until you have a thick batter.
4. Pour batter into baking dish. Smooth top with a wet spatula, if desired. Bake for 20–25 minutes until top of bread is golden-brown and a toothpick inserted in the middle comes out clean.
5. Allow bread to cool for 5–10 minutes before slicing and serving. Serve squares of bread with vegan butter or coconut oil. Store remaining bread in an airtight container on the counter for up to 2 days. Freeze remaining bread for up to 2 months.

"Cheesy" Snack Crackers

*This simple recipe shows how you can use a nondairy cheese
to make your own gluten-free, vegan crispy crackers.*

INGREDIENTS | **YIELDS 40–50 CRACKERS**

1 cup brown rice flour, plus more for
rolling out dough

⅔ cup tapioca starch or arrowroot starch

⅓ cup ground flaxseeds

1 teaspoon sea salt

½ teaspoon baking soda

½ teaspoon cayenne pepper

¼ cup Spectrum Palm Shortening or
vegan butter

¾ cup shredded vegan, gluten-free
cheese, such as Daiya Cheddar Style
Shreds

4–6 tablespoons almond milk

1. Preheat oven to 400°F.
2. In a large bowl whisk together brown rice flour, tapioca starch, flaxseeds, salt, baking soda, and cayenne pepper. Cut in shortening with a pastry blender or a knife and fork until it resembles small peas throughout the dry ingredients.
3. Stir in the vegan cheese until it is thoroughly coated in the dry ingredients and creates a crumbly mixture. Stir in the milk, starting with 4 tablespoons and then an additional tablespoon at a time until you have a thick batter.
4. Place a piece of parchment paper on a hard surface, such as a clean counter. Dust paper with additional brown rice flour and use a rolling pin to roll out the crackers in a large rectangle to ⅛" thickness. Gently move paper to a large rectangular cookie sheet. Use a pizza cutter to score dough into 1"-square crackers. Prick each cracker with a fork 2–3 times to create little holes in the dough.
5. Bake for 10–15 minutes until the crackers are golden-brown. Remove from oven and allow to cool on the pan for 20 minutes. Sprinkle with additional salt, if desired. Once the crackers have cooled completely, break them along the score lines.
6. Store crackers in an airtight container on the counter for up to 1 week. Baked crackers will also freeze for up to 2 months.

Italian Breadsticks

This is another recipe that uses psyllium seed husks instead of gums to give bread structure and texture, without eggs.

INGREDIENTS | YIELDS 20–30 BREADSTICKS

2 cups brown rice flour

1⅓ cups arrowroot starch or tapioca starch

2¼ teaspoons SAF-Instant Yeast, Red Star Quick-Rise or Bread Machine Yeast, or Fleischmann's Bread Machine Yeast

3 tablespoons psyllium seed husks

2 teaspoons sea salt

½ teaspoon baking soda

¼ cup olive oil

2 tablespoons coconut palm sugar or vegan sugar

2 tablespoons unsweetened applesauce

2⅓ cups warm water

2 tablespoons almond milk

Sesame seeds (optional)

1. Preheat oven to 350°F. Line a large cookie sheet with parchment paper and then grease with nonstick cooking spray or light-tasting olive oil.

2. In a large bowl whisk together brown rice flour, arrowroot starch, yeast, psyllium husks, salt, and baking soda. Make a well in the center of the dry ingredients and add olive oil, sugar, applesauce, and warm water. Mix together until you have a pancake-like batter. Batter will be thinner than a regular gluten-free bread dough.

3. Cover dough and let it very slowly rise overnight in the refrigerator, or you can cover it and place it on the counter in a warm place to double in size, about 1–2 hours.

4. When the dough has risen and you are ready to make breadsticks, preheat oven to 450°F. This batter makes a lot of breadsticks, so feel free to only use half the dough and place the rest in the fridge for the next day.

5. Make a breadstick by scooping out 2–4 tablespoons of dough and rolling it in a ball on a brown rice–floured surface. Gently roll the dough out like a snake in a breadstick form. Place the dough 2" apart on the cookie sheet. Cover lightly and allow the dough to rest for 30 minutes before baking. This will allow the breadsticks to rise a bit more.

6. When the breadsticks are ready to bake, brush them lightly with almond milk and sprinkle with sesame seeds, if desired. For soft breadsticks, bake for 10–15 minutes. For more crispy breadsticks, bake for 25–30 minutes. Allow breadsticks to cool for 5 minutes before serving. Store bread in an airtight container on the counter for up to 1 week. Baked breadsticks will also freeze for up to 2 months.

Whole-Grain Vegan Pizza Crust

This crispy, thin crust works great for a vegan pizza.

INGREDIENTS | YIELDS 1 (12") PIZZA CRUST

¾ cup sorghum flour

¼ cup brown rice flour

¼ teaspoon sea salt

1 teaspoon SAF-Instant Yeast, Red Star Quick-Rise or Bread Machine Yeast, or Fleischmann's Bread Machine Yeast

½ teaspoon coconut palm sugar or vegan sugar

½ cup–¾ cup warm water

1 tablespoon olive oil

Other Whole-Grain Options

If you decide to keep a large supply of different gluten-free flours in your pantry, some great options are teff flour and quinoa flour. Both could be used in this recipe in place of the sorghum and brown rice flours. Other options are amaranth flour, buckwheat flour, and millet flour.

1. Preheat oven to 450°F. Place a sheet of parchment paper on a pizza pan or cookie sheet.
2. In a medium-sized bowl whisk together sorghum flour, brown rice flour, salt, yeast, and sugar.
3. Pour warm water into the dry ingredients and stir together with a fork until a ball of dough forms. If ½ cup water is not enough to create a stiff ball of dough, add 1 tablespoon additional warm water at a time until you have a ball of dough.
4. Cover bowl with a kitchen towel and allow to rest for 10 minutes. Prepare topping while dough is resting. When ready to prebake crust, pour 1 tablespoon olive oil onto the parchment paper and spread over paper into a 12" circle. Place ball of dough on parchment paper. Place a piece of plastic wrap over dough and pat out with your hands into a 12" circle.
5. Remove plastic wrap and place pizza crust into oven; bake for 10–12 minutes until golden-brown and crisp. Remove from oven. Add desired toppings and bake for an additional 10 minutes until toppings are heated through and/or cheese substitute is melted.

Savory Rosemary Walnut Cookies

These little savory bites, are nonsweet cookies that are reminiscent of "sausage balls."
They are a great alternative for a meat appetizer, a delicious vegan holiday
meal addition, or just to have a spicy vegan treat to snack on.

INGREDIENTS | YIELDS 22–24 COOKIES

2 tablespoons ground flaxseeds

6 tablespoons hot water

½ cup gluten-free quick-oats

½ cup brown rice flour

½ cup arrowroot starch or tapioca starch

1 teaspoon baking powder

½ teaspoon sea salt

1½ teaspoons dried rosemary, crushed

½ cup applesauce

½ cup melted coconut oil

½ cup walnuts, finely chopped

Coarse sea salt (optional)

1. Preheat oven to 350°F. Line 2 large cookie sheets with parchment paper and set aside.
2. In a small bowl mix together ground flaxseeds and hot water. Stir to combine and set aside to "gel."
3. In a large bowl whisk together gluten-free oats, brown rice flour, arrowroot starch, baking powder, sea salt, and dried rosemary. Make a well in the center of the dry ingredients and add applesauce and coconut oil. Stir the wet ingredients into the dry ingredients until you have a sticky dough. Fold in the chopped walnuts.
4. Scoop 2 tablespoons of cookie dough onto the cookie sheets about 2" apart. Press them down very lightly and shape into a circle. If desired sprinkle the top of each cookie lightly with coarse sea salt!
5. Bake for 15–20 minutes until golden-brown and crisp around the edges. Allow cookies to cool on parchment paper for 10 minutes and then move to a wire rack to cool completely.
6. Store cookies in an airtight container on the counter for 2–3 days. Cookies and cookie dough can also be frozen for up to 1 month.

Mocha Chocolate Chip Cookies

These cookies have just a hint of coffee, which works well with chocolate chips.
These are only slightly sweet and almost have the flavor of biscotti.

INGREDIENTS | YIELDS 22–24 COOKIES

1½ cups sorghum flour

½ cup brown rice flour

½ cup plus 2 tablespoons arrowroot starch

1½ teaspoons baking soda

1 teaspoon xanthan gum

½ teaspoon sea salt

1 teaspoon ground cinnamon

¼ teaspoon freshly grated nutmeg

½ cup Spectrum Palm Shortening or vegan butter

½ cup coconut palm sugar or vegan sugar

¼ cup plus 2 tablespoons double-strength espresso

1 tablespoon vanilla extract

1 cup dairy-free, vegan chocolate chips

1. Preheat oven to 350°F. Line 2 large cookie sheets with parchment paper and set aside.
2. In a large bowl whisk together sorghum flour, brown rice flour, arrowroot starch, baking soda, xanthan gum, salt, cinnamon, and nutmeg.
3. In a smaller bowl cream together shortening and sugar. Add espresso and vanilla and stir until fully incorporated. Mix wet ingredients into dry ingredients until you have a thick dough. Fold in chocolate chips. Chill dough for 10 minutes in the fridge.
4. Scoop cookie dough with a large spoon into rounded balls of dough almost the size of a golf ball. Place the cookies 2" apart on cookie sheets and press them down very lightly (do not press them flat or they will spread too much; just a gentle press with the back of a spoon).
5. Bake for 15–18 minutes until golden-brown and crisp around the edges. Allow cookies to cool on parchment paper for 10 minutes and then move to a wire rack to cool completely.
6. Store cookies in an airtight container on the counter for 2–3 days. Cookies and cookie dough can also be frozen for up to 1 month.

Double Ginger Cookies

*This rich dough can be used to make rolled-out gingerbread cookies
or rolled into a log for slice-and-bake cookies.*

INGREDIENTS | YIELDS 12 VERY LARGE COOKIES

2 cups plus 2 tablespoons brown rice flour

¾ cup plus 1 tablespoon sorghum flour

2 teaspoons baking powder

½ teaspoon sea salt

1½ teaspoons ground ginger

½ teaspoon ground cloves

½ teaspoon ground cinnamon

1½ teaspoons cocoa powder

6 tablespoons light-tasting olive oil or canola oil

6 tablespoons unsweetened applesauce

¾ cup coconut palm sugar or vegan sugar

½ cup molasses

1 tablespoon freshly grated gingerroot

½ cup almond milk

½ cup organic coarse sugar, for rolling cookies

1. Preheat oven to 350°F. Line cookie sheet with parchment paper.
2. In a large bowl whisk together brown rice flour, sorghum flour, baking powder, sea salt, spices, and cocoa powder.
3. In a medium bowl mix together oil, applesauce, coconut palm sugar, molasses, gingerroot, and almond milk. Whisk until frothy. Pour wet ingredients into dry ingredients and mix together until you have a thick dough.
4. Place ½ cup coarse organic sugar in a bowl. Scoop dough out of bowl with a greased ice-cream scoop and roll in the sugar to coat. Place coated cookies on cookie sheets 2" apart. Flatten each cookie gently with the bottom of a glass.
5. Bake for 15–18 minutes until cookies are just turning golden around the edges. Allow cookies to cool completely on the cookie sheets before removing.
6. Store cookies in an airtight container on the counter for 2–3 days. Cookies and cookie dough can also be frozen for up to 1 month.

Vegan Sugar?

Many people who follow a vegan diet avoid sugar that has been refined through a process that uses dead animal bones. The animal parts are not in the final product, but they are used in the processing, which makes the product not vegan. If you want sugar that has not been processed this way, look for the following words and phrases on the package: *vegan, unrefined cane sugar, evaporated cane juice, beet sugar,* or *raw sugar.*

Vegan Peanut Butter Cookies

These easy cookies can be made with any nut, legume, or seed butter.
Add a little more peanut butter or toasted chopped peanuts for a stronger flavor.

INGREDIENTS | YIELDS 2 DOZEN COOKIES

⅔ cup sorghum flour

½ cup plus 1 tablespoon arrowroot starch

½ teaspoon baking soda

½ teaspoon baking powder

½ teaspoon xanthan gum

⅓ cup Spectrum Palm Shortening or vegan butter

½ cup all-natural creamy peanut butter

¾ cup coconut palm sugar or vegan sugar

1 tablespoon ground flaxseeds mixed with 3 tablespoons hot water, set aside to gel

1. Preheat oven to 375°F. Line 2 cookie sheets with parchment paper and set aside.
2. In a large bowl whisk together sorghum flour, arrowroot starch, baking soda, baking powder, and xanthan gum.
3. In a medium bowl cream together shortening, peanut butter, coconut palm sugar, and flaxseed mixture. Pour wet ingredients into dry ingredients and mix together until you have a thick dough.
4. Scoop 1–2 teaspoons of dough per cookie and roll into a ball. Place balls on cookie sheets at least 1" apart. Flatten each cookie gently in a crisscross pattern with a fork.
5. Bake for 7–9 minutes until cookies are just turning golden around the edges. Allow cookies to cool completely on the cookie sheets before removing. These cookies can be a bit fragile if they are taken off the pan before they are cool.
6. Store cookies in an airtight container on the counter for 2–3 days. Cookies and cookie dough can also be frozen for up to 1 month.

Pumpkin Chai Spice Cookies

These soft, delicious cookies are perfect for fall weather. Enjoy them with a mug of hot apple cider.

INGREDIENTS | YIELDS 2–3 DOZEN COOKIES

1½ cups sorghum flour

1¼ cups brown rice flour

1¼ teaspoons baking powder

½ teaspoon sea salt

1 tablespoon chai spice mix

½ teaspoon xanthan gum

½ cup Spectrum Palm Shortening or vegan butter

¾ cup coconut palm sugar or vegan sugar

1¼ cups pure pumpkin purée

1 tablespoon ground flaxseed mixed with 3 tablespoons warm water, set aside to gel

½ cup chopped, toasted pecans (optional)

½ cup unsweetened dried cranberries (optional)

Homemade Chai Spice Mix

Chai spice mix is perfect in a cup of tea or hot chocolate, and it's excellent in these cakelike pumpkin cookies. In a small jar mix together 1 tablespoon ground cinnamon, 1 tablespoon ground cardamom, 1 teaspoon ground ginger, ½ teaspoon ground cloves, and ½ teaspoon ground nutmeg. Close jar with a tight lid. Spice mix will stay fresh for 6 months in your pantry.

1. Preheat oven to 350°F. Line 2 cookie sheets with parchment paper and set aside.
2. In a large bowl whisk together sorghum flour, brown rice flour, baking powder, salt, chai spice mix, and xanthan gum. In a medium bowl cream together shortening, sugar, pumpkin purée, and flaxseed mixture. Pour wet ingredients into dry ingredients and mix together until you have a thick dough. Fold in toasted pecans and dried cranberries, if using.
3. Scoop 1–2 teaspoons of dough per cookie and roll into a ball. Place balls on cookie sheets at least 1" apart. Flatten each cookie gently with the back of a greased spoon.
4. Bake for 10–12 minutes until cookies are just turning golden around the edges. Allow cookies to cool completely on the cookie sheets before removing. These cookies can be a bit fragile if they are taken off the pan before they are cool.
5. Store cookies in an airtight container on the counter for 2–3 days. Cookies and cookie dough can also be frozen for up to 1 month.

Simple Vanilla Wafer Cookies

Sometimes a plain vanilla cookie is all you need to accompany a cup of hot tea.
Use these cookies as the outer layers of sandwich cookies, or crumbled up as a pie crust.

INGREDIENTS | YIELDS 30–40 COOKIES

½ cup Spectrum Palm Shortening or vegan butter, softened
½ cup packed light brown sugar
2 tablespoons vanilla extract
3 tablespoons almond milk or water
1 cup brown rice flour
½ cup arrowroot starch or tapioca starch
½ teaspoon xanthan gum
¾ teaspoon baking powder
⅛ teaspoon baking soda
½ teaspoon sea salt

1. In a large bowl cream together the shortening and brown sugar until thoroughly combined. Add the vanilla extract and almond milk, and stir to combine.
2. In a smaller bowl whisk together the brown rice flour, arrowroot starch, xanthan gum, baking powder, baking soda, and sea salt. Stir the dry ingredients into the sugar-and-butter mixture until batter is very thick and can be formed into a large ball of dough.
3. Divide the dough into 2 smaller balls and place each ball on a separate 12" sheet of plastic wrap. Using plastic wrap to keep dough from sticking to your hands, shape each ball of dough into an 8"–10" long log. Cover each log completely with the plastic wrap and place in the refrigerator for at least 2–3 hours.
4. Heat oven to 350°F. Place parchment paper on 2 large baking sheets. Slice each log of dough into 14–18 cookies. Place cookie slices 1" apart in 4–5 rows on each cookie sheet. Bake for 15–18 minutes until the edges of the cookies appear to be dry. These cookies do not spread much or change their shape.
5. Allow cookies to cool for at least 15 minutes on the baking sheets before moving to a cooling rack. The cookies will easily crumble if moved immediately from the baking sheets. After 15–20 minutes, place cookies on a cooling rack. Allow to cool completely before serving. Store cookies in an airtight container on the counter for up to 1 week or freeze for up to 2 months.

Hamantaschen

This traditional Jewish cookie is often served during the celebration of Purim.
The dough should be chilled at least 6–8 hours or overnight before filling and baking.

INGREDIENTS | YIELDS 2–2½ DOZEN COOKIES

½ cup Spectrum Palm Shortening

1 cup coconut palm sugar or vegan sugar

2 teaspoons vanilla extract

3 tablespoons unsweetened applesauce

1 cup brown rice flour

1 cup arrowroot starch

½ teaspoon xanthan gum

2½ teaspoons baking powder

¼ teaspoon sea salt

½ cup organic, vegan apricot jam

What Is Purim?

Purim is a Jewish holiday that commemorates when the Jews were saved from persecution in the ancient Persian Empire. As noted in the Book of Esther in the Bible, the Jews of Shushan were threatened by the villain Haman, a prime minister who convinced the reigning king to kill all the Jews. Haman cast lots (also known as "purim"—hence the name of the holiday) to determine the date he would massacre the Jews. In the end the people were saved by the heroic Queen Esther.

1. In a large bowl cream together the shortening and sugar until thoroughly combined. Add the vanilla extract and applesauce and stir to combine.
2. In a smaller bowl whisk together the brown rice flour, arrowroot starch, xanthan gum, baking powder, and sea salt. Stir the dry ingredients into the sugar-and-butter mixture until batter is very thick and can be formed into a large ball of dough.
3. Cover dough with plastic wrap and refrigerate 6–8 hours or overnight.
4. When the dough is chilled, remove from refrigerator and roll out on a rice-floured surface to ¼" thickness. Cut dough into 2½" circles. Place a teaspoon of jam in the center of each circle and then pinch the sides of the dough, so the cookies are in a triangle form with three "walls" of dough surrounding the filling.
5. Heat oven to 375°F. Place parchment paper on 2 large baking sheets. Place cookies about 1" apart on the baking sheets. Bake for 10–12 minutes until the edges of the cookies start to brown.
6. Allow cookies to cool completely before serving. Store cookies in an airtight container on the counter for up to 1 week or freeze for up to 2 months.

Vegan Double Chocolate Cake with Vegan Chocolate Frosting

You can double this recipe to make a 9" × 13" sheet cake or a large 2-layer cake. This cake is super moist and no one will know it's gluten-free or vegan.

INGREDIENTS | SERVES 8–10

Cake
⅓ cup brown rice flour

⅓ cup sorghum flour

⅓ cup arrowroot starch or tapioca starch

½ teaspoon xanthan gum

½ cup cocoa powder

¾ cup coconut palm sugar or vegan sugar

2 teaspoons baking powder

¼ teaspoon baking soda

¼ teaspoon sea salt

¾ cup almond milk

½ cup unsweetened applesauce

¼ cup light-tasting olive oil or canola oil

1 tablespoon vanilla extract

⅓ cup mini allergen-free chocolate chips (optional)

Frosting
½ cup Spectrum Palm Shortening, softened

½ cup cocoa powder

1 teaspoon vanilla extract

2 cups sifted vegan confectioners' sugar (such as Wholesome Sweeteners Organic)

2–3 tablespoons water

1. Preheat the oven to 350°F. Line a 9" round baking pan with parchment paper.
2. Sift together the brown rice flour, sorghum flour, arrowroot or tapioca starch, xanthan gum, cocoa powder, sugar, baking powder, baking soda, and salt. Set aside.
3. In another bowl whisk together almond milk, applesauce, oil, and vanilla extract. Mix until well blended. Mix the wet ingredients into the dry ingredients and stir until you have a thick batter. Fold in the chocolate chips, if desired. Pour batter into baking pan.
4. Place on middle rack in preheated oven and bake for 18–25 minutes, or until a toothpick inserted into the middle of the cake comes out clean.
5. Remove cake from oven and allow to sit for 10 minutes before running a knife around the outside of the cake, and inverting the cake onto a wire cooling rack. Cool completely.
6. Make the frosting: With a hand mixer, beat together shortening, ½ cup cocoa powder, vanilla extract, and confectioners' sugar. Slowly add enough water to reach desired consistency. You want the frosting to be stiff enough to hold its shape, but soft enough to easily spread over the cake.
7. Use an offset spatula to frost the cake, as desired.

Vegan Carrot Cake with White "Buttercream" Frosting

This cake is very moist and travels well. It's perfect for potluck dinners and for sharing with neighbors.

INGREDIENTS | SERVES 8–10

Cake

⅔ cup plus 2 tablespoons sorghum flour, divided

⅓ cup arrowroot starch or tapioca starch

½ teaspoon xanthan gum

¾ cup coconut palm sugar or vegan sugar

2 teaspoons baking powder

¼ teaspoon baking soda

1 teaspoon ground cinnamon

2 cups finely shredded carrots

¼ cup light-tasting olive oil or canola oil

½ cup unsweetened applesauce

⅓ cup raisin (optional)

⅓ cup chopped walnuts (optional)

Frosting

½ cup Spectrum Palm Shortening

2 cups vegan confectioners' sugar

½ teaspoon vanilla extract

2–3 tablespoons water

1. Preheat oven to 350°F. Grease a 9" round cake pan (or line with parchment paper). Dust pan lightly with 2 tablespoons of sorghum flour.
2. In a medium-sized bowl, whisk together sorghum flour, arrowroot starch, xanthan gum, coconut palm sugar, baking powder, baking soda, and ground cinnamon. Make a well in center of dry ingredients. Add carrots, oil, and applesauce. Stir wet ingredients into dry ingredients until you have a thick batter. Fold in raisins and chopped walnuts, if desired.
3. Bake for 20–30 minutes until a toothpick inserted in the middle comes out clean. Cool in the pan for 10–15 minutes and then turn out onto a wire rack to cool completely.
4. Make the frosting: In a large bowl mix together shortening, sugar, and vanilla extract. Slowly mix in water, starting with 2 tablespoons and adding more, depending on how thick or thin you prefer the frosting. Frost top and sides of cake.

White Coconut Cake with Coconut Frosting

This rich, coconut cake is decadent, moist, and tropical.
It's a classic cake for weddings and baby showers.

INGREDIENTS | SERVES 8–10

Cake

1½ cups brown rice flour

¾ cup arrowroot starch or tapioca starch

1 teaspoon xanthan gum

1½ cups organic vegan sugar

2½ teaspoons baking powder

1 teaspoon baking soda

½ teaspoon salt

½ cup Spectrum Palm Shortening or vegan butter

¾ cup light coconut milk

½ cup unsweetened applesauce

2 teaspoons vanilla

½ teaspoon coconut extract

Frosting

1 cup Spectrum Palm Shortening

1 teaspoon coconut or vanilla extract

4 cups vegan confectioners' sugar

¼ cup of light coconut milk

1–2 cups flaked sweetened coconut

1. Preheat oven to 350°F. Spray a 13" × 9" pan with non-stick cooking spray and set aside.
2. In a large bowl, combine rice flour, arrowroot or tapioca starch, xanthan gum, sugar, baking powder, baking soda, and salt; mix well with a wire whisk.
3. In a stand mixer fitted with a paddle attachment, beat the shortening until fluffy. Add the flour mixture, along with the milk, applesauce, vanilla, and coconut extract. Beat until blended, and then beat on medium speed for 2 minutes.
4. Pour batter into prepared pan. Bake 35–40 minutes, or until cake is beginning to pull away from edges and is light golden-brown. Cool completely on wire rack.
5. In a large bowl cream together all frosting ingredients except coconut flakes. Stir together well with a whisk or fork until you have a light, smooth, and creamy frosting.
6. Once cake is completely cooled, fill and frost with the coconut frosting, then generously sprinkle sweetened coconut flakes on top. Chill cake for 2–3 hours before serving for the best flavor. Store any remaining cake in the refrigerator for up to 3 days.

Everyday Vanilla Cake

This simple cake is heavily scented with vanilla. Enjoy it plain, dusted with vegan confectioners' sugar, or frosted with the white frosting in the recipe for Vegan Carrot Cake with White "Buttercream" Frosting (see recipe in this chapter).

INGREDIENTS | SERVES 8–10

½ cup Spectrum Palm Shortening or vegan butter, softened

1½ cups coconut palm sugar or vegan sugar

¾ cup unsweetened applesauce

1 cup vanilla almond milk

2 tablespoons vanilla extract

1 cup brown rice flour

1⅓ cups arrowroot starch or tapioca starch

1 teaspoon xanthan gum

1 tablespoon baking powder

1 teaspoon baking soda

½ teaspoon sea salt

1. Preheat oven to 350°F. Line a 9" × 13" baking pan or 2 (8" or 9") cake pans with parchment paper. If you are using a 10" Bundt pan then grease with oil or nonstick cooking spray. (If using a Bundt pan, do not line with parchment paper.)
2. In a large bowl cream together the shortening and sugar thoroughly until light and fluffy. Add the applesauce, almond milk, and vanilla and mix well.
3. In smaller bowl whisk together brown rice flour, arrowroot or tapioca starch, xanthan gum, baking powder, baking soda, and salt.
4. Add the wet ingredients to the dry ingredients and mix together until you have a thick cake batter.
5. Pour batter evenly into the cake pan(s), and bake for 25–35 minutes until a toothpick inserted in the center comes out clean and the top of the cake is golden-brown.
6. Allow cake to cool in the pan(s) for 10 minutes then transfer to a wire rack to cool completely.

Pecan Brownies

Brownies can be a bit tricky without eggs. This recipe uses 2 teaspoons of psyllium seed husks to help give the brownies the right texture, along with adding some healthy fiber.

INGREDIENTS | SERVES 12

½ cup brown rice flour

¼ cup arrowroot starch

2 teaspoons psyllium seed husks

½ teaspoon xanthan gum

½ cup Spectrum Palm Shortening, melted

4 tablespoons cocoa

1 tablespoon light-tasting olive oil or canola oil

1 cup coconut palm sugar or vegan sugar

½ cup unsweetened applesauce

1 teaspoon vanilla

½ cup chopped toasted pecans (optional)

1. Preheat oven to 350°F. Line an 8" × 8" baking pan with parchment paper.
2. In a medium bowl, whisk together brown rice flour, arrowroot starch, psyllium seed husks, and xanthan gum. Set aside.
3. In a small saucepan over medium heat, add the melted shortening. Stir in cocoa, oil, and sugar and mix until simmering. Remove from heat, allow to cool for 5 minutes, and then stir in applesauce and vanilla. Mix to combine. Slowly stir whisked flours into sugar-and-cocoa mixture. If desired, add ½ cup chopped pecans.
4. Fill pan ⅔ full of batter. Bake for 18–20 minutes. Be careful not to over bake as brownies can dry out. Allow to cool for 20 minutes before serving.

Vegan Chocolate Syrup

This thick, creamy chocolate sauce uses coconut milk and cocoa powder. You can store it in your fridge and use it for vegan ice cream, vegan chocolate "milk," or to drizzle over cakes and pies.

INGREDIENTS | YIELDS ABOUT 1½ CUPS

1 (13½-ounce) can full-fat coconut milk

½ cup cocoa powder

¼ cup plus 2 tablespoons coconut palm sugar or vegan sugar

1 tablespoon vanilla extract

½ teaspoon sea salt

1. In a large saucepan heat coconut milk and cocoa powder over medium heat, whisking for 2–3 minutes to thoroughly combine. Add sugar, vanilla extract, and salt and whisk until the mixture is just starting to bubble.
2. Remove from heat and pour into a heat-safe glass jar to cool. Once cool, cover with an airtight lid and store in the refrigerator for up to 1 month.

Vegan Pastry Crust

As with all roll-out pie crusts, this one takes a little practice to learn how to do it well. This is a great pastry to use for the tops of savory vegetable casseroles or the crust of a pumpkin pie.

INGREDIENTS | YIELDS 1 (8" OR 9") PIE CRUST OR TART PASTRY

¾ cup sorghum flour

¾ cup arrowroot starch

½ teaspoon sea salt

¼ teaspoon xanthan gum

½ cup plus 2 tablespoons Spectrum Palm Shortening

3 tablespoons unsweetened applesauce

2 tablespoons ice-cold water, as needed

1. In a large bowl whisk together sorghum flour, arrowroot starch, salt, and xanthan gum. Using a pastry blender or a knife and fork, cut in shortening throughout the flour until it resembles small peas. Make a well in the center of the flour and add the applesauce and 1 tablespoon of water. Mix with a fork until the dough gathers up into a ball. Shape dough into a round disk, cover with plastic wrap, and refrigerate at least 1 hour. Dough can be frozen at this point for up to 1 month.

2. Roll out dough onto a flat surface liberally dusted with sorghum flour.

3. Gently unroll the crust into the pan. It's okay if the dough cracks and doesn't transfer perfectly. This dough is very forgiving and you can patch it with your fingers. Cut off any extra dough around the pan and flute the edges of the crust. You can also mark the edges with a fork for a rustic look. Or, roll scraps of dough and cut out shapes with cookie cutters to decoratively place on top of pie filling right before baking. The crust can also be frozen at this point in an airtight, zip-top plastic bag or container for up to 1 month.

4. To prebake crust, heat oven to 350°F and prick small holes in the bottom of the crust with a fork. Bake for 10–15 minutes until crust is golden-brown. Baked crust can be frozen for up to 1 month.

Homemade Toaster Pastries

One of the most missed foods on a gluten-free diet is toaster pastries. Kids love them because they are sweet and crispy and adults love them because they are quick to prepare. This is a great recipe to make with your kids. Help them roll out the dough and choose their favorite fillings.

INGREDIENTS | YIELDS 4 PASTRIES

¾ cup sorghum flour

¾ cup arrowroot starch

½ teaspoon sea salt

¼ teaspoon xanthan gum

½ cup plus 2 tablespoons Spectrum Palm Shortening

3 tablespoons unsweetened applesauce

2 tablespoons ice-cold water, as needed

8 tablespoons filling of your choice: brown sugar and cinnamon, strawberry jam, peanut butter and jelly

1. In a large bowl whisk together sorghum flour, arrowroot starch, salt, and xanthan gum. Using a pastry blender or a knife and fork, cut in shortening throughout the flour until it resembles small peas. Make a well in the center of the flour and add the applesauce and 1 tablespoon of water. Mix with a fork until the dough gathers up into a ball. Shape dough into a round disk, cover with plastic wrap, and refrigerate at least 1 hour. Dough can be frozen at this point for up to 1 month.

2. Roll out the dough into a 9" × 12" rectangle until it is ⅛" thick. Using a pizza cutter, cut 3" × 4" rectangles (you should be able to get about 9 of them, so you'll have one leftover to make a very small tart).

3. Smear 2 tablespoons of whatever gluten-free vegan filling you want on four of the rectangles, leaving at least ½" of space free around the edges. Place another rectangle of dough on top of the one with filling and then seal edges closed with a fork.

4. Put 5–6 little holes in the top of the pastries decoratively to allow steam to escape the inside. Bake at 350°F for 20–25 minutes until light golden-brown. Cool and serve.

Maple Pecan Pie

This pecan pie is sweetened with maple syrup and coconut palm sugar and thickened without eggs. It needs to be refrigerated at least 8 hours to set after baking, so make the pie at least 1 day ahead of serving.

INGREDIENTS | SERVES 8–10

⅓ cup almond milk

3 tablespoons cornstarch

½ cup coconut palm sugar or vegan sugar

1 cup pure maple syrup (Grade B, if possible)

¼ teaspoon sea salt

½ teaspoon ground nutmeg

½ teaspoon ground cinnamon

2 tablespoons Spectrum Palm Shortening or vegan butter, melted

1 tablespoon vanilla extract

2½ cups chopped pecans

1 unbaked, prepared Vegan Pastry Crust (see recipe in this chapter)

1. Preheat oven to 350°F.
2. In a large bowl whisk together the almond milk and cornstarch for 2–3 minutes until the mixture is foamy. Then add the coconut palm sugar, maple syrup, sea salt, nutmeg, cinnamon, melted shortening, vanilla, and pecans. Stir until the mixture is thoroughly incorporated.
3. Pour the mixture into pie crust. Bake for 30–45 minutes until the filling is bubbling along the edges.
4. Remove from the oven and allow pie to cool on the counter for 30 minutes to 1 hour. Then refrigerate the pie for at least 8 hours before serving. It will set during refrigeration.
5. Store any remaining pie in the refrigerator for up to 1 week.

Does Your Maple Syrup Make the Grade?

Several types of maple syrup are available for sale in the United States and Canada. The most common is Grade A, which is a velvety smooth, light amber color with few impurities. This is a wonderful syrup, but it has a higher sugar/carbohydrate content than Grade B, which is thicker and has a richer maple flavor. Grade B syrup works really well in baking and cooking for these reasons.

Gluten-Free Ingredients

Bob's Red Mill

This is a good source for the gluten-free flours used in this cookbook—brown rice flour, sorghum flour, arrowroot starch, tapioca starch (called tapioca flour on the Bob's Red Mill website)—as well as gluten-free cornmeal, gluten-free rolled oats and quick oats, gluten-free grits, all-purpose gluten-free flour, gluten-free pancake mix, flaxseeds, xanthan gum, guar gum, yeast, and gluten-free baking powder.
www.bobsredmill.com

Amazon.com

Nearly all of the specialty gluten-free ingredients used in this cookbook can be purchased from Amazon.com, including chia seeds, Bob's Red Mill flours, Honeyville flours, Tropical Traditions flours, Spectrum Naturals Palm Shortening, and Bertolli Extra Light Tasting Olive Oil.
www.amazon.com

Blanched Almond Flour

Blanched almond flour is a high-protein flour that's used in several recipes in this cookbook. I prefer Honeyville brand as the quality is always consistently high.
http://store.honeyvillegrain.com/blanchedalmondflour 5lb.aspx

Blue Diamond Almond Breeze

This brand of casein-free, nondairy milk can be purchased at many grocery stores or online in shelf-stable packaging.
www.bluediamond.com/index.cfm?navid=33

Daiya "Cheese" Products

These are excellent dairy-free, soy-free cheese alternatives. This company creates a variety of shredded cheese products, as well as a cream cheese substitute, sandwich cheese product slices, and a gluten-free, dairy-free, and soy-free frozen pizza. Visit the website to find local retailers.
www.daiyafoods.com

Native Forest Organic Coconut Milk

Another nondairy alternative for milk, this can be used in numerous applications in gluten-free cooking and baking.
http://edwardandsons.com/native_shop_coconut.itml

Gluten-Free Website and Book Resources

Websites and Blogs

Adventures of a Gluten Free Mom
www.adventuresofaglutenfreemom.com

The Baking Beauties
www.thebakingbeauties.com

Book of Yum
www.bookofyum.com/blog

Celiac in the City
http://celiacinthecity.wordpress.com

Cook It Allergy Free
www.cookitallergyfree.com

Daily Bites
www.dailybitesblog.com

Daily Dietribe
www.thedailydietribe.com

Elana's Pantry
www.elanaspantry.com

Ginger Lemon Girl
www.gingerlemongirl.com

Gluten-Free-Girl and the Chef
www.glutenfreegirl.com

Gluten Free Gobsmacked
http://glutenfreegobsmacked.com

Gluten-Free Goddess
http://glutenfreegoddess.blogspot.com

Gluten Free Goodness
www.gfgoodness.com

The Gluten-Free Homemaker
www.glutenfreehomemaker.com

Gluten Free in Georgia
http://gfingf.blogspot.com

Harris Whole Heal th
www.harriswholehealth.com

Hunter's Lyonesse
http://hunterslyonesse.wordpress.com

I'm a Celiac
www.imaceliac.com

Lexie's Kitchen
www.lexieskitchen.com

Real Sustenance
www.realsustenance.com

Simply Gluten-Free
www.simplygluten-free.com

Simply Sugar and Gluten-Free
www.simplysugarandglutenfree.com

Spunky Coconut
www.thespunkycoconut.com

Tasty Eats at Home
www.tastyeatsathome.com

The Whole Life Nutrition Kitchen
www.nourishingmeals.com

Gluten-Free and Celiac Support Groups

Celiac.com
Founded by Scott Adams in 1995, it's one of the oldest online resources for gluten-free information including "The Journal of Gluten Sensitivity," an online gluten-free mall, and a host of gluten-free forums.
www.celiac.com

Celiac Disease Foundation
This active gluten-free and celiac disease awareness organization has been in operation since 1990.
www.celiac.org

Celiac Sprue Association (CSA)

This is a great resource for finding local gluten-free support groups, along with basic information on starting a gluten-free diet.
www.csaceliacs.info

Gluten Intolerance Group (GIG)

Here's another resource for finding local gluten-free support groups, as well as information on safe foods that are certified gluten-free by GIG programs.
www.gluten.net

National Foundation for Celiac Awareness

This not-for-profit organization supports raising awareness for celiac disease and gluten intolerance.
www.celiaccentral.org

Books

Amsterdam, Elana. *The Gluten-Free Almond Flour Cookbook*. Celestial Arts; original edition (July 28, 2009)

Amsterdam, Elana. *Gluten-Free Cupcakes*. Celestial Arts (April 26, 2011)

Angell, Brittany and Iris Higgins. *The Essential Gluten-Free Baking Guide, Part 1*. Triumph Dining (March 1, 2012)

Angell, Brittany and Iris Higgins. *The Essential Gluten-Free Baking Guide, Part 2*. Triumph Dining (March 1, 2012)

Barbone, Elizabeth. *Easy Gluten-Free Baking*. Lake Isle Press; Spi edition (March 16, 2009)

Brozyna, Kelly V. *The Spunky Coconut Cookbook, Second Edition: Gluten-Free, Dairy-Free, Sugar-Free*. Apidae Press (July 20, 2011)

Fenster, Carol. *Cooking Free*. Avery Trade (September 22, 2005)

Fenster, Carol. *Gluten-Free Quick and Easy*. Avery Trade; first edition (August 2, 2007)

Fleming, Alisa Marie. *Go Dairy Free*. Fleming Ink; first edition (November 10, 2008)

Green, Amy. *Simply Sugar and Gluten Free*. Ulysses Press; first edition (March 15, 2011)

Hagman, Bette. *The Gluten-Free Gourmet, Revised Edition*. Holt Paperbacks; revised edition (September 1, 2000)

Hagman, Bette. *The Gluten-Free Gourmet Bakes Bread*. Holt Paperbacks; reprint edition (October 1, 2000)

Hagman, Bette. *The Gluten-Free Gourmet Cooks Comfort Foods*. Holt Paperbacks; reprint edition (December 9, 2004)

Klecker, Hallie. *The Pure Kitchen*. Pure Living Press (August 29, 2011)

O'Brien, Susan. *Gluten-free, Sugar-free Cooking*. Da Capo Press; first edition (April 24, 2006)

Pascal, Cybele. *The Allergen-Free Baker's Handbook*. Celestial Arts (December 22, 2009)

Segersten, Alissa. *Nourishing Meals: Healthy Gluten-Free Recipes for the Whole Family*. Whole Life Press; first edition (September 5, 2012)

Baking Equipment Resources and Metric Conversions

Admetior Kitchen Oven Thermometer
http://ow.ly/jhHzN

Beyond Gourmet Paper Baking Cups
http://ow.ly/jhHlx

Beyond Gourmet Unbleached Parchment Paper Roll
http://ow.ly/jhHdj

Chicago Metallic Commercial Large Jelly Roll Pan
http://ow.ly/jhIyT

Metric measuring cups and spoons
http://ow.ly/kUpFo

Parrish Magic Line Loaf Pan
http://ow.ly/jhIGy

Pyrex 2-Cup Glass Measuring Cup
http://ow.ly/jhGFj

Taylor Classic Instant-Read Pocket Thermometer
http://ow.ly/jhHKT

Totally Bamboo 5-Piece Utensil Set
http://ow.ly/jhGLJ

Trudeau Silicone Spatula
http://ow.ly/jhH7i

USA Pans Aluminized Steel Loaf Pan
http://ow.ly/jhIOq

Wilton Cake Pans
http://ow.ly/jhI6q

Wilton Muffin Pans
http://ow.ly/jhIcT

Zak Designs Recycled Mixing Bowls
www.zak.com

Standard U.S./Metric Measurement Conversions

VOLUME CONVERSIONS

U.S. Volume Measure	Metric Equivalent
⅛ teaspoon	0.5 milliliter
¼ teaspoon	1 milliliter
½ teaspoon	2 milliliters
1 teaspoon	5 milliliters
½ tablespoon	7 milliliters
1 tablespoon (3 teaspoons)	15 milliliters
2 tablespoons (1 fluid ounce)	30 milliliters
¼ cup (4 tablespoons)	60 milliliters
⅓ cup	90 milliliters
½ cup (4 fluid ounces)	125 milliliters
⅔ cup	160 milliliters
¾ cup (6 fluid ounces)	180 milliliters
1 cup (16 tablespoons)	250 milliliters
1 pint (2 cups)	500 milliliters
1 quart (4 cups)	1 liter (about)

WEIGHT CONVERSIONS

U.S. Weight Measure	Metric Equivalent
½ ounce	15 grams
1 ounce	30 grams
2 ounces	60 grams
3 ounces	85 grams
¼ pound (4 ounces)	115 grams
½ pound (8 ounces)	225 grams
¾ pound (12 ounces)	340 grams
1 pound (16 ounces)	454 grams

OVEN TEMPERATURE CONVERSIONS

Degrees Fahrenheit	Degrees Celsius
200 degrees F	95 degrees C
250 degrees F	120 degrees C
275 degrees F	135 degrees C
300 degrees F	150 degrees C
325 degrees F	160 degrees C
350 degrees F	180 degrees C
375 degrees F	190 degrees C
400 degrees F	205 degrees C
425 degrees F	220 degrees C
450 degrees F	230 degrees C

BAKING PAN SIZES

U.S.	Metric
8 × 1½ inch round baking pan	20 × 4 cm cake tin
9 × 1½ inch round baking pan	23 × 3.5 cm cake tin
11 × 7 × 1½ inch baking pan	28 × 18 × 4 cm baking tin
13 × 9 × 2 inch baking pan	30 × 20 × 5 cm baking tin
2 quart rectangular baking dish	30 × 20 × 3 cm baking tin
15 × 10 × 2 inch baking pan	30 × 25 × 2 cm baking tin (Swiss roll tin)
9 inch pie plate	22 × 4 or 23 × 4 cm pie plate
7 or 8 inch springform pan	18 or 20 cm springform or loose bottom cake tin
9 × 5 × 3 inch loaf pan	23 × 13 × 7 cm or 2 lb narrow loaf or pâté tin
1½ quart casserole	1.5 liter casserole
2 quart casserole	2 liter casserole

INDEX